Corona SDK Mobile Game Development Beginner's Guide
Second Edition

Learn, explore, and create commercially successful mobile games for iOS and Android

Michelle M. Fernandez

PUBLISHING

BIRMINGHAM - MUMBAI

Corona SDK Mobile Game Development Beginner's Guide
Second Edition

First published: April 2012

Second edition: March 2015

Production reference: 1250315

Published by Packt Publishing Ltd.
Livery Place
35 Livery Street
Birmingham B3 2PB, UK.

ISBN 978-1-78355-934-3

www.packtpub.com

Credits

Author
Michelle M. Fernandez

Reviewers
Oguz Konya
Zeheng Li
Volodymyr Sergeyev
Jason Slater

Commissioning Editor
Usha Iyer

Acquisition Editor
Reshma Raman

Content Development Editor
Sumeet Sawant

Technical Editor
Vivek Arora

Copy Editors
Charlotte Carneiro
Pranjali Chury
Karuna Narayanan
Alfida Paiva
Vikrant Phadke

Project Coordinator
Danuta Jones

Proofreaders
Safis Editing
Maria Gould

Indexer
Priya Sane

Production Coordinator
Shantanu N. Zagade

Cover Work
Shantanu N. Zagade

About the Author

Michelle M. Fernandez is a mobile game developer and cofounder of MobiDojo (`http://www.mobidojo.com`). She is also a mentor to aspiring artists and programmers trying to break into the game industry. After experimenting with several game engines over the years, she was introduced to Corona SDK in late 2010 and has been an avid user of the program ever since. She enjoys creating tutorials and new game frameworks for others to learn from. When Michelle is not developing games, she is spending time with friends and family, playing video games, traveling, and constantly learning new design paradigms.

I would first and foremost like to thank my family and friends for their love and encouragement throughout the production of this book. I'd like to thank David Roper for his support and patience during this project and for always pushing me to do my best and succeed. I'd also like to thank April Quileza and Yanglyn Ou who have always been there for me to help review my work and who become my personal cheerleaders when things get hectic. My greatest appreciation goes out to Carlos Icaza, who has been a wonderful mentor and a great friend. I would like to acknowledge Walter Luh for continuing to give Corona developers an amazing platform to work with. A big thanks to all of the Packt staff for giving me this opportunity to share my love and knowledge of mobile game development through this book.

About the Reviewers

Oguz Konya is a game developer based in Istanbul, Turkey, and holds a master's degree in game technologies. He has been developing games and simulations for the last 4 years and is currently working as a game developer at Dodisoft Games. He is a hardcore gamer and enjoys playing games with his wife, who is scarily getting better and better at beating him at FPS games.

Zeheng Li is a PhD student in computer science at Southern Methodist University. He is interested in the synergy of machine learning and natural language processing in the software engineering domain. He holds a bachelor's degree in computer science and a master's degree in management information systems. Prior to his doctoral study, he worked for a start-up, focusing on mobile and web development. He is passionate about coding and problem solving.

Volodymyr Sergeyev is a software developer and computer science enthusiast.

I would like to thank my wife, Inna; daughter, Vlada; and son, Arsen; for their patience and love. These helps me a lot in everyday work! Also, I want to give my love to my parents, Ludmyla and Volodymyr. I love you all.

Jason Slater is a technology journalist, blogger, and software developer with over 25 years of industrial experience in building, managing, and writing about scalable, distributed, and web-based applications. He is a member of the British Computer Society and holds a master's degree in computer science (Internet technologies) with distinction.

Jason is the editor of a popular technology blog (`http://www.jasonslater.com`) and is a regular contributor to technology-based publications, radio, and television.

You can reach and follow him on Twitter; his Twitter handle is `@jasonslater`.

www.PacktPub.com

Support files, eBooks, discount offers, and more

For support files and downloads related to your book, please visit www.PacktPub.com.

Did you know that Packt offers eBook versions of every book published, with PDF and ePub files available? You can upgrade to the eBook version at www.PacktPub.com and as a print book customer, you are entitled to a discount on the eBook copy. Get in touch with us at service@packtpub.com for more details.

At www.PacktPub.com, you can also read a collection of free technical articles, sign up for a range of free newsletters and receive exclusive discounts and offers on Packt books and eBooks.

https://www2.packtpub.com/books/subscription/packtlib

Do you need instant solutions to your IT questions? PacktLib is Packt's online digital book library. Here, you can search, access, and read Packt's entire library of books.

Why subscribe?

- Fully searchable across every book published by Packt
- Copy and paste, print, and bookmark content
- On demand and accessible via a web browser

Free access for Packt account holders

If you have an account with Packt at www.PacktPub.com, you can use this to access PacktLib today and view 9 entirely free books. Simply use your login credentials for immediate access.

Table of Contents

Preface

This book is designed to introduce you to the basic standards of using the Corona SDK across iOS and Android platforms. You will enhance your learning experience by building three unique games in easy-to-follow steps. Aside from developing games, you will also dive into learning about social network integration, In-App Purchasing, and shipping your applications to the Apple App Store and/or Google Play Store.

What this book covers

Chapter 1, *Getting Started with Corona SDK*, begins by teaching you how to install Corona SDK on both the Mac OS X and Windows operating systems. You will learn how to create your first program in just two lines of code. Lastly, we'll go through the process of building and loading an application to an iOS or Android device.

Chapter 2, *Lua Crash Course and the Corona Framework*, dives into the Lua programming language that is used to develop in Corona SDK. We'll go over the basics of variables, functions, and data structures in Lua. This chapter will also introduce how to implement a variety of display objects within the Corona framework.

Chapter 3, *Building Our First Game – Breakout*, discusses the first half of building your first game, Breakout. You'll learn how to structure game files in a Corona project and create game objects that will be displayed on screen.

Chapter 4, *Game Controls*, continues with the second half of building your first game, Breakout. We'll cover game object movement as well as collision detection between objects in the scene. You will also learn how to create a scoring system that will implement the win and lose conditions of the game.

Chapter 5, *Animating Our Game*, explains how to animate a game using sprite sheets. This chapter will go in-depth with managing motion and transitions while creating a new game framework.

Chapter 6, Playing Sounds and Music, provides information on how to apply sound effects and music to your applications. It is vital to include some type of audio to enhance the sensory experience of your game's development. You will learn how to incorporate audio through loading, executing, and looping techniques with the Corona Audio System.

Chapter 7, Physics – Falling Objects, covers how to implement the Box2D engine in Corona SDK using display objects. You will be able to customize body construction and work with the physical behavior of falling objects. In this chapter, we'll apply the uses of dynamic/static bodies and explain the purpose of post collisions.

Chapter 8, Operation Composer, discusses how to manage all your game scenes with Composer API. We'll also go into detail on menu design, such as creating a pause menu and main menu. In addition, you'll learn how to save high scores within your game.

Chapter 9, Handling Multiple Devices and Networking Your Apps, provides information about integrating your applications with social networks such as Twitter or Facebook. This will enable your app to reach a bigger audience globally.

Chapter 10, Optimizing, Testing, and Shipping Your Games, explains the application submission process for both iOS and Android devices. This chapter will guide you on how to set up a distribution provisioning profile for the Apple App Store and manage your app information in iTunes Connect. Android developers will learn how to sign their applications for publication so they can be submitted to the Google Play Store.

Chapter 11, Implementing In-App Purchases, covers monetization of your game by creating consumable, nonconsumable, or subscription purchases. You will apply for In-App Purchases in the Apple App Store using Corona's store module. We'll take a look at testing purchases on a device to check whether transactions have been applied using the Sandbox environment.

Appendix, Pop Quiz Answers, covers all the answers enlisted in the pop quiz sections of the book.

What you need for this book

You will need the following items before you can start developing games with Corona SDK for Mac:

- ◆ If you are installing Corona for Mac OS X, ensure that your system has:
- ◆ Mac OS X 10.9 or later
- ◆ An Intel-based system that runs Lion, Mountain Lion, Mavericks, or Yosemite
- ◆ 64-bit CPU (Core 2 Duo)

- ◆ OpenGL 2.0 or higher graphics system
- ◆ You must be enrolled in the Apple Developer Program
- ◆ XCode
- ◆ A text editor such as TextWrangler, BBEdit, or TextMate

You will need the following items before you can start developing games with Corona SDK for Windows:

- ◆ If you are running Microsoft Windows, ensure that your system has:
- ◆ Windows 8, Windows 7, Vista, or XP (Service Pack 2) operating system
- ◆ 1 GHz processor (recommended)
- ◆ 80 MB of disk space (minimum)
- ◆ 1 GB of RAM (minimum)
- ◆ OpenGL 2.1 or higher graphics system (available in most modern Windows systems)
- ◆ 32-bit (x86) version of the Java Development Kit (JDK)
- ◆ The Android SDK is not required to create Android device builds with Corona on Mac or Windows
- ◆ Java 6 SDK
- ◆ A text editor such as Notepad ++

You must be enrolled as a Google Play Developer if you want to submit and publish apps for Android devices.

The game tutorials require resource files that are available with this book and can be downloaded from the Packt Publishing website.

Lastly, you will need the latest stable build of Corona SDK. This is applicable for all subscription levels.

Who this book is for

This book is for anyone who wants to have a go at creating commercially successfully games for Android and iOS. You don't need game development or programming experience.

Sections

In this book, you will find several headings that appear frequently (Time for action, What just happened?, Pop quiz, and Have a go hero).

To give clear instructions on how to complete a procedure or task, we use these sections as follows:

Time for action – heading

1. Action 1
2. Action 2
3. Action 3

Instructions often need some extra explanation to ensure they make sense, so they are followed with these sections:

What just happened?

This section explains the working of the tasks or instructions that you have just completed. You will also find some other learning aids in the book, for example:

Pop quiz – heading

These are short multiple-choice questions intended to help you test your own understanding.

Have a go hero – heading

These are practical challenges that give you ideas to experiment with what you have learned.

Conventions

You will also find a number of styles of text that distinguish between different kinds of information. Here are some examples of these styles, and an explanation of their meaning.

Code words in text, database table names, folder names, filenames, file extensions, pathnames, dummy URLs, user input, and Twitter handles are shown as follows: "We can include other contexts through the use of the `include` directive."

A block of code is set as follows:

```
textObject = display.newText( "Hello World!", 160, 80,
native.systemFont, 36 )
textObject: setFillColor ( 1, 1, 1 )
```

When we wish to draw your attention to a particular part of a code block, the relevant lines or items are set in bold:

```
local buyLevel2 = function ( product )
  print ("Congrats! Purchasing " ..product)

 -- Purchase the item
  if store.canMakePurchases then
    store.purchase( {validProducts[1]} )
  else
    native.showAlert("Store purchases are not available,
    please try again later",  { "OK" } ) - Will occur only
    due to phone setting/account restrictions
  end
end
-- Enter your product ID here
-- Replace Product ID with a valid one from iTunes Connect
buyLevel2("com.companyname.appname.NonConsumable")
```

Any command-line input or output is written as follows:

```
keytool -genkey -v -keystore my-release-key.keystore -alias aliasname
-keyalg RSA -validity 999999
```

New terms and **important words** are shown in bold. Words that you see on the screen, in menus or dialog boxes for example, appear in the text like this: "Click on the **Enroll Now** button and follow Apple's instructions to complete the process."

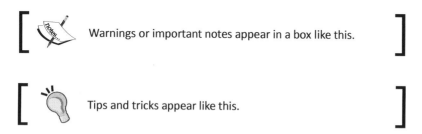

Warnings or important notes appear in a box like this.

Tips and tricks appear like this.

Reader feedback

Feedback from our readers is always welcome. Let us know what you think about this book—what you liked or disliked. Reader feedback is important for us as it helps us develop titles that you will really get the most out of.

To send us general feedback, simply e-mail `feedback@packtpub.com`, and mention the book's title in the subject of your message.

If there is a topic that you have expertise in and you are interested in either writing or contributing to a book, see our author guide at `www.packtpub.com/authors`.

Customer support

Now that you are the proud owner of a Packt Publishing book, we have a number of things to help you to get the most from your purchase.

Downloading the example code

You can download the example code files from your account at `http://www.packtpub.com` for all the Packt Publishing books you have purchased. If you purchased this book elsewhere, you can visit `http://www.packtpub.com/support` and register to have the files e-mailed directly to you.

Downloading the color images of this book

We also provide you with a PDF file that has color images of the screenshots/diagrams used in this book. The color images will help you better understand the changes in the output. You can download this file from `https://www.packtpub.com/sites/default/files/downloads/9343OT_ColoredImages.pdf`.

Errata

Although we have taken every care to ensure the accuracy of our content, mistakes do happen. If you find a mistake in one of our books—maybe a mistake in the text or the code—we would be grateful if you could report this to us. By doing so, you can save other readers from frustration and help us improve subsequent versions of this book. If you find any errata, please report them by visiting `http://www.packtpub.com/submit-errata`, selecting your book, clicking on the **Errata Submission Form** link, and entering the details of your errata. Once your errata are verified, your submission will be accepted and the errata will be uploaded to our website or added to any list of existing errata under the Errata section of that title.

To view the previously submitted errata, go to https://www.packtpub.com/books/content/support and enter the name of the book in the search field. The required information will appear under the **Errata** section.

Piracy

Piracy of copyrighted material on the Internet is an ongoing problem across all media. At Packt, we take the protection of our copyright and licenses very seriously. If you come across any illegal copies of our works in any form on the Internet, please provide us with the location address or website name immediately so that we can pursue a remedy.

Please contact us at copyright@packtpub.com with a link to the suspected pirated material.

We appreciate your help in protecting our authors and our ability to bring you valuable content.

Questions

If you have a problem with any aspect of this book, you can contact us at questions@packtpub.com, and we will do our best to address the problem.

1
Getting Started with Corona SDK

Before we jump right into coding some simple games, we need to install and run the necessary programs that will make our applications come to life. **Corona SDK** *is primarily a 2D development engine. If you've had experience developing for iOS or Android, you will find the experience of working with Corona refreshing. It is also simple to use. In no time, you'll be creating finished products to distribute through the Apple App Store and Google Play Store.*

In this chapter, we will:

- ◆ Set up Corona SDK on Mac OS X and Windows
- ◆ Install Xcode for Mac OS X
- ◆ Create a Hello World program in two lines
- ◆ Add devices in the iOS Provisioning Portal
- ◆ Load an application to an iOS device
- ◆ Load an application to an Android device

Downloading and installing Corona

You have the option of choosing the Mac OS X or Microsoft Windows operating system to develop on. Keep in mind the following system requirements that are needed to run the program. The most compatible version used for this book is Build 2014.2511.

If you are installing Corona for Mac OS X, be sure that your system has the following features:

◆ Mac OS X 10.9 or later

◆ An Intel-based system that runs Lion, Mountain Lion, Mavericks, or Yosemite

◆ A 64-bit CPU (Core 2 Duo)

◆ OpenGL 2.0 or higher graphics system

If you are running Microsoft Windows, be sure that your system has the following features:

◆ Windows 8, Windows 7, Vista, or XP (Service Pack 2) operating system

◆ 1 GHZ processor (recommended)

◆ 80 MB of disk space (minimum)

◆ 1 GB of RAM (minimum)

◆ OpenGL 2.1 or higher graphics system (available in most modern Windows systems)

◆ The 32-bit (x86) version of the **Java Development Kit (JDK)**

◆ The Android SDK is not required to create Android device builds with Corona on Mac or Windows

Time for action – setting up and activating Corona on Mac OS X

Let's begin by setting up the Corona SDK on our desktop:

1. If you haven't downloaded the SDK, please do so from `http://www.coronalabs.com/downloads/coronasdk`. You will have to register as a user before you can access the SDK.

2. The file extension for any Mac program should end in `.dmg`; this is known as an Apple disk image. Once you've downloaded the disk image, double-click on the disk image file to mount it. The name should be similar to `CoronaSDK-XXXX.XXXX.dmg`. Once it is loaded, you should see the mounted disk image folder, as shown in the following screenshot:

3. Next, drag the CoronaSDK folder into the Applications folder. This will copy the contents of the Corona folder into /Applications. You will be prompted to enter an administrator password if you are not the main administrator of the account. You will be able to see the CoronaSDK folder in /Applications once it has been successfully installed. For easy access to the folder contents, create an alias by dragging the CoronaSDK folder to the dock of your Mac desktop:

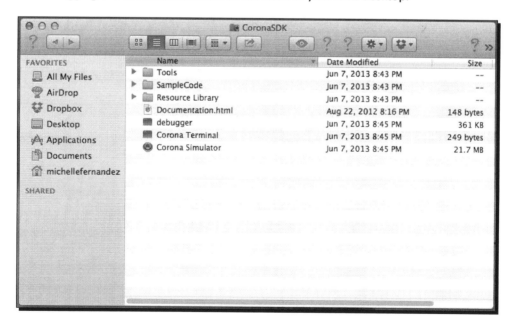

First-time Corona SDK users will have to perform a quick and easy one-time authorization process before it is accessible. You must be connected to the Internet to complete the authorization process.

1. Launch the Corona simulator in the SDK folder.

2. Assuming this is your first time, you will be presented with an **End-user License Agreement (EULA)**. Once you have accepted the agreement, enter the e-mail you used to register for Corona and the password to activate the SDK. Otherwise, click on **Register** to create an account.

 If you register with Corona as a single developer, there is no fee to develop on iOS and/or Android devices.

3. Upon successful login, you will get a confirmation dialog to show that the SDK is ready to use:

4. Click on the **Continue** button, and you'll be presented with the Welcome to Corona screen:

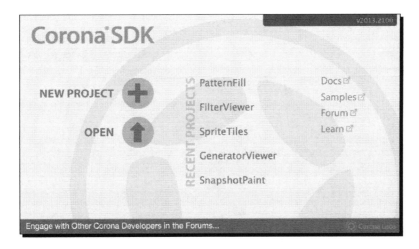

What just happened?

Setting up Corona SDK on your Mac operating system is as simple as installing any other dedicated Mac program. After you have authorized the SDK on your machine and logged in with your e-mail and password, it will be ready for use. From here on out, every time you launch Corona, it will automatically log in to your account. You will notice that you are greeted with a Corona SDK screen when this happens.

Time for action – setting up and activating Corona on Windows

Let's set up the Corona SDK on our desktop using the following steps:

1. Download the Corona SDK from `http://www.coronalabs.com/downloads/coronasdk`. You will have to register as a user before you can access the SDK.

2. The file extension for the Windows version of Corona should end in `.msi`, which is known as a Windows Installer, a component of Windows made to install programs by Microsoft. Double-click on the file. The filename should be similar to `CoronaSDK.msi`.

3. Follow the onscreen directions for installation.

4. Corona will be installed directly into your `Programs` folder by default. On Microsoft Windows, select **Corona Simulator** from the list of programs in your Start menu or double-click on the Corona icon on the desktop. Upon successful activation, you should be greeted with the following screen:

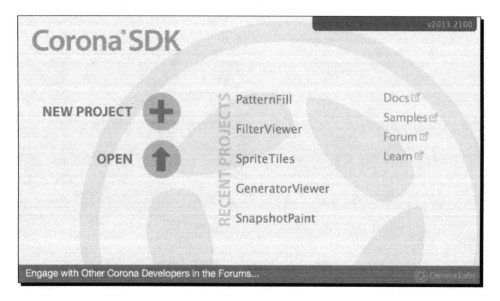

5. The process to activate the SDK should be the same as the Mac procedure once you launch Corona for the very first time.

If you run into issues with images not displaying properly, check to see whether you're using an up-to-date OpenGL graphics driver, 2.1 or higher.

Be aware that Corona SDK on Windows can only build for Android devices, not for iOS devices (iPhone, iPad, or iPod Touch). A Mac can build not only for iOS, but also for Android devices in Corona.

6. To create device builds, you need to install Java 6 SDK on your PC. You will need to go to the Oracle website at `http://www.oracle.com/technetwork/java/javasebusiness/downloads/java-archive-downloads-javase6-419409.html` for the JDK download and click on the **Java SE Development Kit 6u45** link.

7. On the next page, select the **Accept License Agreement** radio button and then click on the **Windows x86** link to download the installer. You will be asked to log in or create a user account on the Oracle website if you don't already have one.

8. As soon as the JDK is downloaded, run the installer. Once installed, you'll be able to create device builds for Android on your PC.

What just happened?

Installing the SDK on Windows is a different setup process compared to on the Mac OS X. While executing the installer file, Windows will automatically present a designated location to install the application, such as the `Programs` folder, so that you won't have to manually choose a destination. Upon successful installation, you will see the Corona SDK icon on your desktop for easy access, or it may be highlighted in the programs list in the Start menu, assuming that you're accessing it for the first time. When you authorize Corona on your machine and sign in with your login information, it is ready for you to use and will log in automatically every time it is launched.

Using the simulator on Mac and Windows

On Mac OS X, launch Corona SDK by either selecting the Corona terminal or Corona simulator from the `Applications` directory. Both selections will access the SDK. The Corona simulator will only open the simulator. The Corona terminal will open both the simulator and the terminal window. The terminal is helpful to debug your programs and display simulator errors/warnings and `print()` messages.

On Microsoft Windows, select the `Corona SDK` folder and click on **Corona Simulator** from the list of programs in your Start menu or double-click on the Corona icon on the desktop. The simulator and terminal are always opened together if you are using Windows.

Let's go over the useful contents contained in the `Corona SDK` folder (located in `Applications/Corona SDK` on Mac and `Start/All Apps/Corona SDK` on Windows):

- **Debugger (Mac)/Corona debugger (Windows)**: This is a tool to find and isolate issues in your code.
- **Corona simulator**: This is the environment used to launch your application for testing. It simulates the mobile device you're developing for on your local computer. On Windows, it will open both the simulator and terminal.
- **Corona terminal**: This launches the Corona simulator and opens a terminal window to display error/warning messages and `print()` statements. It is very helpful to debug your code, but is only available on a Mac.
- **Simulator**: This has the same properties as the Corona terminal, but is called from the command line and is only available on a Mac.
- **Sample code**: This is a set of sample applications to get you started with Corona. It contains code and art assets to work with.

The Corona SDK window opens automatically when you launch the simulator. You can open a Corona project in the simulator, create a device build for testing or distribution, and view some example games and apps to get yourself familiar with the SDK.

Time for action – viewing a sample project in the simulator

Let's take a look at the `HelloPhysics` sample project in the simulator:

1. Click on **Corona Simulator** in the `Corona SDK` folder.

2. Click on the **Samples** link on the Corona SDK window when it launches. In the **Open** dialog that appears, navigate to `Applications/CoronaSDK/SampleCode/Physics/HelloPhysics` **(Mac)** or `C:\Program Files (x86)\Corona Labs\Corona SDK\Sample Code\Physics\HelloPhysics` **(Windows)**. On a Mac, click on **Open**, and it will automatically open `main.lua`. On Windows, double-click on `main.lua` to open the file. The `HelloPhysics` application opens and runs in the simulator.

What just happened?

Accessing the SDK through the Corona terminal or Corona simulator is a matter of preference. Many Mac users prefer to use the Corona terminal so that they can track messages outputted to the terminal. When you launch the SDK through the Corona simulator, the simulator will be displayed, but not the terminal window. When Windows users launch the Corona simulator, it will display both the simulator and the terminal window. This is nice to use when you want play around with any of the example applications that are provided by Corona.

The `main.lua` file is a special filename that tells Corona where to start in a project folder. This file can also load other code files or other program resources such as sounds or graphics.

When you launch the `HelloPhysics` application in Corona, you will observe a box object fall from the top of the screen in the simulator and collide with a ground object. The transition from launching the `main.lua` file to viewing the results in the simulator is almost immediate.

Have a go hero – use a different device shell

As you start getting familiar with the Corona simulator, whether you're in Windows or Mac OS X, a default device is always used when you launch an application. Windows uses the Droid as the default device, while the Mac OS X uses the regular iPhone. Try launching the sample code in a different device shell to view the differences in screen resolution between all the devices the simulator has available.

When porting builds to more than one platform, you'll have to consider the variety of screen resolutions in both iOS and Android devices. A build is a compiled version of all your source code that is converted into one file. Having your game build configured for multiple platforms broadens the audience reach of your application.

Choosing a text editor

Corona does not have a designated program editor to code in, so you will have to find one that suits your needs.

For Mac OS, TextWrangler is a good one, and it is free too! You can download it from `http://www.barebones.com/products/textwrangler/download.html`. Other text editors such as BBEdit at `http://www.barebones.com/thedeck` and TextMate at `http://macromates.com/` are great, but you will need to purchase them in order to use them. TextMate is also compatible with the Corona TextMate Bundle, which is available at `http://www.ludicroussoftware.com/corona-textmate-bundle/index.html`.

For Microsoft Windows, Notepad++ is recommended and can be downloaded from `http://notepad-plus-plus.org/`.

The following are the text editors that are compatible with both Mac OS and Microsoft Windows:

- Sublime Text (`http://www.sublimetext.com`)
- Lua Glider (`http://www.mydevelopersgames.com/Glider/`)
- Outlaw (`http://outlawgametools.com/outlaw-code-editor-and-project-manager/`)

Any text editor, such as TextEdit for Mac or Notepad for Windows, that is already included in the operating system works as well, but it'll be easier to work with one that is designed for programming. For Corona, using an editor that supports the Lua syntax highlighting will work the best when coding. Syntax highlighting adds formatting attributes to keywords and punctuation in a way that makes it easier for the reader to separate code from text.

Developing on devices

It is not necessary to download Apple's developer kit, Xcode, or the Android SDK if you only want to use the Corona simulator. In order to build and test your code on an iOS device (iPhone, iPod Touch, and iPad), you will need to sign up as an Apple developer and create and download the provisioning profiles. If you want to develop on Android, you don't need to download the Android SDK unless you want to use the ADB tool to help with installing builds and viewing debug messages.

The Corona SDK starter version allows you to build Adhoc (for iOS) and debug builds (Android) for testing on your own devices. Corona Pro users also get the benefit of special features, such as access to daily builds, premium features, all plugins, and premium support.

Time for action – downloading and installing Xcode

In order to develop any iOS application, you will need to enroll in the Apple Developer Program, which costs $99 a year, and create an account on the Apple website at `http://developer.apple.com/programs/ios/` by following these steps:

1. Click on the **Enroll Now** button and follow Apple's instructions to complete the process. When adding a program, select **iOS Developer Program**.

2. When you have completed your enrollment, click on the iOS link under the section marked **Dev Centers**.

3. Scroll down to the **Downloads** section and download the current Xcode, or you can download Xcode from the Mac App Store.

4. Once you have fully downloaded Xcode, double-click on Xcode from `/Applications/Xcode`. You will be asked to authenticate as an administrative user:

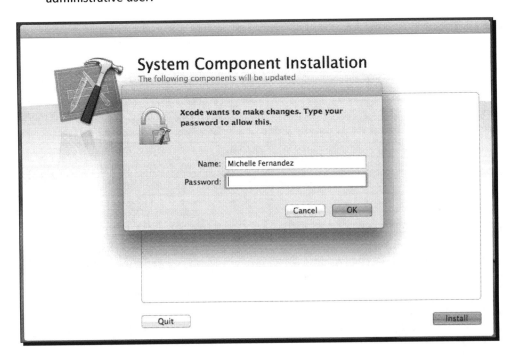

5. After you have entered your credentials, click on the **OK** button to complete the installation. You will see the following screen:

6. When you have installed the Xcode developer tools, you can access the documentation by launching Xcode and choosing any of the items in the **Help** menu. Developer applications such as Xcode and Instruments are installed in `/Applications/Xcode`. You can drag these app icons to your dock for convenient accessibility.

What just happened?

We just went through the steps of how to install Xcode for Mac OS X. By enrolling in the Apple Developer Program, you will have access to up-to-date development tools on the website. Remember that to continue being an Apple developer, *you have to pay* a fee of $99 annually to keep your subscription.

The Xcode file is quite large, so it will take a bit of time to download, depending on how fast your Internet connection is. Once your installation is complete, Xcode will be ready to go.

Time for action – creating a Hello World application in two lines of code

Now that we have the simulator and text editors set up, let's start making our very first Corona program! The first program that we will make is called Hello World. It is a traditional program that many people learn when starting a new programming language.

1. Open your preferred text editor and type the following lines:

```
textObject = display.newText( "Hello World!", 160, 80,
native.systemFont, 36 )
textObject: setFillColor ( 1, 1, 1 )
```

2. Next, create a folder on your desktop called Hello World. Save the preceding text as a file named main.lua to the location of your project folder.

3. Launch Corona. You will be greeted with the Corona SDK screen. Click on **Open** and navigate to the Hello World folder you just created. You should see your main. lua file in this folder:

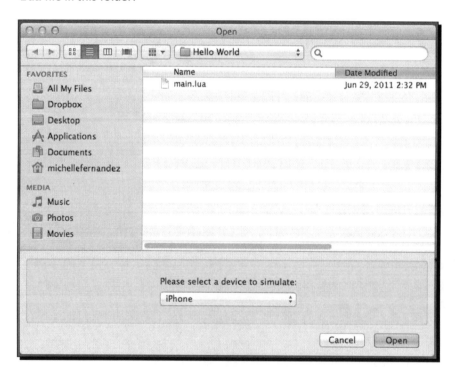

4. On a Mac, click on the **Open** button. On Windows, select the `main.lua` file and click on the **Open** button. You'll see your new program running in the Corona simulator:

Time for action – modifying our application

Before we dive into more complex examples, let's alter some minor things in our program by performing the following steps:

1. Let's alter the second line of `main.lua` to display as follows:

   ```
   textObject = display.newText( "Hello World!", 160, 80,
   native.systemFont, 36 )
   textObject:setFillColor( 0.9, 0.98 ,0 )
   ```

2. Save your file and go back to the Corona simulator. The simulator will detect a change from your file and automatically relaunch with the changes. If the simulator doesn't relaunch automatically upon saving your file, press *Command + R* (Mac) / *Ctrl + R* (Windows). You will see the following output on the screen:

As you continue learning more Corona functions, you'll notice that some of the text values will be optional. In this case, we need to use five values.

Time for action – applying a new font name to our application

Now, let's play around with the font name by performing the following steps:

1. Change the first line to the following line of code:

```
textObject = display.newText( "Hello World!", 160, 80, "Times
New Roman", 36 )
```

2. Be sure to save your `main.lua` file after making any alterations; then, press *Command + R* (Mac) / *Ctrl + R* (Windows) in Corona to relaunch the simulator to view the new font. If you're using a Mac, usually, the simulator automatically relaunches after saving your file, or it may ask you if you want to relaunch the program. You can see the new font in the simulator:

What just happened?

You have now made your first complete mobile application! What's even more amazing is that this is a completed iPhone, iPad, and Android application. This two-line program will actually install and run on your iOS/Android device if you were to create a build. You have now seen what the basic workflow in Corona is like.

If you take a look at line 2 in your `main.lua` file, you will notice that `setFillColor` alters the color of the text for **Hello World!**.

Colors are made up of three sets of RGB numbers that represent the amount of red, green and blue contained within a color. They are displayed with three numbers, with values ranging from 0 to 1. For example, the color black would be (0,0,0), blue would be (0,0,1), and the color white (0.6, 0.4, 0.8).

Continue playing around with different color values to see the different results. You can see the alterations to the code in the simulator when you save your `main.lua` file and relaunch Corona.

When you view the first line from the `main.lua` file, you will notice that `newText()` is called by the display object. The returning reference is `textObject`. The `newText()` function returns an object that will represent the text on the screen. The `newText()` function is a part of the display library.

When you want to access the display properties of `newText`, type in `display.newText`. The two numbers after `Hello World!` control the horizontal and vertical positions of the text on the screen in pixels. The next item specifies the font. We used the name `native.systemFont`, which, by default, refers to the standard font on the current device. For example, the iPhone's default font is Helvetica. You can use any standard font name, such as Times New Roman that is used in the preceding example. The last number used is the font size.

Have a go hero – adding more text objects

Now that you're starting to get a taste of coding, try following these steps in your current project file:

1. Create a new display object using a different font and text color. Ensure it displays below the `Hello World!` text. Make sure that your new display object has a different object name.

2. Continue changing the values of the current display object, `textObject`. Alter the *x* and *y* coordinates, the string text, font name, and even the font size.

3. While `object:setFillColor( r,g,b )` sets the color of the text, there is an optional parameter you can add that controls the opacity of the text. Try using `object:setFillColor( r, g, b [, a] )`. The values available for `a` also range between 0 to 1 (1 is opaque, which is the default value). Observe the results of your text color.

Testing our application on an iOS device

If you are only interested in testing the application on an Android device, skip past this section of the chapter to *Testing our application on an Android device*. Before we can upload our first Hello World application on an iOS device, we need to log in into our Apple developer account so that we can create and install our signing certificates on our development machine. If you haven't created a developer account yet, do so by going to `http://developer.apple.com/programs/ios/`. Remember that there is a fee of $99 a year to become an Apple developer.

The Apple developer account is only applied to users developing on Mac OS X. Make sure that your version of Xcode is the same or newer than the version of the OS on your phone. For example, if you have version 5.0 of the iPhone OS installed, you will need Xcode that is bundled with the iOS SDK version 5.0 or later.

Time for action – obtaining the iOS developer certificate

Make sure that you're signed up for the developer program; you will need to use the Keychain Access tool located in `/Applications/Utilities` so that you can create a certificate request. A valid certificate must sign all iOS applications before they can be run on an Apple device in order to do any kind of testing. The following steps will show you how to create an iOS developer certificate:

1. Go to **Keychain Access | Certificate Assistant | Request a Certificate From a Certificate Authority**:

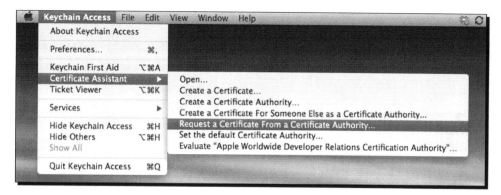

2. In the **User Email Address** field, type in the e-mail address you used when you registered as an iOS developer. For **Common Name**, enter your name or team name. Make sure that the name entered matches the information that was submitted when you registered as an iOS developer. The **CA Email Address** field does not need to be filled in, so you can leave it blank. We are not e-mailing the certificate to a **Certificate Authority (CA)**. Check **Saved to disk** and **Let me specify key pair information**. When you click on **Continue**, you will be asked to choose a save location. Save your file at a destination where you can locate it easily, such as your desktop.

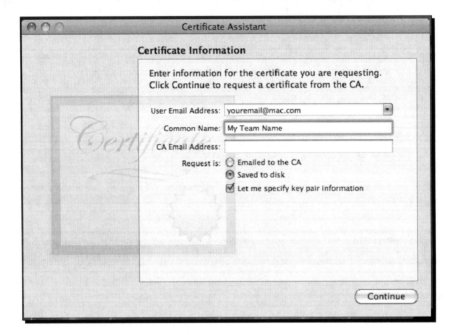

3. In the following window, make sure that **2048 bits** is selected for the **Key Size** and **RSA** for the **Algorithm**, and then click on **Continue**. This will generate the key and save it to the location you specified. Click on **Done** in the next window.

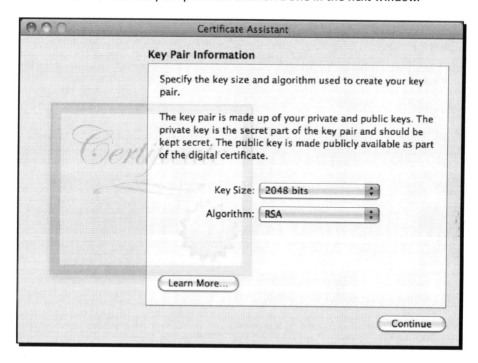

4. Next, go to the Apple developer website at `http://developer.apple.com/`, click on **iOS Dev Center**, and log in to your developer account. Select **Certificates, Identifiers & Profiles** under **iOS Developer Program** on the right-hand side of the screen and navigate to **Certificates** under **iOS Apps**. Select the **+** icon on the right-hand side of the page. Under **Development**, click on the **iOS App Development** radio button. Click on the **Continue** button till you reach the screen to generate your certificate:

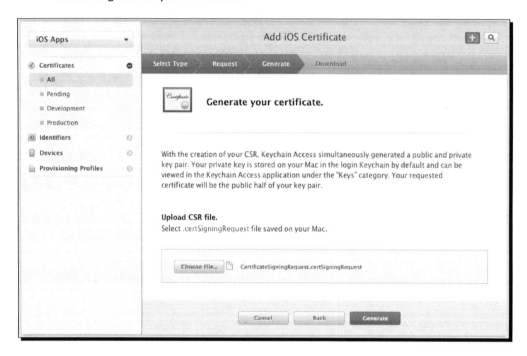

5. Click on the **Choose File** button and locate your certificate file that you saved to your desktop, and then, click on the **Generate** button.

6. Upon hitting **Generate**, you will get the e-mail notification you specified in the CA request form from Keychain Access, or you can download it directly from the developer portal. The person who created the certificate will get this e-mail and can approve the request by hitting the **Approve** button.

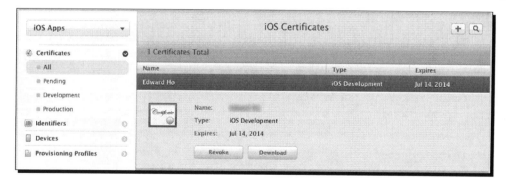

7. Click on the **Download** button and save the certificate to a location that is easy to find. Once this is completed, double-click on the file, and the certificate will be added automatically in the Keychain Access.

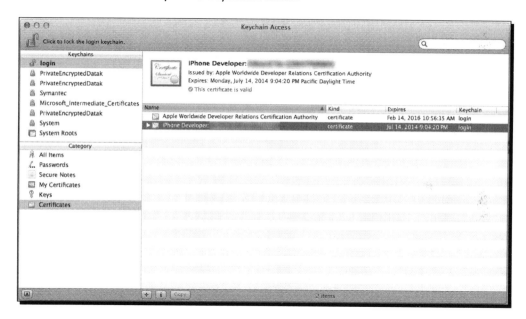

What just happened?

We now have a valid certificate for iOS devices. The iOS Development Certificate is used for development purposes only and valid for about a year. The key pair is made up of your public and private keys. The private key is what allows Xcode to sign iOS applications. Private keys are available only to the key pair creator and are stored in the system keychain of the creator's machine.

Adding iOS devices

You are allowed to assign up to 100 devices for development and testing purposes in the iPhone Developer Program. To register a device, you will need the **Unique Device Identification (UDID)** number. You can find this in iTunes and Xcode.

Xcode

To find out your device's UDID, connect your device to your Mac and open Xcode. In Xcode, navigate to the menu bar, select **Window**, and then click on **Organizer**. The 40 hex character string in the **Identifier** field is your device's UDID. Once the **Organizer** window is open, you should see the name of your device in the **Devices** list on the left-hand side. Click on it and select the identifier with your mouse, copying it to the clipboard.

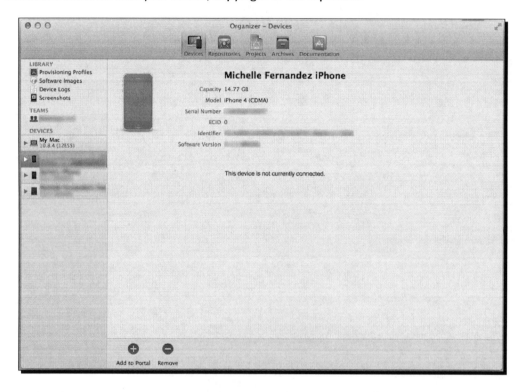

Usually, when you connect a device to **Organizer** for the first time, you'll receive a button notification that says **Use for Development**. Select it and Xcode will do most of the provisioning work for your device in the iOS Provisioning Portal.

iTunes

With your device connected, open iTunes and click on your device in the device list. Select the **Summary** tab. Click on the **Serial Number** label to show the **Identifier** field and the 40-character UDID. Press *Command + C* to copy the UDID to your clipboard.

Time for action – adding/registering your iOS device

To add a device to use for development/testing, perform the following steps:

1. Select **Devices** in the Developer Portal and click on the **+** icon to register a new device. Select the **Register Device** radio button to register one device.

2. Create a name for your device in the **Name** field and put your device's UDID in the **UDID** field by pressing *Command + V* to paste the number you have saved on the clipboard.

3. Click on **Continue** when you are done and click on **Register** once you have verified the device information.

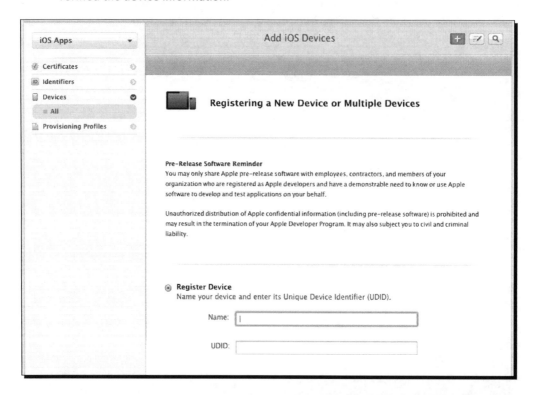

Time for action – creating an App ID

Now that you have added a device to the portal, you will need to create an App ID. An App ID has a unique 10-character Apple ID Prefix generated by Apple and an Apple ID Suffix that is created by the Team Admin in the Provisioning Portal. An App ID could looks like this: `7R456G1254.com.companyname.YourApplication`. To create a new App ID, use these steps:

1. Click on **App IDs** in the **Identifiers** section of the portal and select the **+** icon.

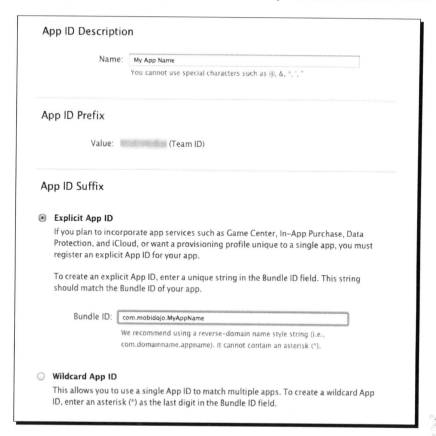

2. Fill out the **App ID Description** field with the name of your application.

3. You are already assigned an Apple ID Prefix (also known as a Team ID).

4. In the **App ID Suffix** field, specify a unique identifier for your app. It is up to you how you want to identify your app, but it is recommended that you use the reverse-domain style string, that is, `com.domainname.appname`. Click on **Continue** and then on **Submit** to create your App ID.

You can create a wildcard character in the bundle identifier that you can share among a suite of applications using the same Keychain access. To do this, simply create a single App ID with an asterisk (*) at the end. You would place this in the field for the bundle identifier either by itself or at the end of your string, for example, `com.domainname.*`. More information on this topic can be found in the App IDs section of the iOS Provisioning Portal at `https://developer.apple.com/ios/manage/bundles/howto.action`.

What just happened?

All UDIDs are unique on every device, and we can locate them in Xcode and iTunes. When we added a device in the iOS Provisioning Portal, we took the UDID, which consists of 40 hex characters, and made sure we created a device name so that we could identify what we're using for development.

We now have an App ID for the applications we want to install on a device. An App ID is a unique identifier that iOS uses to allow your application to connect to the Apple Push Notification service, share keychain data between applications, and communicate with external hardware accessories you wish to pair your iOS application with.

Provisioning profiles

A **provisioning profile** is a collection of digital entities that uniquely ties apps and devices to an authorized iOS Development Team and enables a device to be used to test a particular app. Provisioning profiles define the relationship between apps, devices, and development teams. They need to be defined for both the development and distribution aspects of an app.

Time for action – creating a provisioning profile

To create a provisioning profile, go to the **Provisioning Profiles** section of the Developer Portal and click on the **+** icon. Perform the following steps:

1. Select the **iOS App Development** radio button under the **Development** section and then select **Continue**.

2. Select the **App ID** you created for your application in the pull-down menu and click on **Continue**.

3. Select the certificate you wish to include in the provisioning profile and then click on **Continue**.

4. Select the devices you wish to authorize for this profile and click on **Continue**.

5. Create a **Profile Name** and click on the **Generate** button when you are done:

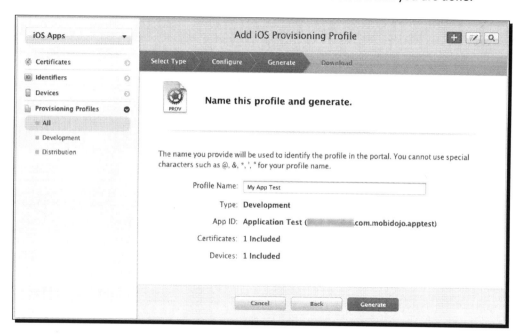

6. Click on the **Download** button. While the file is downloading, launch Xcode if it's not already open and press *Shift + Command + 2* on the keyboard to open **Organizer**.

7. Under **Library**, select the **Provisioning Profiles** section. Drag your downloaded .mobileprovision file to the **Organizer** window. This will automatically copy your .mobileprovision file to the proper directory.

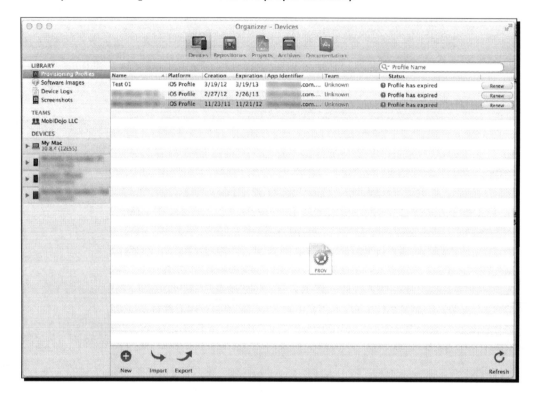

What just happened?

Devices that have permission within the provisioning profile can be used for testing as long as the certificates are included in the profile. One device can have multiple provisioning profiles installed.

Application icon

Currently, our app has no icon image to display on the device. By default, if there is no icon image set for the application, you will see a light gray box displayed along with your application name below it once the build has been loaded to your device. So, launch your preferred creative developmental tool and let's create a simple image.

The application icon for standard resolution iPad2 or iPad mini image file is 76 x 76 px PNG. The image should always be saved as `Icon.png` and must be located in your current project folder. iPhone/iPod touch devices that support retina display need an additional high resolution 120 x 120 px and iPad or iPad mini have an icon of 152 x 152 px named as `Icon@2x.png`.

The contents of your current project folder should look like this:

```
Hello World/          name of your project folder
    Icon.png              required for iPhone/iPod/iPad
    Icon@2x.png     required for iPhone/iPod with Retina display
    main.lua
```

In order to distribute your app, the App Store requires a 1024 x 1024 pixel version of the icon. It is best to create your icon at a higher resolution first. Refer to the *Apple iOS Human Interface Guidelines* for the latest official App Store requirements at `http://developer.apple.com/library/ios/#documentation/userexperience/conceptual/mobilehig/Introduction/Introduction.html`.

Creating an application icon is a visual representation of your application name. You will be able to view the icon on your device once you compile a build together. The icon is also the image that launches your application.

Creating the Hello World build for iOS

We are now set to build our Hello World application for our device. Since we have our provisioning profiles in place, the build process from here on out is pretty simple. Make sure that you are connected to the Internet before creating a device build. You can build your application for testing in the Xcode simulator or on a device.

Time for action – creating an iOS build

Follow these steps to create a new iOS build in Corona SDK:

1. Open the Corona simulator and select **Open**.
2. Navigate to your Hello World application and select your `main.lua` file.

3. Once the application is launched in the simulator, go to the Corona Simulator menu bar and navigate to **File | Build | iOS** or press *Command + B* on your keyboard. The following dialog box will appear:

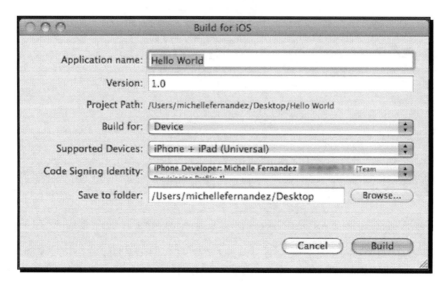

4. Create a name for your app in the **Application Name** field. We can keep the same name, Hello World. In the **Version** field, keep the number at 1.0. In order to test the app in the Xcode simulator, select **Xcode Simulator** from the **Build For** drop-down menu. If you want to build for the device, choose **Device** to build an app bundle. Next, select the target device (iPhone or iPad) from the **Supported Devices** drop-down menu. From the **Code Signing Identity** drop-down menu, choose the provisioning file you created for the specified devices you are building for. It is the same name as **Profile Name** in the iOS Provisioning Portal on the Apple developer website. In the **Save to folder** section, click on **Browse** and choose where you would like your application to be saved.

    If all the information has been confirmed in the dialog box, click on the **Build** button.

> It is more convenient to set your application to save on the Desktop; this way, it is easy to find.

What just happened?

Congratulations! You have now created your very first iOS application file that can be uploaded to your device. As you start developing apps for distribution, you will want to create new versions of your application so that you can keep track of the changes in every new build you make. All the information from your Provisioning Profile was created in the iOS Provisioning Portal and applied to the build. Once Corona has finished compiling the build, the application should be located in the folder you saved it under.

Time for action – loading an app on your iOS device

Select your Hello World build you created and choose either iTunes or Xcode to load your app onto your iOS device. They can be used to transfer the application file.

If using iTunes, drag your build into your iTunes Library and then sync your device normally, as shown in the following screenshot:

Another way to install your app onto your device is to use Xcode, since it provides a convenient method to install iOS device applications. Perform the following steps:

1. With the device connected, open Xcode's **Organizer** from the menu bar by going to **Window | Organizer** and navigate to your connected device under the **Devices** list on the left-hand side.

2. If a proper connection is established, you will see a green indicator. If it is yellow after a couple minutes, try powering the device off and on again or disconnect the device and connect it again. This will usually establish a proper connection.

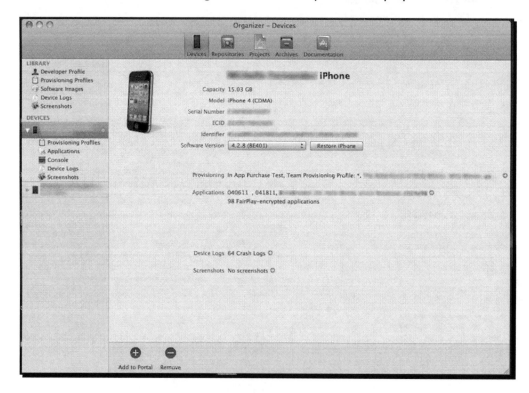

3. Simply drag your build file and drop it into the **Applications** area of the **Organizer** window, and it will automatically install on your device.

What just happened?

We just learned two different ways of loading an application build to an iOS device: using iTunes and using Xcode.

Using iTunes provides a simple drag and drop feature into your library and then allows you to transfer the build as long as your device is synced up.

The Xcode method is probably the easiest and most common way to load a build to a device. As long as your device is connected properly and ready to use in the Organizer, you drag and drop the build to applications and it loads automatically.

Testing our application on an Android device

Creating and testing our builds on an Android device does not require a developer account like how Apple does for iOS devices. The only tools you need to build for Android are a PC or Mac, Corona SDK, JDK6 installed, and an Android device. If you plan on submitting an app to the Google Play Store, you'll need to sign up as a Google Play Developer at `https://play.google.com/apps/publish/signup/`. There is a one-time $25 registration fee you have to pay if you want to publish software on the Google Play Store.

Creating the Hello World build for Android

Building our Hello World application is fairly simple since we do not have to create a unique keystore or key alias for debug builds. When you're ready to submit an application to the Google Play Store, you'll need to create a release build and generate your own private key to sign your app. We'll discuss in further detail about release builds and private keys later on in this book.

Time for action – creating an Android build

Follow these steps to create a new Android build in the Corona SDK:

1. Launch the Corona Simulator and select **Simulator**.
2. Navigate to your Hello World application and select your `main.lua` file.

3. Once your application is running in the simulator, go to the **Corona Simulator** menu bar and navigate to **File | Build For | Android** (Windows) / *Shift + Command + B* on your keyboard (Mac). The following dialog box will appear:

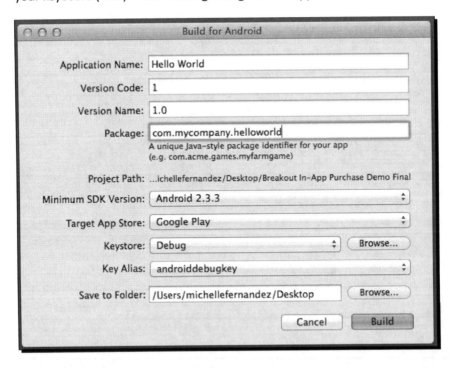

4. Create a name for your app in the **Application Name** field. We can keep the same name, **Hello World**. In the **Version Code** field, set the number to **1** if that is not already the default number. This specific field must always be an integer and is not visible to users. In the **Version Name** field, keep the number at **1.0**. This attribute is the string shown to users. In the **Package** field, you will need to specify a name that uses the traditional Java scheme, which is basically the reverse format of your domain name; for example, **com.mycompany.app.helloworld** would work as a package name. **Project Path** shows the location of your project folder. **Minimum SDK Version** currently supports Android 2.3.3 and newer devices running the ArmV7 processor. In the **Target App Store** pull-down menu, the default store can stay as Google Play. In the **Keystore** field, you will be signing your build with the Debug keystore that is already provided in Corona. In the **Key Alias** field, select androiddebugkey from the pull-down menu if it's not selected. In the **Save to Folder** section, click on **Browse** and choose where you'd like your application to be saved to.

5. If all the information has been confirmed in the dialog box, click on the **Build** button.

 For more information on Java package names, see the section on *Unique Package Names* in the Java documentation at `http://java.sun.com/docs/books/jls/third_edition/html/packages.html#40169`.

What just happened?

You have created your very first Android build! See how simple that was? Since the Corona SDK already provides the `Debug` keystore and `androiddebugkey` key alias in the engine, most of the signing work is already done for you. The only requirement from you is to fill out the build information for your application and click on the **Build** button to make a debug build. Your Hello World application will save as an `.apk` file at the location you designated. The file name will appear as `Hello World.apk`.

Time for action – loading an app on your Android device

There are several ways to load your Hello World build to your Android device, and these ways do not require you to download the Android SDK. Here are some simple methods.

A convenient method is through Dropbox. You can create an account at `https://www.dropbox.com/`. Dropbox is a free service that lets you upload/download files on your PC/Mac and mobile devices. Perform the following steps to load the Hello World build using Dropbox:

1. Download the Dropbox installer and install it on your computer. Also, download the mobile app from the Google Play Store (which is also free) on your device and install it.

2. Log in to your Dropbox account on your computer and mobile device. From your computer, upload your `Hello World.apk` file.

3. Once it has finished uploading, go to the Dropbox app on your device and select your `Hello World.apk` file. You will be greeted with a screen that will ask you if you want to install the application. Select the **Install** button. Assuming that it installs correctly, another screen will appear saying **Application installed**, and you can launch your Hello World app by pressing the **Open** button that is available.

Another method to upload an `.apk` file onto your device is to transfer it to an SD card via the USB interface. If your device doesn't come with some kind of file manager application, a great one you can download from the Google Play Store is ASTRO File Manager, which can be found at `https://play.google.com/store/apps/details?id=com.metago.astro`. You can always do a normal search for the preceding app or similar apk installers through the Google Play app on your device. To transfer the `.apk` file to the SD card, perform the following steps:

1. In your device's **Settings**, select **Applications** and then select **Development**. Tap on **USB Debugging** if the mode is not active.

2. Go back a couple of screens to the **Applications** section. Enable **Unknown Sources** if it is not already active. This will allow you to install any non-market application (that is, debug builds). Select the home button on your device when done.

3. Connect the device to your computer with a USB cable. You will see a new notification that a new drive has connected to your PC or Mac. Access the SD drive and create a new folder. Name the folder to something you can identify easily for your Android builds. Drag and drop your `Hello World.apk` file from the desktop to the folder.

4. Eject the drive from your desktop and disconnect your device from the USB cable. Launch ASTRO File Manager or use whichever app you decided to download from the Google Play Store. In ASTRO, select **File Manager**, search for the folder you added to your SD card, and select it. You will see your `Hello World.apk` file. Select the file, and a prompt will appear asking you to install it. Select the **Install** button, and you should see your Hello World application appear in the **Apps** folder of your device.

One of the easiest methods is through Gmail. If you don't already have a Gmail account, create one at `https://mail.google.com/`. Perform the following steps to send the `.apk` file on your Gmail account:

1. Log in to your account, compose a new e-mail, and attach your `Hello World.apk` file to the message.

2. Address the recipient of the message to your own e-mail address and send it.

3. On your Android device, make sure you have your e-mail account linked. As soon as you receive the message, open the e-mail. You're given the option to install the application on your device. There will be an **Install** button or something similar displayed.

What just happened?

We just learned several ways of loading an `.apk` file to an Android device. The preceding methods are some of the easiest ways to load an application quickly without running into any problems.

Using the file manager method allows you to access your `.apk` files easily without requiring any carrier data or Wi-Fi connection. Using a USB cable that is compatible with your device and connecting it to your computer is a simple drag and drop procedure.

The Dropbox method is the most convenient once you have it set up on your computer and your mobile devices. All you have to do is drag and drop your `.apk` file to your account folder, and it's instantly accessible to any device with the Dropbox app installed. You can also share your files through a download link, which is also another great feature provided by Dropbox.

Setting up a Gmail account and sending your `.apk` files as an attachment to yourself is simple if you don't want to download any file managers or other programs to your device and computer. The only thing you have to remember is that you can't e-mail an attachment over the size of 25 MB in Gmail.

Pop quiz – understanding Corona

Q1. What is true about using the Corona simulator?

1. You need a `main.lua` file to launch your application.

2. The Corona SDK only runs on Mac OS X.

3. The Corona terminal doesn't launch the simulator.

4. None of the above.

Q2. How many iOS devices can you use for development in the iPhone Developer Program?

1. 50.
2. 75.
3. 5.
4. 100.

Q3. What does the version code have to be when building for Android in Corona SDK?

1. A string.
2. An integer.
3. It has to follow the Java scheme format.
4. None of the above.

Summary

In this chapter, we covered some of the necessary tools needed to start developing applications for Corona SDK. Whether you are working on a Mac OS X or Microsoft Windows, you will notice the similarities in working on both operating systems and how simple it is to run the Corona SDK.

To further familiarize yourself with Corona, try doing the following:

- Take time to look into the sample codes provided by Corona to view the capabilities of the SDK
- Feel free to alter any of the sample codes to your liking to get a better understanding of programming in Lua
- Whether you're working on iOS (if you're a registered Apple developer) or Android, try installing any of the sample codes on your device to see how the applications work outside a simulator environment
- Take a look at the Corona Labs Forums at `http://forums.coronalabs.com/` and browse through the latest discussions on Corona development by fellow Corona SDK developers and personnel

Now that you understand the process of how to display objects in Corona, we'll be able to dive into other functions that will help create an operational mobile game.

In the next chapter, we'll look at further details of the Lua programming language, and you will learn simple coding techniques that are similar to the sample code in Corona. You will get a better understanding of the Lua syntax and notice how fast and easy it is to learn compared to other programming languages. So, let's get started!

Local variables

A local variable is accessed from a local scope and usually called from a function or block of code. When we create a block, we are creating a scope in which variables can live or a list of statements, which are executed sequentially. When referencing a variable, Lua must find the variable. Localizing variables helps speed up the look-up process and improves the performance of your code. Using the local statement, it declares a local variable:

```
local i = 5 -- local variable
```

The following lines of code show how to declare a local variable in a block:

```
x = 10      -- global 'x' variable
local i = 1

while i <= 10 do
    local x = i * 2    -- a local 'x' variable for the while block
    print( x )         -- 2, 4, 6, 8, 10 ... 20
    i = i + 1
end

print( x )    -- prints 10 from global x
```

Table fields (properties)

Table fields are groups of variables uniquely accessed by an index. Arrays can be indexed with numbers and strings or any value pertaining to Lua, except nil. You index into the array to assign the values to a field using integers or strings. When the index is a string, the field is known as a property. All properties can be accessed using the dot operator (x.y) or a string (x["y"]) to index into a table. The result is the same:

```
x = { y="Monday" }    -- create table
print( x.y )    -- "Monday"
z = "Tuesday"        -- assign a new value to property "Tuesday"
print( z )    -- "Tuesday"
x.z = 20    -- create a new property
print( x.z )    -- 20
print( x["z"] )    -- 20
```

More information relating to tables will be discussed later in the section called *Tables*.

You may have noticed additional text in certain lines of code in the preceding examples. These are what you call comments. Comments begin with a double hyphen, --, anywhere except inside a string. They run until the end of the line. Block comments are available as well. A common trick to comment out a block is to surround it with --[[.

Here is an example of how to comment one line:

```
a = 2
--print(a)      -- 2
```

This is an example of a block comment:

```
--[[
k = 50
print(k)      -- 50
--]]
```

Assignment conventions

There are rules for variable names. A variable starts with a letter or an underscore. It can't contain anything other than letters, underscores, or digits. It also can't be one of the following reserved words of Lua:

- and
- break
- do
- else
- elseif
- end
- false
- for
- function
- if
- in
- local
- nil
- not
- or
- repeat
- return
- then
- true
- until
- while

The following are valid variables:

- x
- X
- ABC
- _abc
- test_01
- myGroup

The following are invalid variables:

- function
- my-variable
- 123

 Lua is also a case-sensitive language. For example, `else` is a reserved word, but Else and ELSE are two different, valid names.

Types of values

Lua is a dynamically typed language. There is no defined variable type in the language. This allows each value to carry its own type.

As you have noticed, values can be stored in variables. They can be manipulated to give a value of any type. This also allows you to pass arguments to other functions and have them returned as results.

The basic types of values that you'll deal with are as follows:

- **Nil**: This is the only type whose value is `nil`. Any uninitialized variable has `nil` as its value. Like global variables, it is `nil` by default and can be assigned `nil` to delete it.
- **Boolean**: This type has two values: `false` and `true`. You will notice that conditional expressions consider `false` and `nil` as false and anything else as `true`.
- **Numbers**: These represent real (double-precision, floating-point) numbers.
- **String**: This is a sequence of characters. 8-bit characters and embedded zeroes are allowed.

◆ **Tables**: These are data structures in Lua. They are implemented by an associative array, which is an array that can be indexed not only with numbers, but also with strings or any other value, except `nil` (more information on this later in this chapter called *Tables*).

◆ **Functions**: These are known as first-class values of Lua. Typically, functions can be stored in variables, passed as arguments to other functions, and returned as results.

Time for action – printing values using blocks

Let's give it a shot and see how powerful a language Lua is. We're starting to get an idea of how variables work and what happens when you assign values to them. What if you have a variable that has multiple values attached to it? How does Lua differentiate them? We'll use the Corona terminal so that we can see the values outputted in the terminal box. Along the way, you'll pick up other programming techniques as you progress through this section. We will also refer to chunks in this exercise. The unit of execution in Lua is called a **chunk**. A chunk is a block that is executed sequentially. Follow these steps on getting started with Lua:

If you remember, in the previous chapter, you learned how to create your own project folder and `main.lua` file for the Hello World application.

1. Create a new project folder on your desktop and name it `Variables`.

2. Open up your preferred text editor and save it as `main.lua` in your `Variables` project folder.

3. Create the following variables:

```
local x = 10 -- Local to the chunk
local i = 1  -- Local to the chunk
```

4. Add in the `while` loop:

```
while (i<=x) do
  local x = i  -- Local to the "do" body
  print(x)        -- Will print out numbers 1 through 10
  i = i + 1
end
```

5. Create an `if` statement that will represent another local body:

```
if i < 20 then
  local x            -- Local to the "then" body
  x = 20
  print(x + 5)  -- 25
else
```

```
    print(x)            -- This line will never execute since the
above "then" body is already true
    end

    print(x)   -- 10
```

6. Save your script.

7. Launch the Corona terminal. Make sure that you see the Corona SDK screen and a terminal window pop up.

8. Navigate to your `Variables` project folder and open your `main.lua` file in the simulator. You will notice that the device in the simulator is blank, but if you look at your terminal window, there are some results from the code printed out as shown here:

```
1
2
3
4
5
6
7
8
9
10
25
10
```

What just happened?

The first two variables that were created are local ones outside of each block of code. Notice that at the beginning of the `while` loop, `i <= x` refers to the variables in lines 1 and 2. The `local x = i` statement inside the `while` loop is only local to the `do` body and is not the same as `local x = 10`. The `while` loop runs 10 times and prints out a value that is incremented by one each time.

The `if` statement compares `i < 20`, where `i` equals 11 at this point and uses another `local x` variable that is local to the `then` body. Since the statement is true, `x` equals 20 and prints out the value of `x + 5`, which is `25`.

The very last line, `print(x)`, is not attached to any of the blocks of code in the `while` loop or the `if` statement. Therefore, it refers to `local x = 10` and prints out the value of 10 in the terminal window. This may seem confusing, but it's important to understand how local and global variables work in Lua.

Expressions

An **expression** is something that represents a value. It can include numeric constants, quoted strings, variable names, unary and binary operations, and function calls.

Arithmetic operators

+, -, *, /, %, and ^ are called arithmetic operators.

Here is an example of binary arithmetic operators:

```
t = 2*(2-5.5)/13+26
print(t)    -- 25.461538461538
```

An example of the modulo (division remainder) operator is as follows:

```
m = 18%4
print(m)    -- 2
```

An example of the power of operator is as follows:

```
n = 7^2
print(n)    -- 49
```

Relational operators

Relational operators always result in false or true and ask yes or no questions. The relational operators are <, >, <=, >=, ==, ~=.

The == operator tests for equality, and the ~= operator tests for inequality. If the value types are different, then the result is false. Otherwise, Lua compares the values to their types. Numbers and strings are compared in the usual way. Tables and functions are compared by reference as long as two such values are considered equal, only if they are the same object. When a new object is created, the new object is different from the previously existing one.

Here are examples of relational operators. They will display Boolean results and can't be concatenated with strings:

```
print(0 > 1)    --false
print(4 > 2)    --true
```

```
print(1 >= 1)    --true
print(1 >= 1.5)  --false
print(0 == 0)    --true
print(3 == 2)    --false
print(2 ~= 2)    -- false
print(0 ~= 2)    -- true
```

Logical operators

The logical operators in Lua are and, or, and not. All logical operators consider both false and nil as false and anything else as true.

The and operator returns its first argument if the value is false or nil; otherwise, it returns its second argument. The or operator returns its first argument if the value is different from nil and false; otherwise, it returns its second argument. Both and and or use a shortcut evaluation; this means the second operand is evaluated only when necessary. Here are some examples of logical operators:

```
print(10 and 20)       -- 20
print(nil and 1)       -- nil
print(false and 1)     -- false
print(10 or 20)        -- 10
print(false or 1)      -- 1
```

The not operator always returns true or false:

```
print(not nil)     -- true
print(not true)    -- false
print(not 2)       -- false
```

Concatenation

The string concatenation operator in Lua is denoted by two dots, "..". It takes two values as operands and splices them together. If any of its operands is a number, then it is also converted to a string. Some examples of the concatenation operator are as follows:

```
print("Hello " .. "World")    -- Hello World

myString = "Hello"
print(myString .. " World")    -- Hello World
```

The length operator

The # length operator measures the length of a string or size of a table. The length of a string is simply the number of characters in it. A character is considered one byte. Examples of the length operator are as follows:

```
print(#"*") --1
print(#"\n") --1
print(#"hello") --5
myName = "Jane Doe"
print(#myName) --8
```

Precedence

The following list shows the operator precedence in Lua displayed from the highest to the lowest priority:

- ^
- not, #, - (unary)
- *, /
- +, -
- ..
- <, >, <=, >=, ~=, ==
- and
- or

All binary operators are left associative, except for the ^ exponentiation and the .. concatenation, which are right associative. You can use parentheses to change the precedence of an expression.

In cases where two operands of the same precedence compete for operands, the operand belongs to the operator on the left-hand side:

```
print(5 + 4 - 2) -- This returns the number 7
```

The preceding expression shows both the addition and subtraction operators, which have equal precedence. The second element (the number 4) belongs to the addition operator, so the expression is evaluated mathematically as follows:

```
print((5 + 4) - 2) -- This returns the number 7
```

Let's focus on the rules of precedence based on priority. Here is an example:

```
print (7 + 3 * 9) -- This returns the number 34
```

An inexperienced programmer may think that the value of the preceding example is 90 if it were evaluated from left to right. The correct value is 34 because multiplication has a higher precedence than addition, so it is performed first. Adding parentheses to the same expression will make it easier to read:

```
print (7 + (3 * 9)) -- This returns the number 34
```

Strings

Earlier in this chapter, you saw some code examples using sequences of characters. Those sequences of characters are called **strings**. Strings may consist of any character, including numeric values.

Quoting strings

There are three ways to quote strings: with double quotes, with single quotes, and with square brackets.

 When quoting strings, make sure that only straight quotes are used in your code and not curly quotes; or else, it will not compile.

Double quote characters " mark the beginning and end of the string. Here is an example:

```
print("This is my string.")  -- This is my string.
```

You can also quote strings using the single quote character '. Single quotes work the same as double quotes, except that single-quoted strings can contain a double quote. Here is an example:

```
print('This is another string.')  -- This is another string.

print('She said, "Hello!" ')  -- She said, "Hello!"
```

Finally, using a pair of square brackets will also quote strings. They are used mainly for strings when double or single quotes cannot be used. There are not many cases where this occurs, but they will do the job:

```
print([[Is it 'this' or "that?"]]) -- Is it 'this' or "that?"
```

Time for action – getting our hands full of strings

We're starting to familiarize ourselves with several blocks of code and how they interact with each other. Let's see what happens when we add in some expressions using strings and how different they are from just regular strings that you print out in the terminal:

1. Create a new project folder on your desktop and name it `Working With Strings`.

2. Make a new `main.lua` file in your text editor and save it to your folder.

3. Type out the following lines (do not include the line numbers in the code, they are only used for line reference):

```
1 print("This is a string!") -- This is a string!
2 print("15" + 1) -- Returns the value 16
```

4. Add in the following variables. Notice that it uses the same variable name:

```
3 myVar = 28
4 print(myVar)   -- Returns 28


5 myVar = "twenty-eight"
6 print(myVar) -- Returns twenty-eight
```

5. Let's add in more variables with some string values and compare them using different operators:

```
7 Name1, Phone = "John Doe", "123-456-7890"
8 Name2 = "John Doe"

9 print(Name1, Phone)  -- John Doe   123-456-7890
10 print(Name1 == Phone)  -- false
11 print(Name1 <= Phone)  -- false
12 print(Name1 == Name2)  -- true
```

6. Save your script and launch your project in Corona. Observe the results in the terminal window:

```
This is a string!
16
28
twenty-eight
John Doe   123-456-7890
false
false
true
```

What just happened?

You can see that line 1 is just a plain string with characters printed out. In line 2, notice that number 15 is inside the string and then added to the number 1, which is outside of the string. Lua provides automatic conversions between numbers and strings at runtime. Numeric operations applied to a string will try to convert the string to a number.

When working with variables, you can use the same one and have them contain a string and a number at different times, like in lines 3 and 5 (myVar = 28 and myVar = "twenty-eight").

In the last chunk of code (lines 7-12), we compared different variable names using relational operators. First, we printed the strings of Name1 and Phone. The next lines that follow compared Name1, Name2, and Phone. When two strings have the same characters in the exact order, then they are considered the same string and are equal to each other. When you look at print(Name1 == Phone) and print(Name1 <= Phone), the statement returns false because of the ASCII order. Digits are before alphabets, which are smaller when you compare them. In print(Name1 == Name2), both variables contain the same characters, and therefore, it returns true.

Have a go hero – pulling some more strings

Strings are pretty simple to work with since they are just sequences of characters. Try making your own expressions similar to the preceding example with the following modifications:

1. Create some variables with numerical values and another set of variables with numerical string values. Use relational operators to compare the values and then print out the results.

2. Use the concatenation operator, combine several strings or numbers together, and space them out equally. Print out the result in the terminal window.

Tables

Tables are the proprietary data structure in Lua. They represent arrays, lists, sets, records, graphs, and so on. A table in Lua is similar to an associative array. Associative arrays can be indexed with values of any type, not just numbers. Tables implement all these structures efficiently. For example, arrays can be implemented by indexing tables with integers. Arrays do not have a fixed size, but grow as needed. When initializing an array, its size is defined indirectly.

Here is an example of how tables can be constructed:

```
1 a = {}      -- create a table with reference to "a"
2 b = "y"
3 a[b] = 10      -- new entry, with key="y" and value=10
4 a[20] = "Monday"  -- new entry, with key=20 and value="Monday"
5 print(a["y"])     -- 10
6 b = 20
7 print(a[b])       -- "Monday"
8 c = "hello"      -- new value assigned to "hello" property
9 print( c )     -- "hello"
```

You will notice that in line 5, a["y"] is indexing the value from line 3. In line 7, a[b] uses a new value of variable b and indexes the value of 20 to the string, "Monday". The last line, c, is separate from the previous variables, and its only value is the string, "hello".

Passing a table as an array

Keys of a table can be consecutive integers, starting at 1. They can be made into an array (or a list):

```
colors =  {
[1] = "Green",
[2] = "Blue",
[3] = "Yellow",
[4] = "Orange",
[5] = "Red"
}
print(colors[4]) -- Orange
```

Another way of writing table constructors to build arrays in a faster and more convenient way that doesn't require writing out each integer key is shown here:

```
colors = {"Green", "Blue", "Yellow", "Orange", "Red"}
print(colors[4]) -- Orange
```

Altering contents in a table

While working with tables, you can modify or remove the values already in it and also add new values to it. This can be accomplished using the assignment statement. The following example creates a table with three people and their favorite types of drink. You can make an assignment to change one person's drink, add a new person-drink pair to the table, and remove an existing person-drink pair:

```
drinks = {Jim = "orange juice", Matt = "soda", Jackie = "milk"}
drinks.Jackie = "lemonade" -- A change.
drinks.Anne = "water" -- An addition.
drinks.Jim = nil -- A removal.

print(drinks.Jackie, drinks.Anne, drinks.Matt, drinks.Jim)
-- lemonade water soda nil
```

drinks.Jackie = "lemonade" overwrites the original value of drinks.Jackie = "milk".

drinks.Anne = "water" adds a new key and value to the table. The value of drinks. Anne before this line would have been nil.

The value of drinks.Matt = "soda" stays the same since there were no alterations to it.

drinks.Jim = nil overwrites the original value of drinks.Jim = "orange juice" with nil. It removes the Jim key from the table.

Populating a table

Ways to populate a table is to start with an empty table and add things to it one at a time. We'll use constructors, which are expressions that create and initialize tables. The simplest constructor is the empty constructor, {}:

```
myNumbers = {} -- Empty table constructor

for i = 1, 5 do
  myNumbers[i] = i
end

for i = 1, 5 do
print("This is number " .. myNumbers[i])
end
```

The following are the results from the terminal:

```
--This is number 1
--This is number 2
--This is number 3
--This is number 4
--This is number 5
```

The preceding example shows that `myNumbers = {}` is an empty table constructor. A `for` loop is created and calls `myNumbers[i]` 5 times, starting from number 1. Each time it is called, it is incremented by 1 and then printed out.

Objects

Tables and functions are objects; variables do not actually contain these values, only references to them. Tables are also used in what is known as object-oriented programming. Variables and methods that manipulate those variables can be collected together into objects. Such a value is called an **object**, and its functions are called **methods**. In Corona, we'll focus more on display objects since they are essential for game development.

Display objects

Anything drawn on the screen is made by display objects. In Corona, the assets you see displayed in the simulator are instances of display objects. You have probably seen shapes, images, and text, which are all forms of display objects. When you create these objects, you'll be able to animate them, turn them into backgrounds, interact with them using touch events, and so on.

Display objects are created by calling a function known as a factory function. There is a specific kind of factory function for each type of display object. For example, `display.newCircle()` creates a vector object.

Instances of display objects behave in a manner similar to Lua tables. This enables you to add your own properties to an object as long as they do not conflict with the system-assigned properties and method names.

Display properties

The dot operator is used to access properties. Display objects share the following properties:

- `object.alpha`: This is the object's opacity. A value of 0 is transparent and 1.0 is opaque. The default value is 1.0.
- `object.height`: This is in the local coordinates.
- `object.isVisible`: This controls whether the object is visible on the screen. True is visible and false is not. The default is true.
- `object.isHitTestable` This allows an object to continue to receive hit events even if it is not visible. If true, objects will receive hit events regardless of visibility; if false, events are only sent to visible objects. It defaults to false.

- ♦ object.parent: This is a read-only property that returns the object's parent.
- ♦ object.rotation: This is the current rotation angle (in degrees). It can be a negative or positive number. The default is 0.
- ♦ object.contentBounds: This is a table with the xMin, xMax, yMin, and yMax properties in screen coordinates. It is generally used to map the object in a group to the screen coordinates.
- ♦ object.contentHeight: This is the height in screen coordinates.
- ♦ object.contentWidth: This is the width in screen coordinates.
- ♦ object.width: This is in local coordinates.
- ♦ object.x: This specifies the *x* position (in local coordinates) of the object relative to the parent—the parent's origin to be precise. It provides the *x* position of the object's reference point relative to the parent. Changing the value of this will move the object in the *x* direction.
- ♦ object.anchorX: This specifies the *x* position of the object's alignment to the parent's origin. Anchors range from 0.0 to 1.0. By default, new objects have their anchor set to 0.5.
- ♦ object.xScale: This gets or sets the *x* scaling factor. A value of 0.5 will scale the object to 50 percent in the *x* direction. The scaling occurs around the object's reference point. The default reference point for most display objects is center.
- ♦ object.y: This specifies the *y* position (in local coordinates) of the object relative to the parent—the parent's origin to be precise.
- ♦ object.anchorY: This specifies the *y* position of the object's alignment to the parent's origin. Anchors range from 0.0 to 1.0. By default, new objects have their anchor set to 0.5.
- ♦ object.yScale: This gets or sets the *y* scaling factor. A value of 0.5 will scale the object to 50 percent in the *y* direction. The scaling occurs around the object's anchor point. The default reference point for most display objects is center.

Object methods

Corona can create display objects to store object methods as properties. There are two ways this can be done: using the dot operator (" . ") or using the colon operator (" : "). Both are valid ways to create object methods.

This is an example of the dot operator:

```
object = display.newRect(110, 100, 50, 50)
object.setFillColor(1.0, 1.0, 1.0)
object.translate( object, 10, 10 )
```

This is an example of the colon operator:

```
object = display.newRect(110, 100, 50, 50)
object:setFillColor(1.0, 1.0, 1.0)
object:translate( 10, 10 )
```

The call to an object method using the dot operator is passed to the object if it's the first argument. The colon operator method is merely a shortcut with less typing involved to create the function.

Display objects share the following methods:

- `object:rotate(deltaAngle)` or `object.rotate(object, deltaAngle)`: This effectively adds `deltaAngle` (in degrees) to the current rotation property.

- `object:scale(sx, sy)` or `object.scale(object, sx, sy)`: This effectively multiplies the xScale and yScale properties using sx and sy, respectively. If the current xScale and yScale values are 0.5 and sx and sy are also 0.5, the resulting scale will be 0.25 for xScale and yScale. This scales the object from 50 percent of its original size to 25 percent.

- `object:translate(deltaX, deltaY)` or `object.translate(object, deltaX, deltaY)`: This effectively adds deltaX and deltaY to the x and y properties respectively. This will move the object from its current position.

- `object:removeSelf()` or `object.removeSelf(object)`: This removes the display object and frees its memory, assuming that there are no other references to it. This is equivalent to calling `group:remove(IndexOrChild)` on the same display object, but is syntactically simpler. The `removeSelf()` syntax is also supported in other cases, such as removing physics joints in physics.

Images

Many art assets are used in Corona applications images. You will notice that bitmap image objects are a type of display objects.

Loading an image

Using `display.newImage(filename [, baseDirectory] [, left, top])`, an image object is returned. The image data is loaded from a filename you specified for your image and looks in `system.ResourceDirectory` for that file. The acceptable types of image files that are supported are `.png` (PNG-24 or higher only) and `.jpg` files. Avoid high `.jpg` compression as it may take longer to load on a device. The `.png` files have better quality than the `.jpg` files and are used to display transparent images. The `.jpg` files do not save transparent images.

Image autoscaling

The default behavior of `display.newImage()` is to autoscale large images. This is to conserve texture memory. However, there are times when you do not want to have images autoscaled, and there is an optional Boolean flag in the parameter list to control this manually.

To override autoscaling and show the image at its full resolution, use the optional `isFullResolution` parameter. By default, it is false, but if you specify true, then the new image is loaded at its full resolution:

```
display.newImage( [parentGroup,] filename [, baseDirectory] [, x, y]
[,isFullResolution] )
```

The limitations and known issues are as follows:

- ◆ Indexed PNG image files are not supported.

- ◆ Grayscale images are currently not supported; images must be RGB.

- ◆ Images will still be autoscaled if they are larger than the maximum possible texture dimensions of the device. This is usually 2048 x 2048 px (iPad) and bigger for the newer, faster devices.

- ◆ If you reload the same image multiple times, the subsequent calls to `display.newImage` ignore the `isFullResolution` parameter and take on the value passed the first time. In other words, the way you load an image file the first time affects the autoscaling setting the next time you load that same file. This is because Corona conserves texture memory by automatically reusing a texture that has already been loaded. As a result, you can use the same images as many times as you want without consuming additional texture memory.

More information on Corona SDK's documentation is located on Corona's website at `http://coronalabs.com`.

Time for action – placing images on screen

We're finally getting into the visually appealing part of this chapter by starting to add in display objects using images. We don't have to refer to the terminal window for now. So, let's focus on the simulator screen. We'll begin by creating a background image and some art assets by performing the following steps:

1. First off, create a new project folder on your desktop and name it `Display Objects`.

2. In the `Chapter 2 Resources` folder, copy the `glassbg.png` and `moon.png` image files and the `config.lua` file into your `Display Objects` project folder.

3. Launch your text editor and create a new `main.lua` file for your current project.

4. Write out the following lines of code:

```
local centerX = display.contentCenterX
local centerY = display.contentCenterY

local background = display.newImage( "glassbg.png", centerX,
centerY, true)
local image01 = display.newImage( "moon.png", 160, 80 )

local image02 = display.newImage( "moon.png" )
image02.x = 160; image02.y = 200


image03 = display.newImage( "moon.png" )
image03.x = 160; image03.y = 320
```

The background display object should contain the filename of the background image in your project folder. For example, if the background image filename is called `glassbg.png`, then you would display the image like so:

```
local background = display.newImage( "glassbg.png", centerX,
centerY, true)
```

Using `image02.x = 160; image02.y = 200` is the same as the following lines of code:

```
image02.x = 160
image02.y = 200
```

The semicolon (`;`) indicates the end of a statement and is optional. It makes it easier to separate two or more statements in one line and saves adding extra lines in your code.

5. Save your script and launch your project in the simulator.

 If you're using Corona SDK on a Mac OS X, the default device is the iPhone. If you're using Windows, the default device is the Droid.

6. You should see a background image and three other display objects of the same image, as shown in the following screen. The display results will vary depending on which device you use to simulate.

The display objects for the `image01`, `image02`, and `image03` variables should contain the `moon.png` filename. The filenames in your code are case sensitive, so make sure that you write it exactly how it displays in your project folder.

What just happened?

Currently, `background` is scaled to fit within the device screen height and width using `contentCenterX` and `contentCenterY`. The image centered at its local origin since no top or left (*x* or *y*) coordinates were applied. It is also set to full resolution because we specified `true` in the display object.

When you observe the placement of image01, image02, and image03 in the simulator, they're practically in line with each other vertically, though the script styles for image01 versus image02/image03 are written differently. This is because the coordinates for image01 are based on the (left, top) coordinates of the display object. You can optionally specify that the image's top-left corner be located at the coordinate (left, top); if you don't supply both coordinates, the image will be centered about its local origin.

The placement of image02 and image03 are specified from the local origin of the display object and positioned by the local values of the *x* and *y* properties of the device screen. The local origin is at the center of the image; the reference point is initialized to this point. Since we didn't apply (left, top) values to image02 and image03, further access to *x* or *y* properties are referred to the center of the image.

Now, you've probably noticed that the output from the iPhone 4 looks fine and dandy, but the output from the Droid shows that the background image displays at full resolution, while the other objects are lower down the screen. We see that all the objects we specified are there, but the scaling is off. That is because each iOS and Android device has a different screen resolution. The iPhone 4 has a screen resolution of 640 x 960 pixels, and the Droid has a screen resolution of 480 x 854 pixels. What may look fine on one type of device may not look exactly the same on a different one. Don't worry; there is a simple solution to fix all this using a config.lua file that will be discussed in the next couple of sections.

Have a go hero – adjusting display object properties

Now that you know how to add images to the device screen, try testing out the other display properties. Try doing any of the following:

- Changing all the *x* and *y* coordinates of the image01, image02, and image03 display objects
- Choosing any display object and changing its rotation
- Changing the visibility of a single display object

Reference the display properties mentioned earlier in this chapter if you're unsure how to do any of the preceding adjustments.

Runtime configuration

All project files not only contain a main.lua file, but other .lua and related assets as needed for your project. Some Corona projects are configured using a config.lua file that is compiled into your project and accessed at runtime. This allows you to specify dynamic content scaling, dynamic content alignment, dynamic image resolution, frame rate control, and antialiasing, all at the same time, so that the output on every type of device is displayed similarly.

Dynamic content scaling

Corona allows you to specify the screen size you plan to aim your content for. This is done using a file called `config.lua`. You'll be able to scale the assets for your app to run on a device whose screen size is smaller or bigger.

The following values should be used to scale content:

- `width` (number): This is the screen resolution width of the original target device (in portrait orientation)

- `height` (number): This is the screen resolution height of the original target device (in portrait orientation).

- `scale` (string): This is a type of autoscaling from the following values:

    - `letterbox`: This scales up content uniformly as much as possible

    - `zoomEven`: This scales up content to uniformly to fill the screen, while keeping the aspect ratio

    - `zoomStretch`: This scales up content nonuniformly to fill the screen and will stretch it vertically or horizontally

> The `zoomStretch` value works well with Android device scaling, since many of them have different screen resolutions.

Dynamic content alignment

Content that is dynamically scaled is already centered by default. You may find cases where you don't want the content to be centered. Devices such as the iPhone 3G and the Droid have completely different screen resolutions. In order for the content displayed on the Droid to be similar to iPhone 3G, the alignment needs to be adjusted so that the content fills the entire screen without leaving any empty black screen space. The alignment is as follows:

- `xAlign`: This is a string that specifies the alignment in the *x* direction. The following values can be used:

    - `left`

    - `center` (default)

    - `right`

◆ yAlign: This is a string that specifies the alignment in the *y* direction. The following values can be used:

❑ top

❑ center (default)

❑ bottom

Dynamic image resolution

Corona allows you to swap in higher resolution versions of your images to higher resolution devices, without having to change your layout code. This is a case to consider if building for multiple devices with different screen resolutions.

An example where you want to display hi-res images is on an iPhone 4 where the resolution is 640 x 960 pixels. It is double the resolution of the earlier iOS devices, such as iPhone 3GS, which is 320 x 480 pixels. Scaling up the content from the iPhone 3GS to fit the iPhone 4 screen works, but the images will not be as crisp and will look a little fuzzy on the device.

Images of higher resolution can be swapped in for the iPhone 4 by adding a @2x suffix to the end of the filename (but before the period and file extension). For example, if your image filename is myImage.png, then your higher resolution filename should be myImage@2x.png.

In your config.lua file, a table named imageSuffix needs to be added for the image naming convention and image resolutions to take effect. The config.lua file resides in your project folder where all your other .lua files and image files are stored. Look at the following example:

```
application =
{
  content =
  {
    width = 320,
    height = 480,
    scale = "letterbox",

    imageSuffix =
    {
        ["@2x"] = 2,
    },
  },
}
```

When calling your display objects, use `display.newImageRect([parentGroup,]
filename [, baseDirectory] w, h)` instead of `display.newImage()`. The target
height and width need to be set to the dimensions of your base image.

Frame rate control

The frame rate is 30 fps (frames per second) by default. Fps refers to the speed at which
the image is refreshed in games. Thirty fps is standard in mobile games, especially for older
devices. You can set it to 60 fps when you add in the fps key. Using 60 fps makes your app
run smoother. You can easily detect a life-like fluidity in the motion when it comes to running
animations or collision detections.

Time for action – scaling display objects on multiple devices

In our `Display Objects` project, we left off displaying a background image and three
similar display objects in the simulator. When running the project on different devices, the
coordinates and resolution size were most compatible with the iPhone only. When building
applications for multiple devices across iOS and Android platforms, we can configure it
using a `config.lua` file that is compiled into the project and accessed at runtime.
So let's get to it!

1. In your text editor, create a new file and write out the following lines:

```
application =
{
  content =
  {
    width = 320,
    height = 480,
    scale = "letterbox",
    xAlign = "left",
    yAlign = "top"
  },
}
```

2. Save your script as `config.lua` in your `Display Objects` project folder.

3. For Mac users, launch your application in Corona under the iPhone device. Once
    you have done so, under the Corona Simulator menu bar, go to **Window | View As |
    iPhone 4**. You will notice that the display objects fit perfectly on the screen and that
    there are no empty black spaces showing either.

4. Windows users, launch your application in Corona under the Droid device. You will notice that all the content is scaled and aligned properly. Under the Corona Simulator menu bar, go to **Window | View As | NexusOne**. Observe the similarities in the content placement to that of the Droid. In the following screenshot, from left to right, you can see the iPhone 3GS, iPhone 4, Droid, and NexusOne:

What just happened?

You have now learned a way to implement an easy configuration to display your content across a variety of devices on iOS and Android. Content scaling features are useful for multiscreen development. If you look in the config.lua file we created, width = 320 and height = 480. This is the resolution size that the content is originally authored for. In this case, it is the iPhone 3G. Since we used scale = "letterbox", it enabled the content to uniformly scale up as much as possible while still showing the entire content on the screen.

We also set xAlign = "left" and yAlign = "top". This fills in the empty black screen space that shows on the Droid specifically. The content scaling is at the center by default, so aligning the content to the left and top of the screen will take away the additional screen space.

Dynamic resolution images

Earlier, we touched base with dynamic image resolution. The iOS devices are a perfect example for this case. Corona has the capability to use base images (for devices on the 3GS and lower) and double-resolution images (for the iPhone 4 that has a retina display), all in the same project file. Any of your double-resolution images can be swapped to your high-end iOS device without having to alter your code. This will allow your build to work with older devices and lets you handle more complex multiscreen deployment cases. You will notice that dynamic image resolution works in conjunction with dynamic content scaling.

Using the line, `display.newImageRect( [parentGroup,] filename [, baseDirectory] w, h)`, will call out your dynamic resolution images.

Here, `w` refers to the content *width* of the image and `h` refers to the content *height* of the image.

Here is an example:

```
myImage = display.newImageRect( "image.png", 128, 128 )
```

Remember that the two values represent the base image size, *not* the onscreen position of the image. You must define the base size in your code so that Corona knows how to render the higher resolution alternative images. The contents of your project folder would be set up like this:

```
My New Project/       name of your project folder
  Icon.png            required for iPhone/iPod/iPad
  Icon@2x.png         required for iPhone/iPod with Retina display
  main.lua
  config.lua
  myImage.png         Base image (Ex. Resolution 128 x 128 pixels)
  myImage@2x.png      Double resolution image (Ex. Resolution 256 x 256
  pixels)
```

When creating your double-resolution image, make sure that it is *twice* the size of the base image. It's best that you start with the double-resolution image when creating your display assets. Corona lets you select your own image-naming patterns. The @2x convention is one example that can be used, but you have the option of naming suffixes to your personal preference. For now, we'll use the @2x suffix since it distinguishes the double resolution reference. When you create your double-resolution image, name it with the @2x suffix included. Take the same image and resize it to 50 percent of the original size and then use the same filename without the @2x suffix included.

Other examples of naming suffixes can be as follows:

- @2

- -2

- -two

As mentioned earlier in the chapter, you have to define your image suffix for your double-resolution images in the `imageSuffix` table in your `config.lua` file. The content scale you set will allow Corona to determine the ratio between the current screen and base content dimensions. The following example uses the `@2x` suffix to define double-resolution images:

```
application =
{
  content =
  {
    width = 320,
    height = 480,
    scale = "letterbox",

    imageSuffix =
    {
      ["@2x"] = 2,
    },
  },
}
```

Time for some shapes

Another way of creating display objects is using vector objects. You can use vector objects to create shapes such as a rectangle, rounded rectangle, and circle using the following functions:

- `display.newRect([parentGroup,] x, y, width, height)`: This creates a rectangle using width by height. The x and y values determine coordinates for the center of the rectangle. Local origin is at the center of the rectangle, and the anchor point is initialized to this local origin.

- `display.newRoundedRect([parentGroup,] x, y, width, height, cornerRadius)`: This creates a rounded rectangle using width by height. The x and y values determine coordinates for the center of the rectangle. The local origin is at the center of the rectangle, and the anchor point is initialized to this local origin. You can round off the corners using `cornerRadius`.

- `display.newCircle([parentGroup,] xCenter, yCenter, radius)`: This creates a circle using the radius centered at xCenter, yCenter.

Applying stroke width, fill color, and stroke color

All vector objects can be outlined using strokes. You can set the stroke width, fill color, and stroke color using the following methods:

- `object.strokeWidth`: This creates the stroke width in pixels
- `object:setFillColor(red, green, blue, alpha)`: We can use the RGB codes between 0 and 1. The `alpha` parameter, which is optional, defaults to 1.0
- `object:setStrokeColor(red, green, blue, alpha)`: We can use the RGB codes between 0 and 255. The `alpha` parameter, which is optional, defaults to 1.0

Here is an example of displaying vector objects using strokes:

```
local rect = display.newRect(160, 130, 150, 150)
rect:setFillColor(1.0, 1.0, 1.0)
rect:setStrokeColor(0.1, 0.6, 0.2)
rect.strokeWidth = 5
```

You will get on output on the simulator similar to the one shown in the following image:

Text, text, text

In *Chapter 1, Getting Started with Corona SDK*, we created the Hello World application using a text display object. Let's go in detail on how text is implemented onscreen:

- The `display.newText( [parentGroup,] text, x, y, font, fontSize)` method creates a text object using the `x` and `y` values. There is no text color by default. In the `font` parameter, apply any of the font names in the library. The `fontSize` parameter displays the size of the text.

- Some of the following default constants can be used if you don't want to apply a font name:

  - `native.systemFont`

  - `native.systemFontBold`

Applying color and string value

The size, color, and text fields can be set or retrieved in text display objects:

- `object.size`: This is the size of the text.

- `object:setFillColor(red, green, blue, alpha)`: We can use the RGB codes between 0 and 1. The `alpha` parameter, which is optional, defaults to 1.0.

- `object.text`: This contains the text of the text object. It allows you to update a string value for a test object.

What are functions?

Functions can carry out a procedure or compute and return values. We can make a function call as a statement, or we can use it as an expression. You can also use object methods as functions. You have learned that functions can be variables. A table can use these variables to store them as properties.

Functions are the most important means of abstraction in Lua. One function that we have used many times is `print`. In the following example, the `print` function is being told to execute one piece of data—the `"My favorite number is 8"` string:

```
print("My favorite number is 8") -- My favorite number is 8
```

Another way of saying this is that `print` is being called with one argument. The `print` function is only one of the many built-in functions that Lua has, but almost any program you write will involve you defining your own functions.

Defining a function

When trying to define a function, you have to give it a name that you can call out to when you want to return a value. You then have to create a statement or statement block of what the value will output and then apply end to your function after you have finished defining it. Here is an example:

```
function myName()
   print("My name is Jane.")
end


myName()   -- My name is Jane.
```

Notice that the function name is myName, and it is used to call out what's inside the print("My name is Jane.") function definition.

An extension on defining a function is as follows:

```
function myName(Name)
   print("My name is " .. Name .. ".")
end

myName("Jane")    -- My name is Jane.
myName("Cory")    -- My name is Cory.
myName("Diane")   -- My name is Diane.
```

The new myName function has one argument using the Name variable. The "My name is " string is concatenated with Name and then a period as the printed result. When the function is called, we used three different names as an argument, and the result is printed with a new customized name for each line.

More display functions

In Corona, you can change the appearance of the status bar on your device. This is a one-line setting in your code that takes effect once you launch your application. You can change the appearance of your status bar using the display.setStatusBar(mode) method. This hides or changes the appearance of the status bar on iOS devices (iPad, iPhone, and iPod Touch) and Android 2.x devices. Android 3.x devices are not supported.

The argument mode should be one of the following:

◆ display.HiddenStatusBar:To hide the status bar, you can use the following line at the beginning of your code:

```
display.setStatusBar(display.HiddenStatusBar)
```

In the following screenshot, you can see that the status bar is hidden:

- `display.DefaultStatusBar`: To show the default status bar, you can use the following line at the beginning of your code:

```
display.setStatusBar(display.DefaultStatusBar)
```

The code will display the default status bar, as shown in the following screenshot:

- `display.TranslucentStatusBar`: To show the translucent status bar, you can use the following line at the beginning of your code:

```
display.setStatusBar(display.TranslucentStatusBar)
```

The translucent status bar will look like the one shown in the following screenshot:

- `display.DarkStatusBar`: To show the dark status bar, you can use the following line at the beginning of your code:

```
display.setStatusBar(display.DarkStatusBar)
```

The following screenshot is of the dark status bar:

Content size properties

When you want to obtain the display information on your device, you can use the content size properties to return the values. These properties are as follows:

- `display.contentWidth`: This returns the original width of the content in pixels. This will default to the screen width.

- ◆ `display.contentHeight`: This returns the original height of the content in pixels. This will default to the screen height.

- ◆ `display.viewableContentWidth`: This is a read-only property that contains the width of the viewable screen area in pixels, within the coordinate system of the original content. Accessing this property will display how the content is viewed, whether you're in the portrait or landscape mode. Here is an example:

  ```
  print(display.viewableContentWidth)
  ```

- ◆ `display.viewableContentHeight`: This is a read-only property that contains the height of the viewable screen area in pixels, within the coordinate system of the original content. Accessing this property will display how the content is viewed, whether you're in the portrait or landscape mode. Here is an example:

  ```
  print(display.viewableContentHeight)
  ```

- ◆ `display.statusBarHeight`: This is a read-only property that represents the height of the status bar in pixels (only valid on iOS devices). Here is an example:

  ```
  print(display.statusBarHeight)
  ```

Optimize your workflow

So far, we have touched on the vital basics of programming in Lua and the terminology used in Corona SDK. Once you start developing interactive applications to sell in the App Store or Android market, you need to be aware of your design choices and how they affect the performance of your application. This means taking into consideration how much memory your mobile device is using to process the application. Here are some things to look for if you're just starting out with Corona SDK.

Use memory efficiently

In some of our earlier examples, we used global variables in our code. Cases like those are an exception since the examples did not contain a high volume of functions, loops to call out to, or display objects. Once you start building a game that is heavily involved with function calls and numerous display objects, the local variables will increase performance within your application and be placed on the stack so that Lua can interface them faster.

The following code will cause memory leaks:

```
-- myImage is a global variable
myImage = display.newImage( "image.png" )
myImage.x = 160;  myImage.y = 240

-- A touch listener to remove object
```

```
local removeBody = function( event )
  local t = event.target
  local phase = event.phase

  if "began" == phase then
    -- variable "myImage" still exists even if it's not displayed
    t:removeSelf() -- Destroy object
  end

  -- Stop further propagation of touch event
  return true
end

myImage:addEventListener( "touch", removeBody )
```

The preceding code removes myImage from the display hierarchy once it is touched. The only problem is that the memory used by myImage leaks because the myImage variable still refers to it. Since myImage is a global variable, the display object it references will not be freed even though myImage does not display on the screen.

Unlike global variables, localizing variables helps speed up the look-up process for your display object. It also only exists within the block or chunk of code that it's defined in. Using a local variable in the following code will remove the object completely and free memory:

```
-- myImage is a local variable
local myImage = display.newImage( "image.png" )
myImage.x = 160;  myImage.y = 240

-- A touch listener to remove object
local removeBody = function( event )
  local t = event.target
  local phase = event.phase

  if "began" == phase then
    t:removeSelf() -- Destroy object
    t = nil
  end

  -- Stop further propagation of touch event
  return true
end

myImage:addEventListener( "touch", removeBody )
```

Optimize your display images

It's important to optimize your image file size as much as you can. Using full-screen images can impact the performance of your application. They require more time to load on a device and consume a lot of texture memory. When a lot of memory is consumed in an application, in most cases it'll be forced to quit.

The iOS devices vary in the size of their available memory, depending on which one you have out of the following:

- iPhone 3GS, iPad, and iTouch 3G/4G of 256 MB RAM

- iPhone 4/4S, iPad 2, iPad Mini, and iTouch 5G of 512 MB RAM

- iPhone 5/5S/6, 6 Plus, iPad 3G, and iPad 4G of 1 GB RAM

For example, texture memory on the iPhone 3GS should be kept under 25 MB before performance issues start occurring by slowing down your app or even forcing it to quit. An iPad 2 would have no problem going farther down that boundary since it has more memory available.

 Refer to `http://docs.coronalabs.com/api/event/memoryWarning/index.html` to apply memory warnings for iOS devices.

For Android devices, there is around a 24 MB memory limit. So, it's important to be aware of how many display objects you have in your scene and how to manage them when they are not needed in your app any more.

In cases when you no longer need an image to be displayed on screen, use the following code:

```
image.parent:remove( image ) -- remove image from hierarchy
```

Alternatively, you can also use this line of code:

```
image:removeSelf( ) -- same as above
```

If you want to remove an image from the scene completely throughout the lifetime of your app, include the following line after your `image.parent:remove( image )` or `image:removeSelf()` code:

```
image = nil
```

Keeping memory usage low within your application will prevent crashes and improve performance. For more information on optimization, go to `http://developer.coronalabs.com/content/performance-and-optimization`.

Pop quiz – basics of Lua

Q1. Which of the following are values?

1. Numbers
2. nil
3. Strings
4. All of the above

Q2. Which relational operator is false?

1. `print(0 == 0)`
2. `print(3 >= 2)`
3. `print(2 ~= 2)`
4. `print(0 ~= 2)`

Q3. What is the correct way to scale an object in the *x* direction?

1. `object.scaleX`
2. `object.xscale`
3. `object.Xscale`
4. `object.xScale`

Summary

This chapter discussed parts of Lua programming that will send you on your way to start creating your own apps in Corona. As you continue working with Lua, you'll start understanding the terminology better. Eventually, you'll find new programming solutions that will benefit your development process.

Some skills you learned so far include the following:

- Creating variables and assigning values to them
- Establishing expressions using operators
- Using the Corona terminal to output or print results
- Using tables to structure lists, arrays, sets, and so on
- Adding display objects in the simulator
- Configuring your application build to work on different mobile devices
- Implementing dynamic resolution images
- Creating functions to run a block of code

This section was definitely a lot to take in. There is still a lot of information on Lua that we didn't get to touch base on, but you have learned enough to get you started. For more information on programming in Lua, you can refer to `http://www.lua.org/pil/index.html` or the resources section on the Corona website at `http://www.coronalabs.com/resources/`.

In the next chapter, we'll start making our very first game called Breakout! You will get some hands-on experience creating a game framework in Corona and applying all the necessary assets to develop a mobile game. You'll be surprised how fast and simple it is to create one.

3
Building Our
First Game – Breakout

So far, we have gone through some important basics of programming in Lua and applied some code to run in the Corona simulator. Knowing the terminology is a small part of learning how to create an application. We'll need to take a step further and get some hands-on experience of what it's like to structure a project from start to finish. We're going to accomplish this by creating our first game from scratch. This will push you further to understand larger chunks of code and apply some game logic to create a functional game.

By the end of this chapter, you will understand:

- How to structure game files in a Corona project
- How to create variables for the game
- How to add game objects to the screen
- How to create an alert message
- How to display the score and level number

Let the fun begin!

Breakout – bringing back old-school gaming

You have probably seen many forms of the game Breakout in the past couple of decades, especially during the Atari days. To give you a good idea of what the game is about, here is a brief editorial by Big Fish Games about the history of Breakout: `http://www.bigfishgames.com/blog/the-history-of-breakout/`. The following screenshot is an example of Breakout:

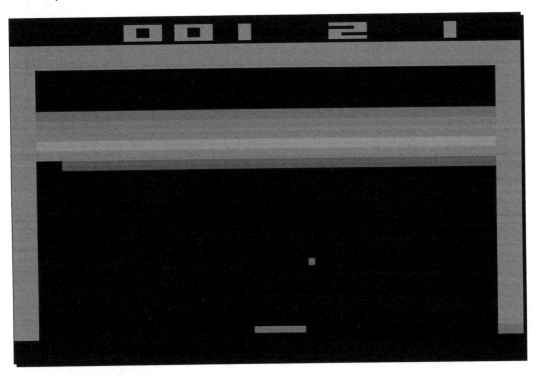

On the game screen, there are several columns and rows of bricks placed near the top of the screen. A ball travels across the screen, bouncing off the top and side walls of the screen. When a brick is hit, the ball bounces away and the brick is destroyed. The player loses the round when the ball touches the bottom of the screen. To prevent this from happening, the player has a movable paddle to bounce the ball upward, keeping it in play.

We're going to create a clone using touch events and the accelerometer for the paddle movement that will be controlled by the player. We'll be adding some physics to the ball so that it can bounce around the screen.

In the next chapter, we'll be adding the movement of the game objects, collision detection, score keeping, and win/lose conditions. Right now, we're going to focus on how to set up the game template of Breakout.

Understanding the Corona physics API

Corona has made it convenient to add physics to your games, especially if you've never worked on one before. The engine uses Box2D and takes only a few lines to incorporate it into your application than what it normally takes to have it set up.

Working with the physics engine in Corona is fairly easy. You use display objects and set them as a physical body in your code. Images, sprites, and vector shapes can be turned into a physical object. This is substantial in visualizing how you want your objects to react in an environment you have created. You can see results right away rather than guessing about how they might act in the physical world.

Setting up the physics world

Making the physics engine available in your app requires the following line:

```
local physics = require "physics"
```

Starting, pausing, and stopping the physics engine

There are three main functions that affect the physics simulation. The following will start, pause, and stop the physics engine:

- `physics.start()`: This will start or resume the physical environment. It is usually activated at the beginning of the application for physics bodies to take effect.
- `physics.pause()`: This stops the physics engine temporarily.
- `physics.stop()`: This basically destroys the physical world altogether.

physics.setGravity

This function sets the x and y parameters of the global gravity vector in units of meters per second square (acceleration units). The default is (0, 9.8) to simulate standard earth gravity, pointing downwards on the y axis. The syntax is `physics.setGravity(gx, gy)`:

```
physics.setGravity( 0, 9.8 ): Standard Earth gravity
```

physics.getGravity

This function returns the x and y parameters of the global gravity vector in units of meter per second square (acceleration units).

The syntax is `gx, gy = physics.getGravity()`.

Tilt-based gravity

When you have `physics.setGravity(gx, gy)` and the accelerometer API applied, implementing tilt-based dynamic gravity is simple. The following is an example of creating the tilt-based function:

```
function movePaddle(event)

   paddle.x = display.contentCenterX - (display.contentCenterX *
(event.yGravity*3))

end

Runtime:addEventListener( "accelerometer", movePaddle )
```

The accelerometer is not present in the Corona simulator; a device build must be created to see the effect.

physics.setScale

This function sets the internal pixels-per-meter ratio used to convert between the onscreen Corona coordinates and simulated physics coordinates. This should be done before any of the physical objects are instantiated.

The default scaling value is 30. For devices of higher resolution, such as iPad, Android, or iPhone 4, you might wish to increase this value to 60 or more.

The syntax is `physics.setScale(value)`:

```
physics.setScale( 60 )
```

physics.setDrawMode

There are three rendering modes for the physics engine. This can be altered at any time.

The syntax is `physics.setDrawMode(mode)`. The three rendering modes are:

- `physics.setDrawMode("debug")`: This mode shows collision engine outlines only, as you can see in the following screenshot:

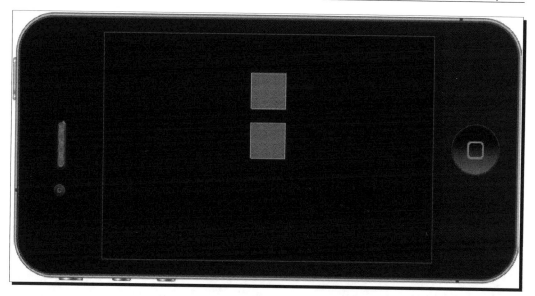

- `physics.setDrawMode("hybrid")`: This mode overlays collision outlines on normal Corona objects, as you can see in the following screenshot:

◆ `physics.setDrawMode("normal")`: This mode is the default Corona renderer with no collision outlines:

The physics data is displayed using color-coded vector graphics, which reflect different object types and attributes:

◆ **Orange**: This is used to denote dynamic physics bodies (the default body type)

◆ **Dark blue**: This is used to denote kinematic physics bodies

◆ **Green**: This is used to denote static physics bodies such as the ground or walls

◆ **Gray**: This is used to denote a body that is in a *sleeping* state due to lack of activity

◆ **Light blue**: This is used to denote joints

physics.setPositionIterations

This function sets the accuracy of the engine's position calculations. The default value is 8, meaning that the engine will iterate through eight position approximations per frame for every object, but will increase processor engagement, so it should be handled carefully, because it might slow down the application.

The syntax is `physics.setPositionIterations(value)`:

```
physics.setPositionIterations(16)
```

physics.setVelocityIterations

This function sets the accuracy of the engine's velocity calculations. The default value is 3, meaning that the engine will iterate through three velocity approximations per frame for every object. However, this will increase processor engagement, so it should be handled carefully because it might slow down the application.

The syntax is `physics.setVelocityIterations( value )`:

```
physics.setVelocityIterations( 6 )
```

Configuring the application

This tutorial is compatible for both iOS and Android devices. The graphics have been designed to accommodate the varying screen dimensions of both platforms.

Build configuration

By default, all items displayed on all device screens are shown in the portrait mode. We'll be creating this game specifically in the landscape mode, so we'll have to alter some build settings and configure how all the items on the screen will be displayed. Playing the game in the landscape mode will actually add more player interactivity since the paddle will have more screen space to move about and less airtime for the ball.

Time for action – adding the build.settings file

The build-time properties can be provided in an optional `build.settings` file, which uses the Lua syntax. The `build.settings` file is used to set the application orientation and autorotation behavior along with a variety of platform-specific build parameters. To add the `build.settings` file in your project folder, perform the following steps:

1. Create a new project folder called `Breakout` on your desktop.
2. In your preferred text editor, create a new file called `build.settings` and save it in your project folder.
3. Type in the following lines:

    ```
    settings =
    {
      orientation =
      {
        default = "landscapeRight",
        supported = { "landscapeLeft", "landscapeRight" },
      }
    }
    ```

4. Save and close the file. The `build.settings` file is completed.

What just happened?

The default orientation setting determines the initial launch orientation on the device and the initial orientation of the Corona simulator.

The default orientation doesn't affect Android devices. The orientation is initialized to the actual orientation of the device (unless only one orientation is specified). Also, the only supported orientations are `landscapeRight` and `portrait`. On a device, you can flip to either `landscapeRight` or `landscapeLeft`, but the operating system only reports one flavor of landscape, and Corona's orientation event chooses `landscapeRight`.

We have created this application to work with landscape orientations that support `landscapeRight`. We have set this orientation as its default so it won't switch to `landscapeLeft` or even any `portrait` mode. While working on an iOS device, if the `build.settings` isn't set before launching the application, it will go to the default portrait mode.

Dynamic scaling

Corona can target builds made for multiple devices across iOS and Android, which display various art assets in different resolutions. Corona can scale upward or downward depending on your starting resolution. It can also substitute higher-resolution image files when needed, ensuring that your app appears clear and sharp on all devices.

Time for action – adding the config.lua file

If no content size is specified, the content width and height returned will be the same as the physical screen width and height of the device. If you specify a different content width and height in `config.lua`, the content width and height will take on those values. To add the config.lua file in your project folder, perform the following steps:

1. In your text editor, create a new file called `config.lua` and save it to your project folder.

2. Type in the following lines:

    ```
    application =
    {
      content =
      {
        width = 320,
        height = 480,
        scale = "letterbox",
        fps = 60,
      },
    }
    ```

3. Save and close your file.

What just happened?

The content width and height allow you to choose a virtual screen size that is independent of the physical device screen size. We have set the size to target the iPhone 3GS since it displays one of the common dimensions across most devices for both iOS and Android platforms.

The scale used for this application is set to `letterbox`. It will uniformly scale up content as much as possible while still displaying all content on the screen.

We set `fps` to `60`. By default, the frame rate is 30 fps. In this application, this will make the movement of the ball appear faster and allow us to increase the speed conveniently. We can stretch the frame rate to 60 fps, which is the maximum that Corona can allow.

Building the application

Now that we have configured our application to the landscape mode and set the display contents to scale on multiple devices, we're ready to start designing the game. Before we start writing some code for the game, we need to add in some art assets that will be displayed on the screen. You can find them in the `Chapter 3 Resources` folder. You can download the project files that accompany this book from the Packt Publishing website. The following are the files that you'll need to add to your `Breakout` project folder:

- `alertBox.png`
- `bg.png`
- `mmScreen.png`
- `ball.png`
- `paddle.png`
- `brick.png`
- `playbtn.png`

Displaying groups

An important function that we'll be introducing in this game is `display.newGroup()`. Display groups allow you to add and remove child display objects and collect the related display objects. Initially, there are no children in a group. The local origin is at the parent object's origin; the anchor point is initialized to this local origin. You can easily organize your display objects in separate groups and refer to them by their group name. For example, in Breakout, we'll combine menu items such as the **Title** screen and **Play** button in a group called `menuScreenGroup`. Every time we access `menuScreenGroup`, any display object contained within the display group will be processed.

display.newGroup()

This function creates a group in which you can add and remove child display objects.

The syntax is `display.newGroup()`.

For example:

```
local rect = display.newRect(0, 0, 150, 150)
rect:setFillColor(1, 1, 1)

local myGroup = display.newGroup()
myGroup:insert(rect)
```

Working with system functions

The system functions that we're going to introduce in this chapter will return information about the system (device information and current orientation) and control system functions (enabling multi-touch and controlling the idle time, accelerometer, and GPS). We'll be using the following system functions to return the environment information that our application will be running in and the response frequency for the accelerometer events.

system.getInfo()

This function returns information about the system on which the application is running.

The syntax is `system.getInfo(param)`:

```
print(system.getInfo("name")) -- display the deviceID
```

Valid values for parameters are as follows:

- ◆ `"name"`: This returns the model name of the device. For example, on the iTouch, this would be the name of the phone as it appears in iTunes, such as "Pat's iTouch".
- ◆ `"model"`: This returns the device type. These include:
    - ❑ iPhone
    - ❑ iPad
    - ❑ iPhone Simulator
    - ❑ Nexus One
    - ❑ Droid
    - ❑ myTouch
    - ❑ Galaxy Tab

- ◆ "deviceID": This returns a hash-encoded device ID of the device.
- ◆ "environment": This returns the environment that the app is running on. These include:
    - ❏ "simulator": The Corona simulator
    - ❏ "device": iOS, Android device, and the Xcode simulator
- ◆ "platformName": This returns the platform name (the OS name), which can be any one of the following:
    - ❏ Mac OS X (Corona simulator on Mac)
    - ❏ Win (Corona simulator on Windows)
    - ❏ iPhone OS (all iOS devices)
    - ❏ Android (all Android devices)
- ◆ "platformVersion": This returns a string representation of the platform version.
- ◆ "build": This returns the Corona build string.
- ◆ "textureMemoryUsed": This returns the texture memory usage in bytes.
- ◆ "maxTextureSize": This returns the maximum texture width or height supported by the device.
- ◆ "architectureInfo": This returns a string that describes the underlying CPU architecture of the device you are running on.

system.setAccelerometerInterval()

This function sets the frequency of accelerometer events. On the iPhone, the minimum frequency is 10 Hz and the maximum is 100 Hz. Accelerometer events are a significant drain on battery, so only increase the frequency when you need faster responses, as in games. Always try to lower the frequency whenever possible to conserve battery life.

The syntax is system.setAccelerometerInterval(frequency):

```
system.setAccelerometerInterval( 75 )
```

The function sets the sample interval in Hertz. Hertz is cycles per second, that is, the number of measurements to take per second. If you set the frequency to 75, then the system will take 75 measurements per second.

After you have the assets from the Chapter 3 Resources folder added in your project folder, we will begin writing some code!

Time for action – creating variables for the game

For any application to start, we'll need to create a `main.lua` file. This has been discussed in *Chapter 2, Lua Crash Course and the Corona Framework*, when we worked with some sample code and ran it with the simulator.

The code will be structured accordingly in your `main.lua` file by the time the game is completed:

- Necessary classes (for example, `physics` or `ui`)
- Variables and constants
- Main function
- Object methods
- Call main function (this has to be called always, or your application will not run)

Arranging your code to make it look like the preceding structure is a good practice on keeping things organized and running your application efficiently.

In this section, we'll be introducing the display group that will show the main menu screen and a **Play** button that the user will be able to interact with in order to move on to the main game screen. All in-game elements such as the paddle, ball, brick objects, and heads-up display elements follow after the player interacts with the **Play** button. We'll also be introducing win and lose conditions that will be referred as `alertDisplayGroup`. All these game elements will be initialized in the beginning of our code.

1. Create a new `main.lua` file in your text editor and save it to your project folder.

2. We're going to hide the status bar (specifically for iOS devices) and load the physics engine. Corona uses the Box2D engine that is already built into the SDK:

```
display.setStatusBar(display.HiddenStatusBar)

local physics = require "physics"
physics.start()
physics.setGravity(0, 0)

system.setAccelerometerInterval(100)
```

> More information on the Corona Physics API can be found on the Corona website at `http://docs.coronalabs.com/guide/physics/physicsSetup/index.html`.
>
> The Box2D physics engine used in Corona SDK was written by Erin Catto of Blizzard Entertainment. More information on Box2D can be found at `http://box2d.org/manual.pdf`.

3. Add in the menu screen objects:

```
local menuScreenGroup  -- display.newGroup()
local mmScreen
local playBtn
```

4. Add in the in-game screen objects:

```
local background
local paddle
local brick
local ball
```

5. Add in HUD elements for the score and level:

```
local scoreText
local scoreNum
local levelText
local levelNum
```

 The HUD is also known as the heads-up display. It is a method of visually representing character information on the game screen.

6. Next, we'll add in the alert display group for the win/lose conditions:

```
local alertDisplayGroup   -- display.newGroup()
local alertBox
local conditionDisplay
local messageText
```

7. The following variables hold the values for the bricks display group, score, ball velocity, and in-game events:

```
local _W = display.contentWidth / 2
local _H = display.contentHeight / 2
local bricks = display.newGroup()
local brickWidth = 35
local brickHeight = 15
local row
local column
local score = 0
local scoreIncrease = 100
local currentLevel
local vx = 3
local vy = -3
local gameEvent = ""
```

8. Accelerometer events can only be tested on a device, so we're going to add a variable for touch events on the paddle by calling the `"simulator"` environment. This is so that we can test the paddle movement in the Corona simulator. If you were to test the application on a device, the event listeners for touch and accelerometer on the paddle won't conflict:

```
local isSimulator = "simulator" ==
system.getInfo("environment")
```

9. Lastly, add in the `main()` function. This will start our application:

```
function main()

end

--[[
This empty space will hold other functions and methods to run
the application
]]--


main()
```

What just happened?

The `display.setStatusBar(display.HiddenStatusBar)` method is only applicable for iOS devices. It hides the appearance of the status bar on the device.

The new Corona API that we added to this game is the physics engine. We'll be adding physics parameters to the main game objects (paddle, ball, and bricks) for collision detection. Having `setGravity(0,0)` will allow the ball to bounce around the playing field freely.

The `local menuScreenGroup`, `local alertDisplayGroup`, and `local bricks` objects are all forms of display groups that we can separate and organize our display objects in. For example, `local menuScreenGroup` is designated for objects that show up on the main menu screen. Hence, they can be removed as a group and not as individual objects.

Some of the variables added already have values that are applied to certain game objects. There is already a set velocity for the ball using `local vx = 3` and `local vy = -3`. The x and y velocities determine how the ball moves on the game screen. Depending on the position the ball collides with an object, the ball will follow a continuous path. The `brickWidth` and `brickHeight` objects have a value that will stay constant throughout the application, so we can line the brick objects evenly onscreen.

`local gameEvent = " "` will store the game events such as `"win"`, `"lose"`, and `"finished"`. When a function checks the game status for any of these events, it will display the proper condition on screen.

We have added some system functions as well. We created `local isSimulator = "simulator" == system.getInfo("environment")` so that it returns information about the system on which the application is running. This will be directed for the paddle touch events so that we can test the application in the simulator. If the build were to be ported on a device, you would only be able to use the accelerometer to move the paddle. The simulator can't test accelerometer events. The other system function is `system.setAccelerometerInterval( 100 )`. It sets the frequency of the accelerometer events. The minimum frequency on an iPhone is 10 Hz and the maximum is 100 Hz.

The `main()` empty function set will start out the display hierarchy. Think of it as a storyboard. The first thing you see is an introduction, and then some action happens in the middle that tells you about the main content. In this case, the main content is the game play. The last thing you see is some kind of ending or closure to tie the story together. The ending is the display of the win/lose conditions at the end of a level.

Understanding events and listeners

Events are sent to listeners that are executed by a touch on the mobile screen, tap, accelerometer, and so on. Functions or objects can be event listeners. When an event occurs, the listener is called by a table that represents the event. All events will have a property name that identifies the kind of event.

Register events

Display objects and global runtime objects can be event listeners. You can add and remove listeners for events using the following object methods:

◆ `object:addEventListener()`: This adds a listener to the object's list of listeners. When the named event occurs, the listener will be invoked and supplied with a table that represents the event.

◆ `object:removeEventListener()`: This removes the specified listener from the object's list of listeners so that it is no longer notified of events that correspond to the specified event.

In the following example, an image display object registers to receive a touch event. Touch events are not broadcast globally. Display objects that register for the event and lie underneath it will be candidates to receive the event:

```
local playBtn = display.newImage("playbtn.png")
playBtn.name = "playbutton"

local function listener(event)
   if event.target.name == "playbutton" then

      print("The button was touched.")

   end
end

playBtn:addEventListener("touch", listener )
```

Runtime events are sent by the system. They broadcast to all listeners. The following is an example of registering for an enterFrame event:

```
local playBtn = display.newImage("playbtn.png")

local function listener(event)
   print("The button appeared.")
end

Runtime:addEventListener("enterFrame", listener )
```

Runtime events

The application that we're creating uses runtime events. Runtime events have no specific target and are only sent to the global runtime. They broadcast to all registered listeners.

Runtime events are sent by the system. They broadcast to all listeners. The following is an example of registering for an enterFrame event:

```
local playBtn = display.newImage("playbtn.png")

local function listener(event)
   print("The button appeared.")
end

Runtime:addEventListener("enterFrame", listener )
```

The following events all have string names and will be applied to the Breakout game.

enterFrame

The `enterFrame` events occur at the frame interval of the application. They are only sent to the global runtime object. For example, if the frame rate is 30 fps, then it will occur approximately 30 times per second.

The following properties are available in this event:

♦ `event.name` is the string `"enterFrame"`

♦ `event.time` is the time in milliseconds since the start of the application

Accelerometer

Accelerometer events let you detect movements and determine the device's orientation in relation to gravity. These events are only sent to devices that support accelerometer. They are only sent to the global runtime object.

The following properties are available for this event:

♦ `event.name` is the string `"accelerometer"`

♦ `event.xGravity` is the acceleration due to gravity in the x direction

♦ `event.yGravity` is the acceleration due to gravity in the y direction

♦ `event.zGravity` is the acceleration due to gravity in the z direction

♦ `event.xInstant` is the instantaneous acceleration in the x direction

♦ `event.yInstant` is the instantaneous acceleration in the y direction

♦ `event.zInstant` is the instantaneous acceleration in the z direction

♦ `event.isShake` is true when the user shakes the device

Touch events

When the user's finger touches the screen, a hit event is generated and dispatched to display objects in the display hierarchy. Only those objects that intersect with the location of the finger on the screen will potentially receive the event.

Touch (single touch)

Touch events are a special kind of hit event. When a user's finger touches the screen, they are starting a sequence of touch events, each with different phases.

♦ `event.name` is the string `"touch"`

♦ `event.x` is the x position in the screen coordinates of the touch

♦ `event.y` is the y position in the screen coordinates of the touch

- `event.xStart` is the *x* position of the touch from the `"began"` phase of the touch sequence

- `event.yStart` is the *y* position of the touch from the `"began"` phase of the touch sequence

- `event.phase` is a string that identifies where in the touch sequence the event occurred:

  - `"began"`: This indicates that a finger touched the screen

  - `"moved"`: This indicates that a finger moved on the screen

  - `"ended"`: This indicates that a finger was lifted from the screen

  - `"cancelled"`: This indicates that the system canceled tracking of the touch

tap

It generates a hit event when the user touches the screen. The event is dispatched to display objects in the display hierarchy. This is similar to the touch event, except that a hit count (number of taps) is available in the event callback and doesn't use event phases. The event APIs are as follows:

- `event.name` is the string `"tap"`

- `event.numTaps` returns the number of taps on the screen

- `event.x` is the *x* position in the screen coordinates of the tap

- `event.y` is the *y* position in the screen coordinates of the tap

Transitions

In this chapter, we'll be touching base with `transition.to()` and `transition.from()`:

- `transition.to()`: This animates a display object's properties over time using the easing transitions.

  The syntax is `handle = transition.to( target, params )`.

- `transition.from()`: This is similar to `transition.to()` except that the starting property values are specified in the function's parameter table, and the final values are the corresponding property values in the target prior to the call. The syntax is `handle = transition.from( target, params )`.

The parameters used are as follows:

- `target`: This is a display object that will be the target of the transition.

- `params`: This is a table that specifies the properties of the display object, which will be animated, and one or more of the following optional non-animated properties:

  - `params.time`: This specifies the duration of the transition in milliseconds. By default, the duration is 500 ms (0.5 seconds).

  - `params.transition`: This is by default `easing.linear`.

  - `params.delay`: This specifies the delay in milliseconds (none by default) before the tween begins.

  - `params.delta`: This is a Boolean that specifies whether non-control parameters are interpreted as final ending values or as changes in value. The default is `nil`, meaning false.

  - `params.onStart`: This is a function or table listener that is called before the tween begins.

  - `params.onComplete`: This is a function or a table listener that is called after the tween completes.

For example:

```
_W = display.contentWidth
_H = display.contentHeight

local square = display.newRect( 0, 0, 100, 100 )
square:setFillColor( 1, 1, 1 )
square.x = _W/2; square.y = _H/2

local square2 = display.newRect( 0, 0, 50, 50 )
square2:setFillColor( 1, 1, 1 )
square2.x = _W/2; square2.y = _H/2

transition.to( square, { time=1500, x=250, y=400 } )
transition.from( square2, { time=1500, x=275, y=0 } )
```

The preceding example shows how two display objects transition throughout the space on a device screen. From its current position, the `square` display object will move to a new location of $x = 250$ and $y = 400$ in 1500 milliseconds. The `square2` display object will transition from $x = 275$ and $y = 0$ to its initial location in 1500 milliseconds.

Creating menu screens

Having menu screens allows the player to transition through different parts of your application. Typically, a game will start out with some kind of screen that displays the game title with an interactive user interface button labeled **Play** or **Start** to give the player the option to play the game. It is standard in any mobile application to have a menu screen before transitioning to the main content.

Time for action – adding the main menu screen

The main menu screen will be the first thing in our menu system that the player interacts with after the application is launched. It's a great way to introduce the title of the game and also give the player an idea of what type of gaming environment they should expect. We wouldn't want the player to jump abruptly into the app without any proper notification. It's important to allow the player to prepare for what is to come when they launch the app.

1. We're going to create a function called `mainMenu()` to introduce the title screen. So after `function main()` ends, add in the following lines:

```
function mainMenu()

end
```

2. We'll be adding in a display group and two display objects to this function. One display object is the image that will represent the main menu screen, and the other will be a UI button called **Play**. Add them inside `function mainMenu()`:

```
menuScreenGroup = display.newGroup()

mmScreen = display.newImage("mmScreen.png", 0, 0, true)
mmScreen.x = _W
mmScreen.y = _H

playBtn = display.newImage("playbtn.png")
playBtn.anchorX = 0.5; playBtn.anchorY = 0.5
playBtn.x = _W; playBtn.y = _H + 50
playBtn.name = "playbutton"

menuScreenGroup:insert(mmScreen)
menuScreenGroup:insert(playBtn)
```

3. Remember the empty `main()` function set? We need to call `mainMenu()` inside it. The entire function should look like this:

```
function main()
   mainMenu()
end
```

4. After the `mainMenu()` function, we're going to create another function called `loadGame()`. This function will initiate the event from `playbtn` to transition to the main game screen. The event will change the alpha of `menuScreenGroup` to 0, which makes it invisible on the screen. Complete the transition by calling the `addGameScreen()` function (`addGameScreen()` will be discussed later in the *Time for action – adding game objects* section of this chapter):

```
function loadGame(event)
   if event.target.name == "playbutton" then

      transition.to(menuScreenGroup,{time = 0, alpha=0,
      onComplete = addGameScreen})

      playBtn:removeEventListener("tap", loadGame)
   end
end
```

5. Next, we need to add in an event listener to `playBtn`, so when it is tapped, it will call the `loadGame()` function. Add the following line in the `mainMenu()` function after the last method:

```
playBtn:addEventListener("tap", loadGame)
```

6. Run the project in the simulator. You should see the main menu screen display **Breakout** and the **Play** button.

What just happened?

Creating a main menu screen only requires a couple of blocks of code. For `loadGame(event)`, we passed a parameter called `event`. When the `if` statement is called, it takes `playbutton`, which references to the display object `playBtn`, and checks to see whether it is true. Since it is, the `menuScreenGroup` will be removed from the stage and called in the `addGameScreen()` function. At the same time, the event listener for `playBtn` is removed from the scene.

Have a go hero – creating a help screen

Right now, the design of the menu system is set up so that from the main menu screen it transitions to the game play screen. You have the option to extend the menu screens without jumping into the game right away. Something additional that can be added is a help menu screen after the main menu screen, which explains to the players how to play the game.

Create a new image in your preferred image editing program and write out the steps for how to play the game. You can then create a new button called **Next** and add both art assets to your project folder. In your code, you'll have to create a new function and event listener for your **Next** button, which will transition to the game play screen.

Creating the game play scene

Now that we have a menu system in place, we can start on the game play elements of the application. We'll start adding all of the main game objects that the player will interact with. One thing to note when adding in game objects is their placement on the screen. Given that this game will be played in the landscape mode, we have to remember that there is plenty of space available in the *x* direction and a smaller amount in the *y* direction. Based on the original design of the game, the bottom wall of the screen causes the player to lose the level or turn if the ball lands in that area. So if we were to pinpoint an area to place the paddle object, we wouldn't set it near the top of the screen. It makes more sense for the paddle to be as close to the bottom of the screen to protect the ball better.

Time for action – adding game objects

Let's add in the display objects the player will see while in game play:

1. After the `loadGame()` function, we're going to create another function that will display all our game objects on screen. The following lines will display the art assets that were created for this tutorial:

    ```
    function addGameScreen()

      background = display.newImage("bg.png", 0, 0, true )
      background.x = _W
      background.y = _H

      paddle = display.newImage("paddle.png")
      paddle.x = 240; paddle.y = 300
      paddle.name = "paddle"

      ball = display.newImage("ball.png")
      ball.x = 240; ball.y = 290
      ball.name = "ball"
    ```

2. Next, we'll add in the text that will display the score and level number during the game:

    ```
    scoreText = display.newText("Score:", 25, 10, "Arial", 14)
    scoreText:setFillColor( 1, 1, 1 )

    scoreNum = display.newText("0", 54, 10, "Arial", 14)
    scoreNum: setFillColor( 1, 1, 1 )
    ```

```
levelText = display.newText("Level:", 440, 10, "Arial", 14)
levelText:setFillColor( 1, 1, 1 )

levelNum = display.newText("1", 470, 10, "Arial", 14)
levelNum:setFillColor( 1, 1, 1 )
```

3. To build the first game level, we're going to call the `gameLevel1()` function, which will be explained later in this chapter. Don't forget to close the `addGameScreen()` function with `end`:

```
gameLevel1()

end
```

What just happened?

The `addGameScreen()` function displays all the game objects shown during game play. We have added the `background`, `paddle`, and `ball` display objects from the art assets provided for this chapter.

We have added text for the score and level at the top of the game screen. `scoreNum` is initially set to `0`. In the next chapter, we'll discuss how to update the score number when a brick collision is made. `levelNum` starts at 1, updates when the level is completed, and moves on to the next one.

We ended the function by calling `gameLevel1()`, which will be implemented in the next section to start the first level.

Time for action – building bricks

The bricks are the last of the game objects we need to add in for this application. We'll be creating two different levels for this game. Each one will have a different brick layout from the other:

1. We're going to create the function for the first level. Let's create a new function, `gameLevel1()`. We will also set `currentLevel` to 1 since the application begins at level 1. Then, we'll add in the `bricks` display group and set it as `toFront()` so that it appears in front of the game background:

```
function gameLevel1()

    currentLevel = 1

    bricks:toFront()
```

The method `object:toFront()` moves the target object to the visual front of its parent group (`object.parent`). In this case, we are setting the `bricks` group to appear as the front-most display group during game play so that it appears in front of the background image.

2. Next, add some local variables that will show how many rows and columns of bricks will be displayed on screen and where each brick will be placed in the playing field:

```
local numOfRows = 4
local numOfColumns = 4
local brickPlacement = {x = (_W) - (brickWidth * numOfColumns
) / 2  + 20, y = 50}
```

3. Create double `for` loops, one for `numOfRows` and the other for `numOfColumns`. Create a brick instance placed according to its width, height, and the number corresponding to `numOfRows` and `numOfColumns`. The art asset for the brick display object is provided with this chapter. Then, close the function with `end`:

```
for row = 0, numOfRows - 1 do
   for column = 0, numOfColumns - 1 do

      local brick = display.newImage("brick.png")
      brick.name = "brick"
      brick.x = brickPlacement.x + (column * brickWidth)
      brick.y = brickPlacement.y + (row * brickHeight)
      physics.addBody(brick, "static", {density = 1, friction =
      0, bounce = 0})
      bricks.insert(bricks, brick)

   end
  end
end
```

4. The setup for level 2 is similar to how level 1 is arranged. The code is almost the same, except that our new function is called `gameLevel2()`, `currentLevel` is set to 2, and the values for `numOfRows` and `numOfColumns` have different values. Add the following block after the `gameLevel1()` function:

```
function gameLevel2()

   currentLevel = 2

   bricks:toFront()

   local numOfRows = 5
   local numOfColumns = 8
   local brickPlacement = {x = (_W) - (brickWidth * numOfColumns )
 / 2  + 20, y = 50}

   for row = 0, numOfRows - 1 do
```

```
for column = 0, numOfColumns - 1 do

    -- Create a brick
    local brick = display.newImage("brick.png")
    brick.name = "brick"
    brick.x = brickPlacement.x + (column * brickWidth)
    brick.y = brickPlacement.y + (row * brickHeight)
    physics.addBody(brick, "static", {density = 1, friction =
    0, bounce = 0})
    bricks.insert(bricks, brick)

  end
 end
end
```

5. Save your file and relaunch the simulator. You'll be able to interact with the **Play** button and see the transition from the main menu screen to the game screen. You will see the game layout for level 1 displayed on screen.

What just happened?

The `bricks` display group is set as `bricks:toFront()`. This means that the group will always be put in front of the display hierarchy, apart from the `background`, `paddle`, and `ball` display objects.

The `gameLevel1()` method has set values for the amount of brick objects displayed in the playing field. They will be centered based on `contentWidth` of the device shell and set at `50` in the y direction. The brick group is placed near the top left-hand corner by `brickPlacement`, takes the middle of the screen, and subtracts it by half the width of all the brick objects put together. Then, we add 20 more pixels in the x direction to center it with the paddle.

We created double `for` loops for `numOfRows` and `numOfColumns`, which start the creation of the brick objects from the left-hand corner of the screen.

Notice that the `brick` display object is given the name `brick`. Just remember that `brick` cannot be used the same way as `brick` when calling the object. The `brick` object is an instance of `brick`. It is merely used as a string when event parameters are called, for example:

```
if event.other.name == "brick" and ball.x + ball.width * 0.5 <
event.other.x + event.other.width * 0.5 then
      vx = -vx
elseif event.other.name == "brick" and ball.x + ball.width * 0.5 >=
event.other.x + event.other.width * 0.5 then
      vx = vx
end
```

The physics body of brick is set to "static", so it is not affected by gravity pulling down. Then, it is added to the bricks group under bricks.insert(bricks, brick).

Have a go hero – focused platform gaming

On completing this chapter and the next one, feel free to redesign the display images to focus on a specific platform. For example, you can easily convert the code to be compatible for all iOS devices. This can be done by converting display objects to display. newImageRect([parentGroup,] filename [, baseDirectory] w, h), so you can substitute image dimensions on devices with larger screen sizes (such as iPhone 5/ Samsung Galaxy S5). Remember that you'll have to adjust your configuration settings to have the changes applied. This pertains to adding a unique image suffix (or your preferred suffix naming convention) to your config.lua file.

Red alert!

In every game, there is some kind of message that tells you the status of your progress when the main action has ended. For this application, we need a way to let the player know if they have won or lost a round, how they can play again, or when the game is officially completed.

Time for action – displaying game messages

Let's set up some win/lose notifications so that we can display these events that occur in game:

1. Create a new function called alertScreen() and pass two parameters called title and message. Add in a new display object called alertbox and have it transition from xScale and yScale of 0.5 using easing.outExpo:

   ```
   function alertScreen(title, message)

       alertBox = display.newImage("alertBox.png")
       alertBox.x = 240; alertBox.y = 160

       transition.from(alertBox, {time = 500, xScale = 0.5, yScale =
       0.5, transition = easing.outExpo})
   ```

2. Store the title parameter in the text object called conditionDisplay:

   ```
   conditionDisplay = display.newText(title, 0, 0, "Arial", 38)
   conditionDisplay:setFillColor( 1, 1, 1 )
   conditionDisplay.xScale = 0.5
   conditionDisplay.yScale = 0.5
   conditionDisplay.anchorX = 0.5
   conditionDisplay.x =  display.contentCenterX
   conditionDisplay.y = display.contentCenterY - 15
   ```

3. Store the `message` parameter in the text object called `messageText`:

```
messageText = display.newText(message, 0, 0, "Arial", 24)
messageText:setFillColor( 1, 1, 1 )
messageText.xScale = 0.5
messageText.yScale = 0.5
messageText.anchorX = 0.5
messageText.x = display.contentCenterX
messageText.y = display.contentCenterY + 15
```

4. Create a new display group called `alertDisplayGroup` and insert all the objects into the group. Close the function:

```
alertDisplayGroup = display.newGroup()
alertDisplayGroup:insert(alertBox)
alertDisplayGroup:insert(conditionDisplay)
alertDisplayGroup:insert(messageText)
end
```

5. Save your file and run the project in the simulator. The functionality of the **Play** button still goes to the game play screen for **Level: 1**. Currently, none of the objects have any movement. We'll be adding touch events, ball movement, and collisions in the next chapter. All the game objects should be laid out as shown in the following screenshot:

What just happened?

We have set up the alert system for the game, but it is not operable at the moment until we add in more game functions to set the game objects in motion. The next chapter will demonstrate how the `alertScreen()` function passes two parameters, `title` and `message`. An `alertBox` display object is added as a background to the alert texts when they pop up after a condition occurs. When the `alertBox` pops up, it transitions from 0.5 of `xScale` and `yScale` to full image scale in 500 milliseconds. This is basically the equivalent of half a second.

The `conditionDisplay` object passes the `title` parameter. This will be the text that displays **You Win** or **You Lose**.

The `messageText` object passes the `message` parameter. The text with this parameter displays a message such as **Play Again** or **Continue** after a condition is reached.

All the objects in this function are then inserted into `alertDisplayGroup = display.newGroup()`. They will act as one group instead of individual objects when they appear on and off the stage.

When running the code in the simulator, if errors pop up in your terminal window, be sure to check the line(s) that caused the errors. Sometimes, a simple capitalization error or even a comma or quotation mark that is missing can keep your app from running in the simulator. Make sure you're aware of those common mistakes. They can be easily overlooked.

You can refer to the `Breakout - Part 1` folder in the `Chapter 3` folder to see how the first half of the code for this tutorial is set up.

Pop quiz – building a game

Q1. When adding the physics engine in your code, which functions are valid to add to your application?

1. `physics.start()`
2. `physics.pause()`
3. `physics.stop()`
4. None of the above

Q2. Which is correct when adding an event listener?

1. `button:addeventlistener("touch", listener)`
2. `button:AddEventListener("touch", listener)`
3. `button:addEventListener(touch, listener)`
4. `button:addEventListener("touch", listener)`

Q3. What is the correct way to make the following display object transition to $x = 300$, $y = 150$, and have the alpha changed to 0.5, in 2 seconds?

```
local square = display.newRect( 0, 0, 50, 50 )
square:setFillColor( 1, 1, 1 )
square.x = 100 square2.y = 300
```

1. `transition.to( square, { time=2000, x=300, y=150, alpha=0.5 })`

2. `transition.from( square, { time=2000, x=300, y=150, alpha=0.5 })`

3. `transition.to( square, { time=2, x=300, y=150, alpha=0.5 })`

4. None of the above

Summary

We have completed the first half of this game tutorial. Understanding how to structure a Corona project properly makes it easier to keep your code organized and tracks your assets better. We have got a taste of working with blocks of code that pertain to a small part of the game logic needed to allow the application to run.

So far we have:

- Specified the build configuration on displaying the content for Android and iOS devices
- Introduced the main variables and constants that will run in the application
- Instantiated the physics engine and started to apply it to the game objects that require physical bodies
- Created transitions from menus to game play screens
- Added display objects and game messages to the screen

It's quite an accomplishment of how much we've done so far, including learning a new API in the process of coding the application. We still have a lot more to add before the game can be fully functional.

In the next chapter, we'll be finishing the second half of this game tutorial. We'll be working with collision detection of the paddle, ball, brick, and wall objects. Also, we'll learn how to update the score when a brick is removed from the scene and get our win/lose conditions active as well. We're in the home stretch. Let's keep going!

4
Game Controls

So far, we have completed the first half of our game in the previous chapter. We started by developing the initial structure for the project by introducing the game objects to the screen. Currently, the paddle and ball movement is inactive, but everything displayed in the simulator is scaled according to the original game design. The last phase of completing this tutorial is to add in all the actions that will occur in the game, including object movement and updating the score.

In this chapter, we will cover the following topics:

◆ Moving the paddle using touch events and accelerometer

◆ Collision detection between all game objects in the scene

◆ Removing objects upon collision detection

◆ Ball movement within the screen boundaries

◆ Calculating the score

◆ Win and lose conditions

Home stretch! We can do it!

Moving in the up direction

If making objects appear on screen is exciting to you, wait till you see them move! The main object of Breakout is to keep the ball above the paddle position to stay in play and have it collide with all the bricks to complete the level. What keeps the suspense going is the anticipation of the ball movement around the game screen. This wouldn't be possible without adding physical boundaries on the game objects to react to collision detection.

Let's get even more physical

In the previous chapter, we talked about how to integrate the physics engine into your code. We also started implementing physical bodies to the brick objects, and now, we'll need to do the same with other active game objects, such as the paddle and ball. Let's continue with this last half of the tutorial. We will continue using our `main.lua` file from the `Breakout` project folder.

physics.addBody()

Corona display objects can be turned into simulated physical objects using one line of code. The following information explains the different forms of physics bodies:

- If no shape information is specified, the display object takes on the form of the actual rectangular boundary of the original image to create the physics body. For example, if a display object is 100 x 100 pixels, then this would be the actual size of the physics body.

- If a shape is specified, then the body boundaries will follow the polygon provided by the shape. The shape coordinates must be defined in a clockwise order, and the resulting shape must be convex only.

- If a radius is specified, then the body boundaries will be circular, centered at the middle of the display object used to create the physics body.

A body shape is a table of local (x,y) coordinates relative to the center of the display object.

The syntaxes for the body shapes are as follows:

- Circular shapes:

```
physics.addBody(object, [bodyType,] {density=d, friction=f,
bounce=b [,radius=r]})
```

- Polygon shapes:

```
physics.addBody(object, [bodyType,] {density=d, friction=f,
bounce=b [,shape=s]})
```

The following are the examples of the body shapes:

◆ Circular bodies:

```
local ball = display.newImage("ball.png")
physics.addBody( ball, "dynamic" { density = 1.0, friction =
0.3, bounce = 0.2, radius = 25 } )
```

◆ Polygon bodies:

```
local rectangle = display.newImage("rectangle.png")
rectangleShape = { -6,-48, 6,-48, 6,48, -6,48 }
physics.addBody( rectangle, { density=2.0, friction=0.5,
bounce=0.2, shape=rectangleShape } )
```

Now, we will discuss the parameters of the preceding methods:

◆ Object: This is a display object.

◆ bodyType: This is a string that specifies that the body type is optional. It uses a string parameter before the first body element. The possible types are "static", "dynamic", and "kinematic". The default type is "dynamic" if no value is specified. Let's talk about these types:

   ❏ Static bodies don't move unless manually moved in code, and they don't interact with each other; examples of static objects would include the ground or the walls of a pinball machine.

   ❏ Dynamic bodies are affected by gravity and collisions with the other body types.

   ❏ Kinematic objects are affected by forces but not by gravity, so you should generally set draggable objects to kinematic, at least for the duration of the drag event.

◆ Density: This is a number that is multiplied by the area of the body's shape to determine mass. It is based on a standard value of 1.0 for water. Lighter materials (such as wood) have a density below 1.0, and heavier materials (such as stone) have a density greater than 1.0. The default value is 1.0.

◆ Friction: This is a number. This may be any non-negative value; a value of 0 means no friction, and 1.0 means fairly strong friction. The default value is 0.3.

◆ Bounce: This is a number that determines the object's velocity that is returned after a collision. The default value is 0.2.

◆ Radius: This is a number. This is the radius of the bounding circle in pixels.

- ◆ Shape: This is a number. It is the shape value in the form of a table of the shape vertices, that is, {x1, y1, x2, y2, ..., xn, yn}, for example, `rectangleShape = { -6,-48, 6,-48, 6,48, -6,48 }`. The coordinates must be defined in a clockwise order, and the resulting shape must be convex only. Physics assumes that the (0,0) point of an object is the center of the object. A *-x* coordinate will be to the left of object's center and *-y* coordinate will be at the top of object's center.

Time for action – starting physics for the paddle and ball

Right now, our display objects are rather stagnant. In order for the game play to initiate, we have to activate physics for collision detection to occur between the paddle and ball. Perform the following steps:

1. Above the `gameLevel1()` function, create a new function called `startGame()`:

   ```
   function startGame()
   ```

2. Add in the following lines to instantiate the physics for the paddle and ball:

   ```
   physics.addBody(paddle, "static", {density = 1, friction = 0,
   bounce = 0})
   physics.addBody(ball, "dynamic", {density = 1, friction = 0,
   bounce = 0})
   ```

3. Create an event listener that uses the background display object to remove the `"tap"` event for `startGame()`. Close the function with `end`:

   ```
   background:removeEventListener("tap", startGame)
   end
   ```

4. In the `addGameScreen()` function that we created in the previous chapter, we have to add the following line after the call to the `gameLevel1()` function. This starts the actual game when the background is touched:

   ```
   background:addEventListener("tap", startGame)
   ```

What just happened?

The paddle object has a `"static"` body type, so it is not affected by any collision that occurs against it.

The ball object has a `"dynamic"` body type because we want it to be affected by the collisions on the screen due to directional changes caused by the wall borders, bricks, and paddle.

The event listener on the background is removed from the `startGame()` function; this way, it doesn't affect any of the other touch events that are applied in the game.

Paddle movement

Getting the paddle to move side to side is one of the key actions that needs to be accomplished. Part of the game design is to prevent the ball from reaching the bottom of the screen. We will be separating the paddle movement in the simulator and the accelerometer. The movement in the simulator enables us to test with touch events since accelerometer actions cannot be tested in the simulator.

Time for action – dragging the paddle in the simulator

Right now, the paddle does not move at all. There are no coordinates set that will allow the paddle to move side to side on the screen. So let's create them by performing the following steps:

1. Underneath the `addGameScreen()` function, create a new function called `dragPaddle(event)`:

   ```
   function dragPaddle(event)
   ```

2. Next, we'll focus on moving the paddle side to side within the boundary of the game screen. Add in the following block of code to enable paddle movement in the simulator and then close the function. The reason for adding this block is because the simulator does not support accelerometer events:

   ```
   if isSimulator then

     if event.phase == "began" then
       moveX = event.x - paddle.x
     elseif event.phase == "moved" then
       paddle.x = event.x - moveX
     end

     if((paddle.x - paddle.width * 0.5) < 0) then
       paddle.x = paddle.width * 0.5
     elseif((paddle.x + paddle.width * 0.5) >
     display.contentWidth) then
       paddle.x = display.contentWidth - paddle.width * 0.5
     end

   end

   end
   ```

See the following image of the ball colliding with the bricks and the paddle and anticipate where the ball will move towards next:

What just happened?

We have created a function where the drag event only works in the simulator. For `if event.phase == "began"`, a touch event has been made to the paddle. On `elseif event.phase == "moved"`, a touch event where the paddle moved from its original position has been made.

In order to keep the paddle from moving past the wall boundaries, `paddle.x` does not go less than `0` in the *x* direction when it hits the coordinate. When the paddle slides to the right-hand side of the screen, `paddle.x` does not go greater than `display.contentWidth` in the *x* direction.

There is no designated coordinate for the right-hand side of the screen since the code is supposed to be universal for all screen sizes on iOS and Android devices. Both platforms have varying screen resolutions, so `display.contentWidth` takes this into account.

Time for action – moving the paddle with the accelerometer

As mentioned earlier, accelerometer events cannot be tested in the simulator. They only work when a game build is uploaded to a device to see the results. The paddle movement will stay within the wall borders of the level across the *x* axis. To move the paddle, follow the steps:

1. Below the `dragPaddle()` function, create a new function called `movePaddle(event)`:

    ```
    function movePaddle(event)
    ```

2. Add in the accelerometer movement using `yGravity`. It provides acceleration due to gravity in the *y* direction:

    ```
    paddle.x = display.contentCenterX - (display.contentCenterX *
    (event.yGravity*3))
    ```

3. Add in the wall borders for the level and close the function:

    ```
    if((paddle.x - paddle.width * 0.5) < 0) then
       paddle.x = paddle.width * 0.5
    elseif((paddle.x + paddle.width * 0.5) >
    display.contentWidth) then
       paddle.x = display.contentWidth - paddle.width * 0.5
    end
    end
    ```

What just happened?

To make the accelerometer movement work with a device, we have to use `yGravity`.

 Accelerometer events are based on portrait scale when `xGravity` and `yGravity` are used accordingly. When display objects are designated for the landscape mode, the `xGravity` and `yGravity` values are switched to compensate for the events to work properly.

We have applied the same code for the paddle from `function dragPaddle()`:

```
if((paddle.x - paddle.width * 0.5) < 0) then
   paddle.x = paddle.width * 0.5
elseif((paddle.x + paddle.width * 0.5) > display.contentWidth) then
   paddle.x = display.contentWidth - paddle.width * 0.5
end
```

This still keeps the paddle from going past any wall boundaries.

Ball collision with the paddle

The motion of the ball has to flow in a fluid manner every time it collides with the paddle. This means proper direction changes on all sides of the game field.

Time for action – making the ball bounce against the paddle

We will check which side of the paddle the ball has hit to choose the side where it will move next. It's important to have the motion to follow through any directional hits as it would in a realistic environment. With every paddle collision, we want to make sure that the ball goes in the up direction. For this, follow these steps:

1. Create a new function called `bounce()` for the ball after the `movePaddle()` function:

   ```
   function bounce()
   ```

2. Add in a value of `-3` for velocity in the *y* direction. This will make the ball move in an upward motion:

   ```
   vy = -3
   ```

3. Check when a collision is made with the `paddle` and `ball` objects and close the function:

   ```
   if((ball.x + ball.width * 0.5) < paddle.x) then
      vx = -vx
   elseif((ball.x + ball.width * 0.5) >= paddle.x) then
      vx = vx
   end
   end
   ```

What just happened?

When the ball collides with the paddle, the motion follows through, depending on what side of the paddle is touched by the ball. In the first part of the `if` statement, the ball travels toward 0 in the *x* direction. The last part of the `if` statement shows the ball travelling toward the opposite side of the screen in the *x* direction.

Removing objects from the scene

There are limited resources on a device. As much as we wish they were as powerful as a desktop to hold so much memory, it's not at that point yet. This is why it is important to remove display objects from the display hierarchy when you no longer use them in your application. This helps overall system performance by reducing memory consumption and eliminates unnecessary drawing.

When a display object is created, it is added by default to the root object of the display hierarchy. This object is a special kind of group object known as the **stage** object.

In order to keep an object from rendering on screen, it needs to be removed from the scene. The object needs to be removed explicitly from its parent. This removes the object from the display hierarchy. This can be done in either in the following way:

```
myImage.parent:remove( myImage ) -- remove myImage from hierarchy
```

Alternatively, this can be done using the following line of code:

```
myImage:removeSelf( ) -- same as above
```

This does not free all the memory from the display object. To make sure that the display object is removed properly, we need to eliminate all the variable references to it.

Variable references

Even though a display object has been removed from the hierarchy, there are situations in which the object continues to exist. To do this, we will set the property to `nil`:

```
local ball = display.newImage("ball.png")
local myTimer = 3

function time()
  myTimer = myTimer - 1
  print(myTimer)

  if myTimer == 0 then

    ball:removeSelf()
    ball = nil

  end
end

timer.performWithDelay( 1000, time, myTimer )
```

Brick by brick

The bricks in the game are the main obstacles, since they have to be cleared in order to move on to the next round. In this version of Breakout, the player must destroy all the bricks in one turn. Failure to do so results in starting over from the beginning of the current level.

Time for action – removing the bricks

When the ball collides with a brick, we will use the same technique applied to the paddle to determine the path the ball will follow. When a brick is hit, we'll need to figure out which brick has been touched and then remove it from both the stage and the bricks group. Each brick removal will increment 100 points to the score. The score will be taken from the `score` constant and added to the current score as text. To remove the bricks from the game, follow these steps:

1. Below the `gameLevel2()` function, create a function called `removeBrick(event)`:

```
function removeBrick(event)
```

2. Check which side of the brick the ball hits by using the `if` statement. When checking for an event, we'll refer the event to the object name, `"brick"`. This is the name we gave our `brick` display object:

```
if event.other.name == "brick" and ball.x + ball.width * 0.5
< event.other.x + event.other.width * 0.5 then
    vx = -vx
elseif event.other.name == "brick" and ball.x + ball.width *
0.5 >= event.other.x + event.other.width * 0.5 then
    vx = vx
end
```

3. Add in the following `if` statement to remove the brick from the scene when the ball collides with one. After a collision has been made, increase `score` by 1. Initiate `scoreNum` to take the value of the score and multiply it by `scoreIncrease`:

```
if event.other.name == "brick" then
    vy = vy * -1
    event.other:removeSelf()
    event.other = nil
    bricks.numChildren = bricks.numChildren - 1

    score = score + 1
    scoreNum.text = score * scoreIncrease
    scoreNum.anchorX = 0
    scoreNum.x = 54
end
```

4. When all the bricks in the level are destroyed, create an `if` statement that pops up the alert screen for a win condition and set the `gameEvent` string to `"win"`;

```
if bricks.numChildren < 0 then
    alertScreen("YOU WIN!", "Continue")
    gameEvent = "win"
end
```

5. Close the function with `end`:

```
end
```

The following is a screenshot of the ball colliding with the paddle:

What just happened?

If you remember from the previous chapter, we gave the `brick` objects a name called "brick".

When the ball hits the left-hand side of any of the individual bricks, it travels towards the left. When the ball hits the right-hand side of the bricks, it travels toward the right. The width of each object is taken as a whole to calculate the direction in which the ball travels.

When a brick is hit, the ball bounces upward (the *y* direction). After every collision the ball makes with a brick, the brick is removed from the scene and destroyed from the memory.

The `bricks.numChildren - 1` statement subtracts the count from the total number of bricks it started out with originally. When a brick is removed, the score increments 100 points each time. The `scoreNum` text object updates the score every time a brick is hit.

When all the bricks are gone, the alert screen pops up with a notification that the player has won the level. We also set `gameEvent` equal to `"win"`, which will be used in another function that will transition the event to a new scene.

Directional changes

Apart from the ball motion against the paddle, the other factor is the collision state against the wall borders. When a collision occurs, the ball diverts its direction in the opposite way. For every action, there is a reaction, just like real-world physics.

Time for action – updating the ball

The ball needs to move in a continuous motion without gravity affecting it. We'll have to take into account the side walls and the top and bottom walls. The velocity in the *x* and *y* direction have to reflect the other way when a collision happens on any of the boundaries. We need to set coordinates so that the ball is only allowed to move through and alert when it passes through the area below the paddle region. Let's perform the following steps:

1. Create a new function called `function updateBall()` below the `removeBrick(event)` function:

    ```
    function updateBall()
    ```

2. Add in the ball movement:

    ```
    ball.x = ball.x + vx
    ball.y = ball.y + vy
    ```

3. Add in the ball movement for the *x* direction:

    ```
    if ball.x < 0 or ball.x + ball.width > display.contentWidth
    then
      vx = -vx
    end
    ```

    The following screenshot shows the movement of ball in the *x* direction:

4. Add in the ball movement for the *y* direction:

```
if ball.y < 0 then
    vy = -vy
end
```

The following screenshot shows the movement of the ball in the *y* direction:

5. Add in the ball movement when it collides with the bottom of the game play screen. Create the lost alert screen and a game event for `"lose"`. Close the function with `end`:

```
if ball.y + ball.height > paddle.y + paddle.height then
    alertScreen("YOU LOSE!", "Play Again") gameEvent = "lose"
end
end
```

The following screenshot shows the lost alert screen when the ball collides with the bottom of the game play screen:

What just happened?

Everywhere the ball travels, proper direction change is needed when it hits the wall. Any time the ball hits the side walls, we used vx = -vx. When the ball hits the top boundary, vy = -vy is used. The only time the ball doesn't reflect the opposite direction is when it hits the bottom of the screen.

The alert screen displays the lose condition, which emphasizes to the player to play again. The gameEvent = "lose" statement will be used in another if statement to reset the current level.

Transitioning levels

When a win or lose condition occurs, the game needs a way to transition to the next level or repeat the current one. The main game objects have to be reset to their starting position and the bricks redrawn. It's pretty much the same idea as when you first start a game.

Time for action – resetting and changing levels

We'll need to create functions that set up the first and second levels in the game. If a level needs to be replayed, only the current level the user lost in can be accessed. Follow these steps to transition between the levels:

1. Create a new function called `changeLevel1()`. This will be placed below the `updateBall()` function:

    ```
    function changeLevel1()
    ```

2. Clear the `bricks` group when the player loses the round, and then reset them:

    ```
    bricks:removeSelf()

    bricks.numChildren = 0
    bricks = display.newGroup()
    ```

3. Remove `alertDisplayGroup`:

    ```
    alertBox:removeEventListener("tap", restart)
    alertDisplayGroup:removeSelf()
    alertDisplayGroup = nil
    ```

4. Reset the `ball` and `paddle` positions:

    ```
    ball.x = (display.contentWidth * 0.5) - (ball.width * 0.5)
    ball.y = (paddle.y - paddle.height) - (ball.height * 0.5) -2

    paddle.x = display.contentWidth * 0.5
    ```

5. Redraw the bricks for the current level:

    ```
    gameLevel1()
    ```

6. Add an event listener to the `background` object for `startGame()`. Close the function:

    ```
    background:addEventListener("tap", startGame)
    end
    ```

7. Next, create a new function called `changeLevel2()`. Apply the same code used for `changeLevel1()`, but make sure that the bricks are redrawn for `gameLevel2()`:

```
function changeLevel2()

    bricks:removeSelf()

    bricks.numChildren = 0
    bricks = display.newGroup()

    alertBox:removeEventListener("tap", restart)
    alertDisplayGroup:removeSelf()
    alertDisplayGroup = nil


    ball.x = (display.contentWidth * 0.5) - (ball.width * 0.5)
    ball.y = (paddle.y - paddle.height) - (ball.height * 0.5) -2

    paddle.x = display.contentWidth * 0.5

    gameLevel2() -- Redraw bricks for level 2

    background:addEventListener("tap", startGame)
end
```

What just happened?

When a level needs to be reset or changed, the display objects have to be wiped from the screen. In this case, we removed the `bricks` group using `bricks:removeSelf()`.

When any alert screen pops up, whether win or lose, the entire `alertDisplayGroup` is removed during the reset as well. The `ball` and `paddle` objects are set back to their starting position.

The `gameLevel1()` function is called to redraw the bricks for level 1. The function holds the initial setup for the `brick` display objects and `bricks` group.

The `background` object is used again to call the `startGame()` function with an event listener. When level 2 needs to be set up, the same procedure like in function `changeLevel1()` is used, but `changeLevel2()` and `gameLevel2()` are called to redraw the bricks.

Have a go hero –add more levels

Right now, the game only has two levels. What can be done to extend this game is to add more levels. They can be created using the same logic used for `gameLevel1()` and `gameLevel2()`, by adjusting the numbers used to create rows and columns of bricks. You'll have to create a new function that resets the level. We can use the same method followed for `changeLevel1()` and `changeLevel2()` to recreate a level and reset it.

You win some, you lose some

Nothing is more exhilarating than the anticipation of winning. That is until you make that one small mistake, and it causes you to start over. Don't worry; it's not the end of the world; you can always try again and learn from your errors to beat the level.

Game events such as a win or lose condition will alert the player of their progress. The game has to have some way of guiding the player about what action they need to take next to replay the level or move on to the next one.

Time for action –making win and lose conditions

For any game alerts to even appear during game play, we need to create some `if` statements for every possible scenario available in each level. When this occurs, the score needs to be reset back to zero. To make the win and lose conditions, follow these steps:

1. Below the `alertScreen()` function, create a new function called `restart()`:

   ```
   function restart()
   ```

2. Create an `if` statement for a `"win"` game event when the first level has been completed and transitions to level 2:

   ```
   if gameEvent == "win" and currentLevel == 1 then
       currentLevel = currentLevel + 1
       changeLevel2()
       levelNum.text = tostring(currentLevel)
   ```

The `tostring()` method converts any argument to a string. In the preceding example, the `currentLevel` value changes from 1 to 2 when a `"win"` game event occurs. The value will convert to a string format that the `levelNum` text object can display on screen for level 2.

3. Add an `elseif` statement for a `"win"` game event when the second level has been completed and when it notifies the player that the game has been completed:

```
elseif gameEvent == "win" and currentLevel == 2 then
    alertScreen(" Game Over", " Congratulations!")
    gameEvent = "completed"
```

4. Add another `elseif` statement for the `"lose"` game event at the first level. Reset the score to zero and replay level 1:

```
elseif gameEvent == "lose" and currentLevel == 1 then
    score = 0
    scoreNum.text = "0"
    changeLevel1()
```

5. Add another `elseif` statement for a `"lose"` game event at the second level. Reset the score to zero and replay level 2:

```
elseif gameEvent == "lose" and currentLevel == 2 then
    score = 0
    scoreNum.text = "0"
    changeLevel2()
```

6. Finally, add another `elseif` statement for `gameEvent = "completed"`. Close the function with `end`:

```
elseif gameEvent == "completed" then
    alertBox:removeEventListener("tap", restart)
  end
end
```

7. Now, we need to backtrack and add an event listener to the `alertScreen()` function using the `alertBox` object. We will add it to the bottom of the function. This will activate the `restart()` function:

```
alertBox:addEventListener("tap", restart)
```

What just happened?

The `restart()` function checks all the `gameEvent` and `currentLevel` variables that occur during game play. When a game event checks for the `"win"` string, it also goes down the list of statements to see what comes out true. For example, if the player wins and is currently on level 1, then the player moves on to level 2.

If the player loses, `gameEvent == "lose"` becomes true, and the code checks what level the player lost in. For any level the player loses in, the score reverts to 0, and the current level the player was on is set up again.

Activating event listeners

The event listeners in this game basically turn the movements of the objects on and off. We have already coded the functions that carry out the actions of our game objects to run the level. Now, it's time to activate them using a certain type of events. As you've noticed from the previous chapter, we can add event listeners to display objects or have them run globally.

Collision events

Collision events within the physics engine occur through Corona's event listener model. There are three new event types, which are as follows:

- "collision": This event includes phases for "began" and "ended", which signify the moments of initial contact and broken contact. These phases exist for both normal two-body collisions and body-sensor collisions. If you do not implement a "collision" listener, this event will not fire.

- "preCollision": This is an event type that fires right before the objects start to interact. Depending on your game logic, you may wish to detect this event and conditionally override the collision. It may also result in multiple reports per contact and affect the application's performance.

- "postCollision": This is an event type that fires right after the objects have interacted. This is the only event in which the collision force is reported. If you do not implement a "postCollision" listener, this event will not fire.

Collisions are reported between pairs of objects and can be detected either globally, using a runtime listener, or locally within an object, using a table listener.

Global collision listeners

When detected as a runtime event, each collision event includes event.object1, which contains the table ID of the Corona display object involved.

Here is an example:

```
local physics = require "physics"
physics.start()

local box1 = display.newImage( "box.png" )
physics.addBody( box1, "dynamic", { density = 1.0, friction = 0.3,
bounce = 0.2 } )
box1.myName = "Box 1"
```

```
local box2 = display.newImage( "box.png", 0, 350)
physics.addBody( box2, "static", { density = 1.0, friction = 0.3,
bounce = 0.2 } )
box2.myName = "Box 2"

local function onCollision( event )
  if event.phase == "began" and event.object1.myName == "Box 1" then

    print( "Collision made." )

  end
end
```

```
Runtime:addEventListener( "collision", onCollision )
```

Local collision listeners

When detected with a table listener within an object, each collision event includes `event.other`, which contains the table ID of the other display object involved in the collision.

Here is an example:

```
local physics = require "physics"
physics.start()

local box1 = display.newImage( "box.png" )
physics.addBody( box1, "dynamic", { density = 1.0, friction = 0.3,
bounce = 0.2 } )
box1.myName = "Box 1"

local box2 = display.newImage( "box.png", 0, 350)
physics.addBody( box2, "static", { density = 1.0, friction = 0.3,
bounce = 0.2 } )
box2.myName = "Box 2"

local function onCollision( self, event )
  if event.phase == "began" and self.myName == "Box 1" then

    print( "Collision made." )

  end
end
```

```
box1.collision = onCollision
box1:addEventListener( "collision", box1 )

box2.collision = onCollision
box2:addEventListener( "collision", box2 )
```

Time for action – adding game listeners

For many of the functions we have created for our game objects, we need to activate the event listeners so that they will run the code and then disable them when game play has stopped. To add game listeners, follow these steps:

1. The last function we need to create in order to complete this game is called gameListeners(), which will also have a parameter called event. This should be added right after the gameLevel2() function:

    ```
    function gameListeners(event)
    ```

2. Add in the following event listeners that will start several events in the application, using an if statement:

    ```
    if event == "add" then
        Runtime:addEventListener("accelerometer", movePaddle)
        Runtime:addEventListener("enterFrame", updateBall)
        paddle:addEventListener("collision", bounce)
        ball:addEventListener("collision", removeBrick)
        paddle:addEventListener("touch", dragPaddle)
    ```

3. Next, we'll add in an elseif statement for the event listeners that will remove the events and then close the function:

    ```
    elseif event == "remove" then
        Runtime:removeEventListener("accelerometer", movePaddle)
        Runtime:removeEventListener("enterFrame", updateBall)
        paddle:removeEventListener("collision", bounce)
        ball:removeEventListener("collision", removeBrick)
        paddle:removeEventListener("touch", dragPaddle)

    end
    end
    ```

4. In order for function gameListeners() to work properly, we need to instantiate it in the startGame() function using the "add" string in the parameter. Place it before the end of the function:

    ```
    gameListeners("add")
    ```

5. In the `alertScreen()` function, add the `"remove"` string in the parameter and place it at the start of the function:

```
gameListeners("remove")
```

6. All the code has been written! Go ahead and run the game in the simulator. The application is also device ready. Make a simple icon image that fits the required dimensions for the device you're developing on. Compile a build and run it on your device.

What just happened?

There are two sets of `if` statements for the `event` parameter: `"add"` and `"remove"`.

All the event listeners in this function play an important role in making the game run. The `"accelerometer"` and `"enterframe"` events are used as runtime events since they have no specific target.

Both the `paddle` and `ball` objects have `"collision"` events that will carry out their purpose in any object contact made.

The `"touch"` event allows the user to touch and drag the paddle so that it can move back and forth in the simulator.

Notice that when `event == "remove"`, it removes all the event listeners that were active in the game. When the game starts, `gameListeners("add")` is activated. When a win or lose condition is achieved, `gameListeners("remove")` is activated.

Have a go hero – let's turn everything upside down

What if we decided to flip the game upside down, that is, have the paddle placed near the top of the screen, the ball below the paddle, and the group of bricks closer to the bottom of the screen?

Things you'll have to consider are as follows:

- The top wall is now the area you have to keep the ball from entering
- The y direction is where the ball travels when it collides with the bricks
- The ball has to reflect off the bottom wall when it collides with it

As you can see, there are a couple of things to consider before switching values from negative to positive and vice versa. Be sure to verify your logic and ensure that it makes sense when creating this new variation.

The results are in!

Let's summarize what has been made to make sure that you have everything added into your game. You can also refer to the `Breakout Final` folder in the `Chapter 4` folder to see the final code. You made sure that the necessary variables were introduced in the game. You also initialized the `main()` function that starts the game play. A main menu screen was implemented with the game title and a play button.

Next, you transitioned the `menuScreenGroup` away from the screen to load the main playing field. The main display objects of the game, such as the paddle, ball, and bricks, were added. The score and level number were displayed as the UI elements and updated throughout game play. Paddle movement in both the simulator and accelerometer were added as well as the collision detection with the paddle and the ball.

The physical properties of the paddle and ball were added at the start of the game. The brick layouts for each of the two levels were created. You have also added event listeners to all our game objects from the point when they need to be activated during the game and removed when game play is over.

Every time the ball collides with a brick, the brick is removed from the scene. The directional changes of the ball are updated for every wall, paddle, or brick collision made. Every time a win or lose condition occurred, all game objects are reset to begin the start of the current or new level.

When a condition occurs, an alert screen pops up, notifying the player of what has happened. The display objects that initiate the alerts are created in a function. Finally, the win and lose arguments are created to determine whether the current level has to be replayed, whether the player goes to the next level, or whether the game has been completed.

Beware of case-sensitive variables and functions in case you run into errors. Also, be sure to check whether you're missing any punctuation required in your code. These can be easily overlooked. Refer to your terminal window in the simulator for any error references.

Pop quiz – working with game controls

Q1. How do you properly remove a display object from the stage?

1. `remove()`

2. `object: remove()`

3. `object:removeSelf()`

   `object = nil`

4. None of the above.

Q2. What is the correct way to make the following display object into a physics object?

```
local ball = display.newImage("ball.png")
```

1. `physics.addBody( ball, { density=2.0, friction=0.5, bounce=0.2,radius = 25 })`

2. `physics.addBody( ball, "dynamic", { density=2.0, friction=0.5, bounce=0.2,radius = 15 } )`

3. 1 and 2.

4. d. None of the above.

Q3. What best represents what "began" means in the following function?

```
local function onCollision( event )
    if event.phase == "began" and event.object1.myName == "Box 1" then

        print( "Collision made." )

    end
end
```

1. A finger was moved on the screen.

2. A finger was lifted from the screen.

3. The system cancelled tracking the start touch.

4. A finger touched the screen.

Summary

Congratulations! You have completed making your very first game! You should be very proud of yourself. Now, you have experienced how simple it is to make an application with Corona SDK. It can take just a few hundred lines of code to make an application.

In this chapter, we did the following:

- Added movement to the paddle with touch events
- Introduced the accelerometer features
- Implemented collision event listeners for all game objects affected
- Removed objects from memory when they weren't needed on the game screen
- Implemented movement of the ball as a physical object
- Updated a scoreboard for every brick collision
- Learned how to handle win and lose conditions

The last two chapters weren't so bad now, were they? You're getting familiar with the workflow as you continue programming in Lua. It will definitely get easier to understand as long as you keep progressing and working with different game frameworks.

The next chapter holds another game that will surely catch your attention. You'll create animated sprite sheets for your display objects. How's that for eye candy?

5
Animating Our Game

We're off to a great start in our mobile game development journey. We have already gone through a great deal of programming, from game logic to displaying objects on screen. One of the most powerful things about the Corona SDK is that any display object can be animated. This is a testament to the flexible graphics model that Corona offers.

Animation adds a lot of character to the user experience in a game. This is accomplished by generating a sequence of frames that evolve smoothly from frame to frame. We'll be learning this skill and applying it to the new game that we're going to create.

In this chapter, we will:

- ◆ Work with motion and transitions
- ◆ Animate with image sheets
- ◆ Create a game loop for display objects
- ◆ Build our next game framework

Let's animate!

Panda Star Catcher

This section involves creating our second game called Panda Star Catcher. The main character is a panda named Ling Ling, who needs to be launched toward the skies and catch as many stars as possible before the timer runs out. The panda will be animated and have separate movements for every course of action that is applied, such as during the setup before launch and while it's in the air. The slingshot mechanics will also be applied to launch Ling Ling into the air. You might have seen similar features in games such as *Angry Birds* and *Crush the Castle*.

Let's get everything moving

We have introduced transitions in *Chapter 3, Building Our First Game – Breakout*, and briefly touched base with it. Let's go into more detail.

Transitions

The transition library allows you to create animations with only a single line of code by allowing you to tween one or more properties of a display object. We have discussed the basics of transitions back in *Chapter 3, Building Our First Game – Breakout*.

This can be done through the `transition.to` method, which takes a display object and a table that contains the control parameters. The control parameters specify the duration of the animation and the final values of properties for the display object. The intermediate values for a property are determined by an optional easing function, which is also specified as a control parameter.

The `transition.to()` method animates a display object's properties over time, using the "easing" algorithm.

The syntax is `handle = transition.to( target, params )`.

The return function is an object. The parameters are as follows:

- `target`: This is an object that will be the target of the transition. This includes display objects.
- `params`: This is a table that specifies the properties of the display object, which will be animated, and one or more of the following optional non-animated properties:
  - `params.time`: This specifies the duration of the transition in milliseconds. By default, the duration is 500 ms (0.5 seconds).
  - `params.transition`: By default, this is `easing.linear`.
  - `params.delay`: This specifies the delay in milliseconds (none by default) before the tween begins.

□ `params.delta`: This is a Boolean that specifies whether non-control parameters are interpreted as final ending values or as changes in value. The default is `nil`, meaning false.

□ `params.onStart`: This is a function or a table listener called before the tween begins.

□ `params.onComplete`: This is a function or a table listener called after the tween completes.

Easing

The easing library is a collection of interpolation functions used by the transition library. One example is opening a drawer. The first movement at first is fast and then a slow precise movement before it stops. The following are some easing examples:

◆ `easing.linear(t, tMax, start, delta)`: This defines a constant motion with no acceleration

◆ `easing.inQuad(t, tMax, start, delta)`: This performs a quadratic interpolation of animated property values in a transition

◆ `easing.outQuad(t, tMax, start, delta)`: This starts the motion quickly and then decelerates to zero velocity as it executes

◆ `easing.inOutQuad(t, tMax, start, delta)`: This starts the animation from a zero velocity, accelerates, and then decelerates to zero velocity

◆ `easing.inExpo(t, tMax, start, delta)`: This starts the motion from zero velocity and then accelerates as it executes

◆ `easing.outExpo(t, tMax, start, delta)`: This starts the motion quickly and then decelerates to zero velocity as it executes

◆ `easing.inOutExpo(t, tMax, start, delta)`: This starts the motion from zero velocity, accelerates, and then decelerates to zero velocity using an exponential easing equation

You can create your own easing function to interpolate between a start and a final value. The arguments of the function are defined as follows:

◆ `t`: This is the time in milliseconds since the transition started

◆ `tMax`: This is the duration of the transition

◆ `start`: This is the starting value

◆ `delta`: This is the change in value (final value = `start` + `delta`)

For example:

```
local square = display.newRect( 0, 0, 50, 50 )
square:setFillColor( 1,1,1 )
square.x = 50; square.y = 100

local square2 = display.newRect( 0, 0, 50, 50 )
square2:setFillColor( 1,1,1 )
square2.x = 50; square2.y = 300

transition.to( square, { time=1500, x=250, y=0 } )
transition.from( square2, { time=1500, x=250, y=0, transition =
easing.outExpo } )
```

The value of timed functions

Using a function that can be called at a later time can be helpful when organizing the timing of your game objects' appearance in an application. The timer library will allow us to handle our functions in a timely manner.

Timers

The timer function enables you to trigger events at a specific delay (in milliseconds) of your choosing.

- `timer.performWithDelay(delay, listener [, iterations])`: This invokes the listener after a delay in milliseconds and returns a handle to an object that you can pass to `timer.cancel()` in order to cancel the timer before it invokes the listener. For example:

```
local function myEvent()
  print( "myEvent called" )
end
timer.performWithDelay( 1000, myEvent )
```

- `timer.cancel(timerId)`: This cancels a timer operation initiated with `timer.performWithDelay()`. The parameter is as follows:

  - `timerId`: This is an object handle returned by the call to `timer.performWithDelay()`. For example:

```
local count = 0

local function myEvent()
  count = count + 1
```

```
    print ( count )

    if count >= 3 then
      timer.cancel( myTimerID )  -- Cancels myTimerID
      end
    end
```

♦ `timer.pause(timerId)`: This pauses a timer object started with `timer.performWithDelay()`. The parameter is:

  ❏ `timerId`: This is the timer ID object from `timer.performWithDelay()`. For example:

```
local count = 0

local function myEvent()
  count = count + 1
  print ( count )

  if count >= 5 then
    timer.pause( myTimerID )  -- Pauses myTimerID
    end
end

myTimerID = timer.performWithDelay(1000, myEvent, 0)
```

♦ `timer.resume(timerId)`: This resumes a timer that was paused with `timer.pause(timerId)`. The parameter is as follows:

  ❏ `timerID`: This the timer ID from `timer.performWithDelay()`. For example:

```
local function myEvent()
  print ( "myEvent called" )
end

myTimerID = timer.performWithDelay( 3000, myEvent )  -- wait
3 seconds

result = timer.pause( myTimerID )  -- Pauses myTimerID
print ( "Time paused at " .. result )

result = timer.resume( myTimerID )  -- Resumes myTimerID
print ( "Time resumed at " .. result )
```

What are image sheets?

Corona SDK includes an image sheet feature to construct animated sprites (also known as sprite sheets).

 For more information on image sheets, refer to the following link at `http://docs.coronalabs.com/guide/media/imageSheets/index.html`.

Image sheets are an efficient way to save texture memory. They are recommended for complex character animation or when numerous types of animations are involved.

Image sheets require more coding and have more of an advanced setup. They require the construction of a large sheet of animation frames.

It's sprite mania!

Image sheets are 2D animations that compile multiple frames into a single texture image. This is an efficient way to save on texture memory. It is beneficial for mobile devices and minimizes the loading time.

Image sheet API

The `graphics.newImageSheet` function creates a new image sheet. Refer to the following code:

```
graphics.newImageSheet( filename, [baseDir, ] options )
```

For example, the number of frames in the image sheet is assumed to be `floor(imageWidth/frameWidth) * floor(imageHeight/frameHeight)`. The first frame is placed at the top-left position and reads left to right and follows the next row, if applicable. The following image sheet has five frames that are 128 x 128 pixels each. The image sheet image is 384 pixels x 256 pixels altogether. If it were to be integrated in Corona, a sample method would be displayed like this:

```
local options =
{
  width = 128,
  height = 128,
  numFrames = 5,
```

```
    sheetContentWidth=384,
    sheetContentHeight=256
}
local sheet = graphics.newImageSheet( "mySheet.png", options )
```

The `display.newSprite(imageSheet, sequenceData)` function creates a new sprite from an image sheet. A sprite defines the collection of frames that belong to the same character or other moving asset, which may then be subdivided into different animation sequences for playback. The `sequenceData` parameter is an array of animation sequences that you set up. Sequences can be shared between multiple sprite objects. The following are some examples:

◆ Single sequence (consecutive frames):

```
local sequenceData =
{
    name="run", start=1, count=5, time=200, loopCount=0
}

local myCharacter = display.newSprite(imageSheet, sequenceData)
```

◆ Single sequence (non-consecutive frames):

```
local sequenceData =
{
    name="jump",
    frames= { 6, 7, 8 },
    time=200,
    loopCount=0
}

local myCharacter = display.newSprite(imageSheet, sequenceData)
```

♦ Multiple sequences (both consecutive and non-consecutive frames):

```
local sequenceData =
{
   { name="run", start=1, count=5, time=200 },
   {name="jump", frames= { 6, 7, 8 }, time=200, loopCount=0 }
}

local myCharacter = display.newSprite(imageSheet, sequenceData)
```

♦ `object:pause()`: This pauses the current animation. The frame remains on the current displayed frame.

♦ `object:play()`: This plays an animation sequence, starting at the current frame.

♦ `object:setFrame()`: This sets the frame in the currently loaded sequence.

♦ `object:setSequence()`: This loads an animation sequence by name.

Game time!

Now that we have learned how to set up image sheets, let's try to incorporate them into Panda Star Catcher! You can download the project files that accompany this book from the Packt Publishing website. There is a project folder called `Panda Star Catcher` in the `Chapter 5` folder. It already has the `config.lua` and `build.settings` files set up for you. The art assets are included in the folder as well. From *Chapters 3, Building our First Game – Breakout* and *Chapter 4, Game Controls*, you might have noticed that the build and runtime configuration has a similar setup. This tutorial is compatible for both iOS and Android devices. The graphics included in the project folder have been designed to display properly on both platforms. The welcome screen of the game will look like the following:

Time for action – setting up the variables

Let's start off with introducing all the variables needed to run the game:

1. Create a brand new `main.lua` file and add it in the `Panda Star Catcher` project folder.

2. Let's hide the status bar from the devices and set all the variables needed in game:

```
display.setStatusBar( display.HiddenStatusBar ) -- Hides the
status bar in iOS only

-- Display groups
local hudGroup = display.newGroup() -- Displays the HUD
local gameGroup = display.newGroup()
local levelGroup = display.newGroup()
local stars = display.newGroup() -- Displays the stars

-- Modules
local physics = require ("physics")

local mCeil = math.ceil
local mAtan2 = math.atan2
local mPi = math.pi
local mSqrt = math.sqrt

-- Game Objects
local background
local ground
local powerShot
local arrow
local panda
local poof
local starGone
local scoreText
local gameOverDisplay

-- Variables
local gameIsActive = false
local waitingForNewRound
local restartTimer
local counter
local timerInfo
local numSeconds = 30 -- Time the round starts at
```

```
local counterSize = 50
local gameScore = 0 -- Round starts at a score of 0
local starWidth = 30
local starHeight = 30
```

What just happened?

We hid the status bar at the start of the application. This is only applicable for iOS devices. There are four different groups set up, and all of them play an important role in the game.

Notice that `gameIsActive` is set as `false`. This enables us to activate properties of the application to affect the round when the display objects need to stop animating, appear on screen, and become affected by touch events.

The elements for the timer have also been set in the beginning of the code as well. Setting `numSeconds` to `30` denotes how long the round will count down from, in seconds. `starWidth` and `starHeight` depict the dimensions of the object.

Let's start the round

We'll need to load the panda to the game screen before it can launch. The panda will transition from the bottom of the screen and move upward on the screen before any touch event can occur.

Time for action – starting the game

Right now, we need to set the offscreen position for the panda and have it transition to its starting launch location, so the user can interact with it.

1. After adding the variables, create a new local function called `startNewRound()` and add an `if` statement to initiate the `panda` object into the scene:

```
local startNewRound = function()
    if panda then
```

2. Add a new local function called `activateRound()` within `startNewRound()`. Set the starting position of the `panda` display object on screen and add `ground:toFront()`, so that the ground appears in front of the panda character:

```
local activateRound = function()

    waitingForNewRound = false

    if restartTimer then
      timer.cancel( restartTimer )
    end

    ground:toFront()
    panda.x = 240
    panda.y = 300
    panda.rotation = 0
    panda.isVisible = true
```

3. Create another local function called `pandaLoaded()`. Set `gameIsActive` to `true` and set the `panda` object's air and hit properties to `false`. Add `panda:toFront()` so that it appears in front of all the other game objects on screen and set the body type to `"static"`:

```
local pandaLoaded = function()

    gameIsActive = true
    panda.inAir = false
    panda.isHit = false
    panda:toFront()

    panda.bodyType = "static"

end
```

4. Transition the panda to y=225 in 1,000 milliseconds. When the tween is completed, call the pandaLoaded() function using the onComplete command. Close the activateRound() function with end and call out to it. Close the if statement for panda and the startNewRound() function with end:

```
transition.to( panda, { time=1000, y=225,
onComplete=pandaLoaded } )
end

activateRound()

end
end
```

What just happened?

When the level is activated, the panda is placed below the ground before it is visible to the player. For pandaLoaded(), the game is activated by gameIsActive = true, and the panda is ready for launch by the player. The panda transitions from the ground level to an area on the screen where it can be accessed.

Poof! Be gone!

The panda needs to disappear from the stage after a turn has been made. Instead of having it disappear into thin air, we'll be adding a "poof" effect when it collides with any object on the screen.

Time for action – reloading the panda on the stage

When the panda has been in the air for a certain amount of time or has hit any out-of-bounds areas off the screen, it will turn into a cloud of smoke. The panda will be replaced with a "poof" image when a collision event occurs with the edge of the screen or the ground. The visible properties of the panda have to be turned off for the "poof" effect to work. When the collision has been made, the panda needs to be reloaded back onto the screen while the game is still activated.

1. Create a local function called `callNewRound()`. Include a local variable called `isGameOver` and set it to `false`:

```
local callNewRound = function()
   local isGameOver = false
```

2. Within the current function, create a new local function called `pandaGone()`. Add in the new properties for the panda, so it no longer displays on the game stage:

```
local pandaGone = function()

   panda:setLinearVelocity( 0, 0 )
   panda.bodyType = "static"
   panda.isVisible = false
   panda.rotation = 0

   poof.x = panda.x; poof.y = panda.y
   poof.alpha = 0
   poof.isVisible = true
```

3. Add in a new function for the `poof` object called `fadePoof()`. With the `onComplete` command, transition with `time` set to `50` and `alpha` set to `1`. Have the `poof` object fade out with `time` set to `100` and `alpha` set to `0`. Close the `pandaGone()` function and call out to it using `timer.performWithDelay`:

```
local fadePoof = function()
   transition.to( poof, { time=100, alpha=0 } )
end
transition.to( poof, { time=50, alpha=1.0,
onComplete=fadePoof } )

restartTimer = timer.performWithDelay( 300, function()
   waitingForNewRound = true;
   end, 1)

end

local poofTimer = timer.performWithDelay( 500, pandaGone, 1 )
```

4. When `isGameOver` is still `false`, add in a `timer.performWithDelay` method for `startNewRound()`. Close the `callNewRound()` function:

```
if isGameOver == false then
  restartTimer = timer.performWithDelay(1500, startNewRound,
  1)
end
end
```

What just happened?

A new round is called when the panda is no longer displayed on the screen and the clock is still counting down. When `isGameOver` is still `false`, then the panda reloads by calling `startNewRound()`.

The panda collision occurs through `pandaGone()`. All physical properties become inactive by applying `panda.isVisible = false`.

The smoke appears exactly where the panda disappeared. This happens when `poof.x = panda.x; poof.y = panda.y`. `poof` becomes visible for a short while through `fadePoof()`. Once it has faded, a new round awaits, which sets `waitingForNewRound` to `true`.

Earning some points

Points are earned when the panda catches any stars in the sky. The game is run on a timer, so it is the player's job to catch as many stars as they can, before the time runs out. Let's rack up some points!

Time for action – tracking the score

The score updates through a parameter called `scoreNum` and displays it during the game play. The score number is received through `gameScore`.

1. The next function that will be created is called `setScore` with a parameter called `scoreNum`:
   ```
   local setScore = function( scoreNum )
   ```

2. Use a local variable called `newScore` and set it as `scoreNum`. Set the `gameScore = newScore`. Provide an `if` statement for `gameScore`, so that the score during game play is set to 0:
   ```
   local newScore = scoreNum
   gameScore = newScore

   if gameScore < 0 then gameScore = 0; end
   ```

3. Add the `scoreText` display object and make it equal to `gameScore`. Close the function:

```
scoreText.text = gameScore
scoreText.xScale = 0.5; scoreText.yScale = 0.5
scoreText.x = (480 - (scoreText.contentWidth * 0.5)) - 15
scoreText.y = 20
end
```

What just happened?

For `setScore = function(scoreNum)`, we set a parameter called `scoreNum`. The `scoreNum` parameter will update the game score continuously through `local newScore`. `newScore` will update through `gameScore`, which provides the basis of the score keeping. At the same time, `scoreText` will display the value of `gameScore` during the game.

When the game ends

There are no losers in this game. Everyone wins! You'll still keep your adrenaline pumping by trying to catch as many stars as you can before the timer runs out. When it's all over, we still need to be notified that the time is up.

Time for action – displaying the game over screen

We need to set up the game over screen and have it display the final score that the player has achieved at the end of the round:

1. Create a new local function called `callGameOver()`:

   ```
   local callGameOver = function()
   ```

2. Set `gameIsActive` as `false` and pause the physics engine. Remove the `panda` and `stars` objects from the stage:

   ```
   gameIsActive = false
   physics.pause()

   panda:removeSelf()
   panda = nil
   stars:removeSelf()
   stars = nil
   ```

3. Display the game over objects and insert them into the `hudGroup` group. Use the `transition.to` method to display the game over objects on the screen:

```
local shade = display.newRect( 0, 0, 480, 320 )
shade:setFillColor( 0, 0, 0, 0.5)
shade.x = display.contentCenterX
shade.y = display.contentCenterY

gameOverDisplay = display.newImage( "gameOverScreen.png")
gameOverDisplay.x = 240; gameOverDisplay.y = 160
gameOverDisplay.alpha = 0

hudGroup:insert( shade )
hudGroup:insert( gameOverDisplay )

transition.to( shade, { time=200 } )
transition.to( gameOverDisplay, { time=500, alpha=1 } )
```

4. Update the final score with a local variable called `newScore`. Set `isVisible` to `false` for the `counter` and `scoreText`. Introduce `scoreText` again to display the final score in a different location on the device screen. Close the function:

```
local newScore = gameScore
setScore( newScore )

counter.isVisible = false

scoreText.isVisible = false
scoreText.text = "Score: " .. gameScore
scoreText.xScale = 0.5; scoreText.yScale = 0.5
scoreText.x = 280
scoreText.y = 160
scoreText:toFront()
timer.performWithDelay( 1000, function() scoreText.isVisible
= true; end, 1 )

end
```

What just happened?

The `callGameOver()` method displays the game over screen when time runs out or if all the stars are collected. We have set `gameIsActive` to `false` and paused all the physics so the panda cannot be moved with any other screen touches. The panda and stars are then removed from the scene. The `shade` and `gameOverDisplay` objects are visible through `transition.to`, so it notifies the player that the round is over. The final score will display at the end of the round in front of the `gameOverDisplay` object.

Background display

The panda needs a general setting of where it's located in the game. Let's set the background and ground objects.

Time for action – adding the background elements

1. Add in the `background` and `ground` display objects to the `drawBackground()` function. Insert the objects in the group called `gameGroup`:

```
local drawBackground = function()

   background = display.newImage( "background.png" )
   background.x = 240; background.y = 160
```

```
gameGroup:insert( background )

ground = display.newImage( "ground.png" )
ground.x = 240; ground.y = 300

local groundShape = { -240,-18, 240,-18, 240,18, -240,18 }
physics.addBody( ground, "static", { density=1.0, bounce=0,
friction=0.5, shape=groundShape } )

gameGroup:insert( ground )

end
```

What just happened?

The `background` and `ground` display objects are placed in the function called `drawBackground()`. The `ground` object has a customized physical shape that is not the same size as the original display object. So if the panda happens to hit the ground, it will collide with it but not fall through.

Heads up!

Before the game can be played, we need a general idea of how to operate the controls of the game. Luckily, we'll be adding a help screen that explains how to play. The **heads-up display (HUD)** needs to be displayed as well, so that the player can be updated on the time left on the clock and see how many points they have accumulated.

Time for action – displaying the timer and score

Let's set up the help screen and HUD elements that need to be displayed during the game:

1. Create a new local function called `hud()`:

    ```
    local hud = function()
    ```

2. Display `helpText` at the start of the game for 10 seconds. Have it transition by sliding it to the left and turning visibility to `false`. Add `helpText` to the `hudGroup` group:

    ```
    local helpText = display.newImage("help.png")
    helpText.x = 240; helpText.y = 160
    helpText.isVisible = true
    hudGroup:insert( helpText )
    ```

```
timer.performWithDelay( 10000, function() helpText.isVisible
= false; end, 1 )

transition.to( helpText, { delay=9000, time=1000, x=-320,
transition=easing.inOutExpo })
```

3. Display `counter` and `scoreText` near the top of the screen. Add `scoreText` to the `hudGroup` group as well. Close the function with `end`:

```
counter = display.newText( "Time: " .. tostring(numSeconds),
0, 0, "Helvetica-Bold", counterSize )
counter:setFillColor( 1, 1, 1 )
counter.xScale = 0.5; counter.yScale = 0.5
counter.x = 60; counter.y = 15
counter.alpha = 0

transition.to( counter, { delay=9000, time=1000, alpha=1,
transition=easing.inOutExpo })

hudGroup:insert( counter )

scoreText = display.newText( "0", 470, 22, "Helvetica-Bold",
52 )
scoreText: setFillColor( 1, 1, 1 )--> white
scoreText.text = gameScore
scoreText.xScale = 0.5; scoreText.yScale = 0.5
scoreText.x = (480 - (scoreText.contentWidth * 0.5)) - 15
scoreText.y = 15
scoreText.alpha = 0

transition.to( scoreText, { delay=9000, time=1000, alpha=1,
transition=easing.inOutExpo })

hudGroup:insert( scoreText )

end
```

What just happened?

The `helpText` object appears before the game starts and stays on the main device display for 9 seconds and transitions to -320 in the *x* direction in 1 second. This happens through `transition.to( helpText, { delay=9000, time=1000, x=-320, transition=easing.inOutExpo })`.

The `counter` object displays `"Time: " .. tostring( numSeconds )`, where `numSeconds` denotes the seconds that are counted down, starting from 30. It is located near the top-left corner of the screen.

The `scoreText` object displays `gameScore` and is updated for every star collision made. This will be placed on the top-right corner of the screen. All the objects in `local hud = function()` are inserted in `hudGroup`.

Time after time

This game has a timer that the player has to work against, in order to catch as many stars as possible before it runs out. We're going to start the countdown as soon as the help text leaves the stage.

Time for action – setting up the timer

We'll need to create a couple of functions that activate the countdown and also stop at 0 seconds when the game is over:

1. Set up the timer countdown for the game with a local function called `myTimer()`:

   ```
   local myTimer = function()
   ```

2. Increment the seconds for the timer countdown by 1. With the `counter` text object, display the time using `numSeconds`. Print out `numSeconds` to see the countdown in the terminal window:

   ```
   numSeconds = numSeconds - 1
   counter.text = "Time: " .. tostring( numSeconds )
   print(numSeconds)
   ```

3. Create an `if` statement for when the timer runs out or if all the stars are gone. Within the block, cancel the timer and call `callGameOver()` to end the round. Close the `myTimer()` function with `end`:

   ```
   if numSeconds < 1 or stars.numChildren <= 0 then
     timer.cancel(timerInfo)
     panda:pause()
     restartTimer = timer.performWithDelay( 300, function()
     callGameOver(); end, 1 )
   end

   end
   ```

4. Initiate the `myTimer()` function with a new local function called `startTimer()`. This will start the countdown at the beginning of the game play:

```
local startTimer = function()
  print("Start Timer")
  timerInfo = timer.performWithDelay( 1000, myTimer, 0 )
end
```

What just happened?

The main timer function is within `myTimer()`. We count down the seconds using `numSeconds = numSeconds - 1`. The seconds will update in the `counter` display object. `print(numSeconds)` will be updated in the terminal window to see how fast the countdown runs inside the code.

When time runs out or all the stars have been collected, an `if` statement is created to check if any of the arguments are true. When any statement evaluates to true, the timer stops counting down, the panda animation pauses, and the `callGameOver()` function is called. This will call the function to display the game over screen.

The timer initiates the countdown through `local startTimer = function()` at a rate of 1,000 milliseconds, which is equivalent to 1 second.

It's so glowy

The panda needs another element that will display how much force is required to launch it into the sky. We're going to add a subtle glow-like display object that will represent this.

Time for action – making the power shot

We need to create a separate function for `powerShot`, so that it can be called when the panda is set for launch:

1. Display the `powerShot` object through a new local function called `createPowerShot()`. Insert it in the `gameGroup` group:

```
local createPowerShot = function()
  powerShot = display.newImage( "glow.png" )
  powerShot.xScale = 1.0; powerShot.yScale = 1.0
  powerShot.isVisible = false

  gameGroup:insert( powerShot )
end
```

What just happened?

The `powerShot` object is created through the `createPowerShot()` function and is called when the panda is setting up for launch.

Pandas!

It will be exciting to see something animated on the screen. Our main character will have designated animations for every action applied during the game play.

Time for action – creating the panda character

We need to set up the panda collision event and animate it accordingly, using the image sheet:

1. We need to create a local function that will introduce the collision and touch events for the panda. We shall call it `createPanda()`:

    ```
    local createPanda = function()
    ```

2. When the panda collides with the stars, use `onPandaCollision()` with the parameters `self` and `event`. Reload `panda` every time a collision occurs with the stars or the edge of the screen, by using `callNewRound()`:

    ```
    local onPandaCollision = function( self, event )
      if event.phase == "began" then

        if panda.isHit == false then

          panda.isHit = true

          if event.other.myName == "star" then
            callNewRound( true, "yes" )
          else
            callNewRound( true, "no" )
          end

          if event.other.myName == "wall" then
            callNewRound( true, "yes" )
          else
            callNewRound( true, "no" )
          end
    ```

```
        elseif panda.isHit then
            return true
        end
    end
end
```

3. Create a directional arrow to allow the user to aim for an area to launch the panda. Insert it to the gameGroup group:

```
arrow = display.newImage( "arrow.png" )
arrow.x = 240; arrow.y = 225
arrow.isVisible = false

gameGroup:insert( arrow )
```

4. Create the image sheet for the panda that has three different animation sequences called "set", "crouch", and "air":

```
local sheetData = { width=128, height=128, numFrames=5,
sheetContentWidth=384, sheetContentHeight=256 }
local sheet = graphics.newImageSheet( "pandaSprite.png",
sheetData )

local sequenceData =
{
   { name="set", start=1, count=2, time=200 },
   { name="crouch", start=3, count= 1, time=1 },
   { name="air", start=4, count=2, time=100 }
}

panda = display.newSprite( sheet, sequenceData )

panda:setSequence ("set")
panda:play()
```

5. Add the following properties to panda before it launches into the air:

```
panda.x = 240; panda.y = 225
panda.isVisible = false

panda.isReady = false
panda.inAir = false
panda.isHit = false
```

```
panda.isBullet = true
panda.trailNum = 0

panda.radius = 12
physics.addBody( panda, "static", { density=1.0, bounce=0.4,
friction=0.15, radius=panda.radius } )
panda.rotation = 0
```

6. Set up collisions for `panda` using `"collision"` and apply an event listener:

```
panda.collision = onPandaCollision
panda:addEventListener( "collision", panda )
```

7. Create the `poof` object:

```
poof = display.newImage( "poof.png" )
poof.alpha = 1.0
poof.isVisible = false
```

8. Insert the `panda` and `poof` objects into the `gameGroup` group. Close the function:

```
gameGroup:insert( panda )
gameGroup:insert( poof )
end
```

9. We'll need to scroll up to the `activateRound()` function and add the `"set"` animation sequence for the panda:

```
panda:setSequence("set")
panda:play()
```

What just happened?

The collision events that occur for the panda start with `if event.phase == "began"`. The panda reloads on screen through several cases of `if` statements. `event.other. myName == "star"` will call a new round when the panda launches off screen towards the right, left, or top sides of the stage.

The image sheet for the panda has three sets of animations. They are called `"set"`, `"air"`, and `"crouch"`. There are a total of five frames in the image sheet.

The physical properties of the panda are set before launch. The body type is set to `"static"` and will change when it's in the air.

The collision event for the panda is called by `panda:addEventListener( "collision", panda )`.

Now that the image sheet has been set up, the `"set"` animation needs to be added in the `activateRound()` function to initiate movement.

Starry skies

The stars play a big part in the game. They are the main obstacle that the panda has to get past in order to achieve points before the clock runs out.

Time for action – creating star collisions

Star collisions need to be made and removed from the stage so that points can be accumulated for the player.

1. Create a function for the star collision called `onStarCollision()` and have a `self` and `event` parameter:

    ```
    local onStarCollision = function( self, event )
    ```

2. Add the `if` statements that remove the `stars` children from the game screen when a collision is made. Increment the score by 500 for each star removed from the screen. Close the function with `end`:

    ```
    if event.phase == "began" and self.isHit == false then

      self.isHit = true
      print( "star destroyed!")
      self.isVisible = false

      stars.numChildren = stars.numChildren - 1

      if stars.numChildren < 0 then
        stars.numChildren = 0
      end

      self.parent:remove( self )
      self = nil
    ```

```
        local newScore = gameScore + 500
        setScore( newScore )
    end
end
```

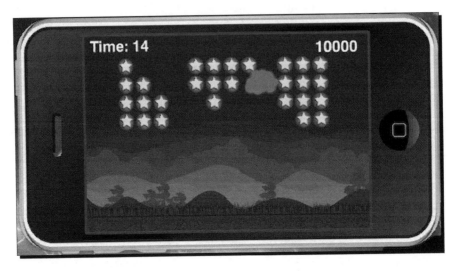

What just happened?

The star collision occurs on first contact with `if event.phase == "began"` and `self.isHit == false`, assuming the star has not been touched by the panda. The stars are removed from the screen by `self.parent:remove( self )` and `self = nil`. The score is incremented by 500 through `gameScore` and updated to `setScore = (scoreNum)`.

Have a go hero – tracking the star count

Try tracking how many stars the panda catches during game play. The logic is similar to how the game score was created. Each star that is caught will have to increment by 1 as the count for every collision made. The star count is placed within the `onStarCollision()` function. A new function and method will have to be created to display the text of the star count, and will have to be updated every time the count changes.

Screen touches

The panda will have to get across the playing field to reach the stars by creating a launch mechanic similar to a slingshot. Force will play a big role in pushing the panda upward.

Time for action – launching the panda

Let's add a touch event for the panda so that it flings toward the stars. The `powerShot` object will play a role in helping the player visualize how much power needs to be applied to the panda, before it launches into the air.

1. Implement touch events for the panda. Create a local function called `onScreenTouch()` with an event parameter:

```
local onScreenTouch = function( event )
```

2. With `gameIsActive` initiated, add in an `if` statement for when the touch event starts, by using `event.phase == "began"`. During this event, use the "crouch" animation set to prepare `panda` for launch:

```
if gameIsActive then
   if event.phase == "began" and panda.inAir == false then

      panda.y = 225
      panda.isReady = true
      powerShot.isVisible = true
      powerShot.alpha = 0.75
      powerShot.x = panda.x; powerShot.y = panda.y
      powerShot.xScale = 0.1; powerShot.yScale = 0.1

      arrow.isVisible = true

      panda:setSequence("crouch")
      panda:play()
```

3. Add an `elseif` statement for when the touch event ends by using `event.phase == "ended"`. Create a new local function called `fling()`, which will hold the properties of `panda` when it is launched toward the `star` objects. Apply a force opposite to where the touch event is dragged. Scale the `powerShot` display object outward when the touch event is pulled farther from the character:

```
   elseif event.phase == "ended" and panda.isReady then

      local fling = function()
        powerShot.isVisible = false
        arrow.isVisible = false

        local x = event.x
        local y = event.y
        local xForce = (panda.x-x) * 4
```

```
        local yForce = (panda.y-y) * 4

        panda:setSequence("air")
        panda:play()

        panda.bodyType = "dynamic"
        panda:applyForce( xForce, yForce, panda.x, panda.y )
        panda.isReady = false
        panda.inAir = true

    end

    transition.to( powerShot, { time=175, xScale=0.1,
    yScale=0.1, onComplete=fling} )

    end

    if powerShot.isVisible == true then

        local xOffset = panda.x
        local yOffset = panda.y

        local distanceBetween = mCeil(mSqrt( ((event.y - yOffset)
        ^ 2) + ((event.x - xOffset) ^ 2) ))

        powerShot.xScale = -distanceBetween * 0.02
        powerShot.yScale = -distanceBetween * 0.02

        local angleBetween = mCeil(mAtan2( (event.y - yOffset),
        (event.x - xOffset) ) * 180 / mPi) + 90

        panda.rotation = angleBetween + 180
        arrow.rotation = panda.rotation
    end

    end
end
```

What just happened?

Once the game is active and the panda has been loaded on the screen, a touch event to launch the panda can be initiated. The panda will go from a `"static"` physics state to a `"dynamic"` physics state. The `powerShot` display object size increases the farther back the panda is pulled by an event touch.

The force from the panda launch is applied by `local fling = function()`. Launch force is created by `xForce` and `yForce`. The panda object is propelled by `panda:applyForce( xForce, yForce, panda.x, panda.y )`. Notice that the body type changes to `"dynamic"`, so gravity can affect the object.

Organizing display objects

When the round has been set, the display hierarchy of the game objects needs to be rearranged. The most important objects are displayed towards the front of the screen.

Time for action – reordering layers

1. A new local function `reorderLayers()` needs to be created to organize the display hierarchy of objects on screen during game play:

```
local reorderLayers = function()

    gameGroup:insert( levelGroup )
    ground:toFront()
    panda:toFront()
    poof:toFront()
    hudGroup:toFront()

end
```

What just happened?

The `gameGroup`, `hudGroup`, and other display objects are reorganized in the display hierarchy of the game screen. The most significant object is set to the front, while the least important one is towards the back.

Creating stars

The sky background needs to be filled with stars, so that the panda can catch as many stars as possible.

Time for action – creating stars in the level

We need to add the layout of the stars in the game and have them moving so as to add a little effect to show that they're active. A collision event will need to be applied, which would remove them when the panda collides with them.

1. Create a new function called `createStars()` and lay out the `star` objects in a `for` loop. Add in the `"collision"` event that will be called by `onStarCollision()` to remove the stars when they are hit by the panda. Rotate the stars forward and backward at 10 seconds and 1,080 and -1,080 degrees each. This will allow the stars to rotate three full intervals backward and forward. Create the walls for the left and right sides of the screen:

```
local createStars = function()

    local numOfRows = 4
    local numOfColumns = 12
```

```
    local starPlacement = {x = (display.contentWidth  * 0.5) -
(starWidth * numOfColumns ) / 2  + 10, y = 50}

  for row = 0, numOfRows - 1 do
    for column = 0, numOfColumns - 1 do

      -- Create a star
      local star = display.newImage("star.png")
      star.name = "star"
      star.isHit = false
      star.x = starPlacement.x + (column * starWidth)
      star.y = starPlacement.y + (row * starHeight)
      physics.addBody(star, "static", {density = 1, friction =
      0, bounce = 0, isSensor = true})
      stars.insert(stars, star)

      star.collision = onStarCollision
      star:addEventListener( "collision", star )

      local function starAnimation()
        local starRotation = function()
          transition.to( star, { time=10000, rotation = 1080,
          onComplete=starAnimation })
        end

        transition.to( star, { time=10000, rotation = -1080,
        onComplete=starRotation })
      end

      starAnimation()

    end
  end

local leftWall  = display.newRect (0, 0, 0,
display.contentHeight)
leftWall.name = "wall"

local rightWall = display.newRect (display.contentWidth, 0,
0, display.contentHeight)
  rightWall.name = "wall"

  physics.addBody (leftWall, "static", {bounce = 0.0,
  friction = 10})
```

```
        physics.addBody (rightWall, "static", {bounce = 0.0,
        friction = 10})

        reorderLayers()
end
```

What just happened?

The number of stars displayed on screen is set by numOfRows and numOfColumns. A for loop is made to display each individual star object and is placed in the stars group. The collision for star is detected by an event listener through onStarCollision().

The leftWall and rightWall objects have physical properties as well and will take into account the collision detection with the panda.

The stars are animated by starAnimation() and starRotation(). Each function rotates each star object for 10 seconds (10,000 milliseconds), and alternates between 1,080 and -1,080 degrees.

Starting the game

The game starts when the clock starts counting down and the panda is loaded on the screen. Once the panda is set on screen, the player needs to aim and launch it quickly so that reloading of the panda can occur immediately.

Time for action – initializing the game

The physics and the remaining game functions need to be initialized to run the game. All game actions need to be delayed until the help screen has left the stage.

1. Start the game by creating a new function called gameInit(), which will hold the physics properties and activate the display objects on the stage:

```
local gameInit = function()
  physics.start( true )
  physics.setGravity( 0, 9.8 )

  drawBackground()
  createPowerShot()
  createPanda()
  createStars()
  hud()
```

2. Add in a Runtime event listener, using "touch" for onScreenTouch():

```
Runtime:addEventListener( "touch", onScreenTouch )
```

3. Have the level and timer start 10 seconds later so that the user has time to read through the help text. Close the function and start the game with `gameInit()`:

```
local roundTimer = timer.performWithDelay( 10000, function()
startNewRound(); end, 1 )
local gameTimer = timer.performWithDelay( 10000, function()
startTimer(); end, 1 )
end


gameInit()
```

All the code is completed! Run the game in the simulator and see for yourself how it works. Make sure to check for any typos in your code if errors occur.

What just happened?

The round is initialized through `gameInit()`. The physics engine and the remaining functions are run at this time. The event listener for `onScreenTouch()` is added as well. The `startNewRound()` and `startTimer()` functions initiate 10 seconds after launching the application through `timer.performWithDelay`.

Pop quiz – animating graphics

Q1. What is the proper way to pause the animation of an image sheet?

1. `object:stop()`

2. `object:pause()`

3. `object:dispose()`

4. None of the above

Q2. How do you make an animation sequence loop forever?

1. ```
   local sequenceData =
       {
          name="run", start=1, count=5, time=100, loopCount=1
       }
   ```

2. ```
   local sequenceData =
       {
          name="run", start=1, count=5, time=100, loopCount=0
       }
   ```

3. ```
   local sequenceData =
       {
          name="run", start=1, count=5, time=100, loopCount=-1
       }
   ```

4. ```
   local sequenceData =
       {
          name="run", start=1, count=5, time=100, loopCount=100
       }
   ```

Q3. How do you create a new image sheet?

1. ```
   myCharacter = display.newSprite(sequenceData)
   ```

2. ```
   myCharacter = display.newSprite(imageSheet, sequenceData)
   ```

3. ```
   myCharacter = sprite.newSpriteSheet("myImage.png", frameWidth,
   frameHeight)
   ```

4. None of the above

Summary

Our second game, Panda Star Catcher, is finally complete! We're now getting a great grasp on writing more functions and different types of game logic, and we also have animation under our belt! Way to go!

In this chapter, we did the following:

- Took a more in-depth look at transitions and applied easing techniques
- Understood image sheets and sprite animation
- Created a game loop for display objects that have to be reloaded continuously on screen
- Applied force to a display object that propels it to a designated direction
- Added a collision event that switches from one display object to another

We have pushed through making another game in one whole chapter! Working in Corona SDK is so simple and fast to learn. It doesn't even require thousands of lines of code to create a simple game.

In the next chapter, we'll be learning another vital element to create games, sound effects, and music! You're in for a treat.
   ```

6

Playing Sounds and Music

We hear sound effects and music in almost every type of media we encounter daily. Many notable games such as Pac-Man, Angry Birds, and Fruit Ninja can be recognized just by their theme music or sound effects alone. Aside from the visual imagery we see in games, sounds help impact the mood conveyed in the storyline and/or during game play. Quality sound effects and music that pertain to the theme of your game helps give a realistic feel to the experience.

In this chapter, you will learn how to apply sound effects and music that can be added to your applications. You have the visual appeal down from creating Breakout and Panda Star Catcher in the previous chapters. Now, let's enhance the sensory experience for our ears!

The main points you'll be going over are:

- ◆ Loading, playing, and looping audio
- ◆ Understanding how to play, pause, resume, rewind, and stop the audio
- ◆ Memory management (disposing audio)
- ◆ Volume control
- ◆ Performance and encoding tips

Let's create some more magic!

Corona audio system

The Corona audio system has advanced **Open Audio Library (OpenAL)** features. OpenAL is designed for the efficient rendering of multichannel three-dimensional positional audio. The general functionality of OpenAL is encoded in source objects, audio buffers, and a single listener. A source object contains a pointer to a buffer, the velocity, position and direction of the sound, and the intensity of the sound. Buffers contain audio data in the PCM format, either 8- or 16-bit, in either mono or stereo format. The listener object contains the velocity, position and direction of the listener, and the general gain applied to all sounds.

 For more information on the Corona audio system, you can go to `http://developer.coronalabs.com/partner/audionotes`. General information on OpenAL can be found at `http://www.openal.org`.

Sound formats

The following are the sound formats that are compatible with iOS and Android platforms:

- All platforms support files that are 16-bit, little endian, linear, and in `.wav` format
- iOS supports the `.mp3`, `.aif`, `.caf`, and `.aac` formats
- The Mac simulator supports the `.mp3`, `.aif`, `.caf`, `.ogg`, and `.aac` formats
- The Windows simulator supports the `.mp3` and `.ogg` formats
- Android supports the `.mp3` and `.ogg` formats

Sound filename limitations on Android

File extensions are ignored when building in Android, so files are considered the same regardless of the extension. The workaround for the mean time is to change the filenames to differentiate between file extensions. See the examples listed here:

- `tap_aac.aac`
- `tap_aif.aif`
- `tap_caf.caf`
- `tap_mp3.mp3`
- `tap_ogg.ogg`

Mono sounds at their best

Using mono sounds takes half the amount of memory than stereo sounds. Since the Corona audio system uses OpenAL, it will only apply spatialized/3D effects to mono sounds. OpenAL does not apply 3D effects stereo samples.

Maximum number of simultaneous channels

The maximum number of channels that can be run is 32. This allows up to 32 distinct sounds to be played simultaneously. The API to see the resulting number of channels in your code is `audio.totalChannels`.

Time to play

Audio can be loaded in two different ways, as follows:

* `loadSound()`: This preloads an entire sound into the memory
* `loadStream()`: This prepares the sound to be played by reading small chunks at a time to save memory

audio.loadSound()

The `audio.loadSound()` function loads an entire file completely into the memory and returns a reference to the audio data. Files that are loaded completely into the memory can be reused, played, and shared simultaneously on multiple channels. So, you only need to load one instance of the file. Sounds that you would use as sound effects in your game will fit in this category.

The syntax is `audio.loadSound(audiofileName [, baseDir ])`.

The parameters are as follows:

* `audiofileName`: This specifies the name of the audio file you want to load. The supported file formats are determined by the platform the file is being run on.
* `baseDir`: By default, sound files are expected to be in the application resources directory. If the sound file is in the application documents directory, use `system.DocumentsDirectory`.

For example:

* `tapSound = audio.loadSound("tap.wav")`
* `smokeSound = audio.loadSound("smoke.mp3")`

audio.loadStream()

The `audio.loadStream()` function loads a file to be read as a stream. Streamed files are read in small chunks at a time to minimize memory use. Files that are large in size and have a long duration would be ideal for this. These files cannot be shared simultaneously across multiple channels. If need be, you must load multiple instances of the file.

The syntax is `audio.loadStream( audioFileName [, baseDir ] )`

The parameters are as follows:

- `audiofileName`: This specifies the name of the audio file you want to load. The supported file formats are determined by the platform the file is being run on.

- `baseDir`: By default, sound files are expected to be in the application resources directory. If the sound file is in the application documents directory, use `system.DocumentsDirectory`.

For example:

- `music1 = audio.loadStream("song1.mp3")`
- `music2 = audio.loadStream("song2.wav")`

audio.play()

The `audio.play()` function plays the audio specified by the audio handle on a channel. If a channel is not specified, an available channel will be automatically chosen for you. The function returns the channel number the audio is playing on.

The syntax is `audio.play( audioHandle [, options ] )`

The parameters are as follows:

- `audioHandle`: This is the audio data you want to play
- `options`: This is an additional option for playback, formatted as a table

Parameters for `options`:

- `channel`: This option lets you select the channel number that you want the audio to play on. 1 to the maximum number of channels, which is 32, are valid channels. If you specify 0 or omit, this parameter will have a channel automatically picked for you.

- `loops`: This option lets you select the number of times you want the audio to loop. 0 means the audio will loop zero times, which means that the sound will play once and not loop. Passing -1 will tell the system to infinitely loop the sample.

- ◆ `duration`: This option is measured in milliseconds, this option will cause the system to play the audio for the specified amount of time.

- ◆ `fadein`: This option is measured in milliseconds, this will start playing a sound at the minimum channel volume and transition to the normal channel volume over the specified number of milliseconds.

- ◆ `onComplete`: This is a callback function that you will call when playback ends. The `onComplete` callback function passes back an event parameter.

For example:

```
backgroundMusic = audio.loadStream("backgroundMusic.mp3")
backgroundMusicChannel = audio.play( backgroundMusic, { channel=1,
loops=-1, fadein=5000 }  )
-- play the background music on channel 1, loop infinitely, and fadein
over 5 seconds
```

Looping

Highly compressed formats, such as MP3, AAC, and Ogg Vorbis, can remove samples at the end of an audio sample and possibly break a clip that is looped correctly. If you experience gaps in looping during playback, try using WAV (compatible with iOS and Android). Make sure your lead-in and ending points are clean.

Simultaneous playback

Sounds loaded via `loadSound()` can be played back simultaneously on multiple channels. For example, you can load a sound effect as follows:

```
bellSound = audio.loadSound("bell.wav")
```

If you want to make a variety of bell sounds to occur for multiple objects, you can. The audio engine is highly optimized to handle this case. Call `audio.play()` using that same handle as many times as you need it (up to the maximum channels):

```
audio.play(bellSound)
audio.play(bellSound)
audio.play(bellSound)
```

Time for action – playing audio

We're going to learn how sound effects and music are implemented in Corona to get an idea of how it really works. To play an audio follow the steps:

1. Create a new project folder on your desktop called `Playing Audio`.

2. In the `Chapter 6 Resources` folder, copy the `ring.wav` and `song1.mp3` sound files into your project folder and create a new `main.lua` file. You can download the project files that accompany this book from the Packt Publishing website.

3. Preload the following audio with `loadSound()` and `loadStream()`:

    ```
    ringSound = audio.loadSound( "ring.wav" )
    backgroundSound = audio.loadStream( "song1.mp3" )
    ```

4. Play `backgroundSound` by setting it to channel 1, loop it infinitely, and fade in after 3 seconds:

    ```
    mySong = audio.play( backgroundSound, { channel=1, loops=-1,
    fadein=3000 }  )
    ```

5. Add in `ringSound` and play it once:

    ```
    myRingSound = audio.play( ringSound )
    ```

6. Save and run the project in the Corona Simulator to hear the results.

What just happened?

For audio that is merely a short sound effect, we used `audio.loadSound()` to prepare the sound. For audio that is large in size or long in duration, `audio.loadStream()` is used.

The `backgroundSound` file is set to channel 1, and fades in at 3 seconds when it starts playing. The `loops = -1` statement means that the file loops infinitely from beginning to the end.

Have a go hero – repeating audio with delay

As you can see, loading and playing an audio is really simple. It only takes two lines of code to play a simple sound. Let's see if you can take it up a notch.

Use the `ring.wav` file and load it through `loadSound()`. Create a function that plays the audio. Have the sound play at an interval of 2 seconds, repeating five times.

Time to take control

We have the ability to control our sounds, now that we can play them in the simulator. If you think back to the days of cassette tape players, it had the ability to use functions such as pause, stop, and rewind. Corona's audio API library can do just that.

audio.stop()

The `audio.stop()` function stops playback on a channel and clears the channel, so it can be played on again.

The syntax is `audio.stop( [channel] )` or `audio.stop( [ { channel = c } ] )`.

Having no parameters stops all active channels. The `channel` parameter specifies the channel to stop. Specifying 0 stops all channels.

audio.pause()

The `audio.pause()` function pauses playback on a channel. This has no effect on channels that aren't playing.

The syntax is `audio.pause( [channel] )` or `audio.pause( [ {channel = c} ] )`.

Having no parameters pauses all active channels. The `channel` parameter specifies the channel to pause. Specifying 0 pauses all channels.

audio.resume()

The audio.resume() function resumes playback on a channel that is paused. This has no effect on channels that aren't paused.

The syntax is `audio.pause( [channel] )` or `audio.pause( [ {channel = c} ] )`.

Having no parameters resumes all paused channels. The `channel` parameter specifies the channel to resume. Specifying 0 resumes all channels.

audio.rewind()

The `audio.rewind()` function rewinds audio to the beginning position on either an active channel or directly on the audio handle.

The syntax is `audio.rewind( [, audioHandle ] [, { channel=c } ] )`.

The parameters are as follows:

◆ `audioHandle`: The `audioHandle` parameter lets you rewind the data you want. It's best for audio loaded with `audio.loadStream()`. Don't try using it with the `channel` parameter in the same call.

◆ `channel`: The `channel` parameter lets you select the channel you want the rewind operation to apply to. It's best for audio loaded with `audio.loadSound()`. Don't try using with the `audioHandle` parameter in the same call.

Time for action – controlling audio

Let's simulate our own little music player by creating user interface buttons that will control the audio calls as follows:

1. In the `Chapter 6` folder, copy the `Controlling Audio` project folder to your desktop. You will notice several art assets, a `ui.lua` library, `config.lua` file, and a `song2.mp3` file inside. You can download the project files accompanying this book from the Packt Publishing website.

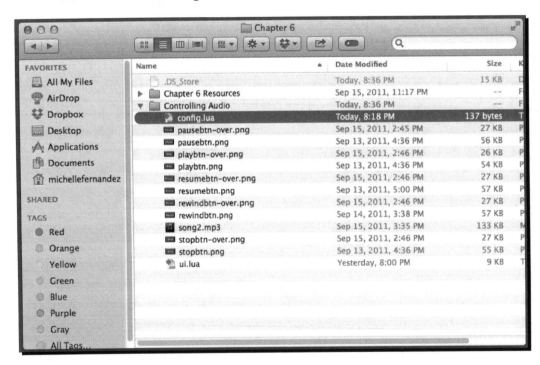

2. In the same project folder, create a brand new `main.lua` file.

3. Load the audio file via `loadStream()`, name it `music`, and call the UI library. Also add it in a local variable called `myMusic`:

```
local ui = require("ui")
local music = audio.loadStream( "song2.mp3" ) local myMusicChannel
```

4. Create a local function called `onPlayTouch()` with an `event` parameter to play the audio file. Add an `if` statement that contains `event.phase == "release"` so that the music starts playing when the button releases. Apply the `playBtn` display object as a new UI button:

```
local onPlayTouch = function( event )
  if event.phase == "release" then
    myMusicChannel = audio.play( music, { loops=-1 }  )
  end
end

playBtn = ui.newButton{
  defaultSrc = "playbtn.png",
  defaultX = 100,
  defaultY = 50,
  overSrc = "playbtn-over.png",
  overX = 100,
  overY = 50,
  onEvent = onPlayTouch,
  id = "PlayButton",
  text = "",
  font = "Helvetica",
  size = 16,
  emboss = false
}

playBtn.x = 160; playBtn.y = 100
```

5. Create a local function called `onPauseTouch()` with an `event` parameter to pause the audio file. Add an `if` statement when `event.phase == "release"` so that the music pauses. Apply the `pauseBtn` display object as a new UI button:

```
local onPauseTouch = function( event )
  if event.phase == "release" then
    audio.pause( myMusicChannel )
    print("pause")
  end
end
```

```
pauseBtn = ui.newButton{
  defaultSrc = "pausebtn.png",
  defaultX = 100,
  defaultY = 50,
  overSrc = "pausebtn-over.png",
  overX = 100,
  overY = 50,
  onEvent = onPauseTouch,
  id = "PauseButton",
  text = "",
  font = "Helvetica",
  size = 16,
  emboss = false
}

pauseBtn.x = 160; pauseBtn.y = 160
```

6. Add a local function called onResumeTouch() with an event parameter to resume the audio file. Add an if statement when event.phase == "release" so that the music resumes. Apply the resumeBtn display object as a new UI button:

```
local onResumeTouch = function( event )
  if event.phase == "release" then
    audio.resume( myMusicChannel )
    print("resume")
  end
end

resumeBtn = ui.newButton{
  defaultSrc = "resumebtn.png",
  defaultX = 100,
  defaultY = 50,
  overSrc = "resumebtn-over.png",
  overX = 100,
  overY = 50,
  onEvent = onResumeTouch,
  id = "ResumeButton",
  text = "",
  font = "Helvetica",
  size = 16,
  emboss = false
}

resumeBtn.x = 160; resumeBtn.y = 220
```

7. Add a local function called `onStopTouch()` with an `event` parameter to stop the audio file. Create an `if` statement when `event.phase == "release"` so that the music stops. Apply the `stopBtn` display object as a new UI button:

```
local onStopTouch = function( event )
  if event.phase == "release" then
    audio.stop()
    print("stop")

  end
end

stopBtn = ui.newButton{
  defaultSrc = "stopbtn.png",
  defaultX = 100,
  defaultY = 50,
  overSrc = "stopbtn-over.png",
  overX = 100,
  overY = 50,
  onEvent = onStopTouch,
  id = "StopButton",
  text = "",
  font = "Helvetica",
  size = 16,
  emboss = false
}

stopBtn.x = 160; stopBtn.y = 280
```

8. Add a local function called `onRewindTouch()` with an `event` parameter to rewind the audio file. Create an`if` statement when `event.phase == "release"` so that the music rewinds to the beginning of the track. Apply the `rewindBtn` display object as a new UI button:

```
local onRewindTouch = function( event )
  if event.phase == "release" then
    audio.rewind( myMusicChannel )
    print("rewind")
  end
end

rewindBtn = ui.newButton{
  defaultSrc = "rewindbtn.png",
  defaultX = 100,
  defaultY = 50,
  overSrc = "rewindbtn-over.png",
```

```
    overX = 100,
    overY = 50,
    onEvent = onRewindTouch,
    id = "RewindButton",
    text = "",
    font = "Helvetica",
    size = 16,
    emboss = false
}

rewindBtn.x = 160; rewindBtn.y = 340
```

9. Save your project and run it in the simulator. You have now created a functional media player!

What just happened?

We added a UI library for our user interface buttons by calling `require("ui")`. This produces the on press look when a button has been pushed down.

A variety of functions were created to run each button. They are as follows:

◆ `onPlayTouch()`: This calls out `myMusicChannel = audio.play( music, { loops=-1 } )` when the event is triggered by the user pressing the button

◆ `onPauseTouch()`: This calls out `audio.pause( myMusicChannel )` to pause the song when the button is pressed

◆ `onResumeTouch()`: This calls out `audio.resume( myMusicChannel )` to resume the song if it has been paused

◆ `onStopTouch()`: This calls out `audio.stop()` if the song is currently playing and will stop the audio

◆ `onRewindTouch()`: This calls out `audio.rewind( myMusicChannel )` to rewind the song to the beginning of the track.

 When a song is paused, it resumes only by pressing the **Resume** button. The **Play** button will have no effect when the **Pause** button is pressed.

Memory management

It is important to call `audio.dispose()` on your loaded audio when you are completely done with the audio file. Doing so allows you to recover the memory.

audio.dispose()

The `audio.dispose()` function releases the audio memory associated with the handle.

The syntax is `audio.dispose( audioHandle )`.

The parameter is as follows:

◆ `audioHandle`: The handle returned by the `audio.loadSound()` or `audio.loadStream()` functions that you want to free.

You must not use the handle once the memory is freed. The audio should not be playing or paused on any channel when you try to free it.

For example:

```
mySound = audio.loadSound( "sound1.wav" )
myMusic = audio.loadStream( "music.mp3" )

audio.dispose( mySound )
audio.dispose( myMusic )

mySound = nil
myMusic = nil
```

Have a go hero – disposing audio

You have just learned how to dispose audio files properly to recover memory in your application. Try the following:

- Load your audio file and have it play for a specified time. Create a function that will dispose the file when calling an `onComplete` command.
- In the `Controlling Audio` project file, dispose the audio in the `onStopTouch()` function.

Alterations to audio

The audio system also has the ability to alter the minimum and maximum states of audio volume, as well as fading the audio when needed.

Volume control

The volume of the audio can be set with values ranging from 0 to 1.0. This setting can be adjusted at any time before or during the extended sound playback.

audio.setVolume()

The `audio.setVolume` function sets the volume.

The syntax is `audio.setVolume( volume [, [options] ] ) --upon success, should return true.`

The parameters are as follows:

◆ volume: This lets you set the volume level you want to apply. Valid numbers range from 0.0 to 1.0, where 1.0 is the maximum volume value. The default volume is based on your device ringer volume and will vary.

◆ options: This is a table that supports the channel number you want to set the volume on. You can set the volume on any channel between 1 to 32. Specify 0 to apply the volume to all the channels. Omitting this parameter entirely sets the master volume, which is different from the channel volume.

For example:

◆ ```
audio.setVolume(0.75) -- set master volume
```
◆ ```
audio.setVolume( 0.5, { channel=2 } ) -- set volume on channel
scaled to the volume on the master channel
```

audio.setMinVolume()

The audio.setMinVolume() function clamps the minimum volume to the set value. Any volumes that go below the minimum volume will be played at the minimum volume level.

The syntax is audio.setMinVolume(volume, options).

The parameters are as follows:

◆ volume: This lets you set the new minimum volume level you want to apply. Valid numbers range from 0.0 to 1.0, where 1.0 is the maximum volume value.

◆ options: This is a table that supports a single key channel number you want to set the minimum volume on. 1 to the minimum number of channels are valid channels. Specify 0 to apply the minimum volume to all the channels.

The example is mentioned as follows:

```
audio.setMinVolume( 0.10, { channel=1 } ) -- set the min volume on
channel 1
```

audio.setMaxVolume()

The audio.setMaxVolume() function clamps the maximum volume to the set value. Any volumes that exceed the maximum volume will be played at the maximum volume level.

The syntax is audio.setMaxVolume(volume, options).

The are parameters are as follows:

◆ volume: This lets you set the new maximum volume level you want to apply. Valid numbers range from 0.0 to 1.0, where 1.0 is the maximum value.

◆ options: This is a table that supports a single key channel number you want to set the maximum volume on. 1 to the maximum number of channels are valid channels. Specify 0 to apply the maximum volume to all the channels.

The example is mentioned as follows:

```
audio.setMaxVolume( 0.9, { channel=1 } ) -- set the max volume on
channel 1
```

audio.getVolume()

The audio.getVolume() function gets the volume either for a specific channel or the master volume.

The syntax is audio.getVolume({ channel=c }).

The parameter is as follows:

◆ channel: This sets the channel number you want to get the volume on. There can be a maximum number of 32 channels that are valid. Specifying 0 will return the average volume across all channels. Omitting this parameter entirely gets the master volume, which is different than the channel volume.

Some example are mentioned as follows:

◆ masterVolume = audio.getVolume() -- get the master volume
◆ channel1Volume = audio.getVolume({ channel=1 }) -- get the volume on channel 1

audio.getMinVolume()

The audio.getMinVolume() function gets the minimum volume for a specific channel.

The syntax is audio.getMinVolume({ channel=c }).

The parameter is as follows:

◆ channel: This sets the channel number you want to get the minimum volume on. There can be a maximum number of 32 channels that are valid. Specifying 0 will return the average minimum volume across all channels.

The example is mentioned as follows:

```
channel1MinVolume = audio.getMinVolume( { channel=1 } ) -- get the min
volume on channel 1
```

audio.getMaxVolume()

The `audio.getMaxVolume()` function gets the maximum volume for a specific channel.

The syntax is `audio.getMaxVolume( { channel=c } )`.

The parameter is as follows:

◆ `channel`: This sets the channel number you want to get the maximum volume on. There can be a maximum number of 32 channels that are valid. Specifying 0 will return the average volume across all channels.

The example is mentioned as follows:

```
channel1MaxVolume = audio.getMaxVolume( { channel=1 } ) -- get the max
volume on channel 1
```

Fading audio

You can fade in the volume at the time any audio starts playing, but there are other ways to control it as well.

audio.fade()

The `audio.fade()` function fades a playing sound in a specified amount to a specified volume. The audio will continue playing after the fade completes.

The syntax is `audio.fade( [ { [channel=c] [, time=t] [, volume=v ] } ] )`.

The parameters are as follows:

◆ `channel`: This sets the channel number you want to fade on. 1 to the maximum number of channels are valid channels. Specify 0 to apply fade to all the channels.

◆ `time`: This sets the amount of time from now that you want the audio to fade out and stop. Omitting this parameter invokes a default fade time, which is 1,000 milliseconds.

◆ `volume`: This sets the target volume you want to change the fade to. Valid numbers are 0.0 to 1.0, where 1.0 is the maximum volume. If this parameter is omitted, the default value is 0.0.

See the following example:

```
audio.fade({ channel=1, time=3000, volume=0.5 } )
```

audio.fadeOut()

The `audio.fadeOut()` function stops playing the sound in a specified amount of time and fades to the minimum volume. The audio will stop at the end of the time and the channel will be freed.

The syntax is `audio.fadeOut( [ { [channel=c] [, time=t] } ] )`.

The parameters are as follows:

◆ `channel`: This sets the channel number you want to fade out on. 1 to the maximum number of channels are valid channels. Specify 0 to apply fade out to all the channels.

◆ `time`: This sets the amount of time from now that you want the audio to fade out over and stop. Omitting this parameter invokes a default fade out time, which is 1,000 milliseconds.

The example is mentioned as follows:

```
audio.fadeOut({ channel=1, time=5000 } )
```

Performance tips

When creating good quality audios for your games, refer to the helpful notes mentioned here.

Preloading phase

It is best to preload the files you regularly use on startup of your application. While `loadStream()` is generally fast, `loadSound()` may take a while since it must load and decode the entire file the instant it needs to be used. Generally, you don't want to be calling `loadSound()` in the parts of your application that users expect it to be running smoothly when events occur, such as during game play.

audioPlayFrequency

In the `config.lua` file, you may specify a field called `audioPlayFrequency`:

```
application =
{
  content =
  {
```

```
      width = 480,
      height = 960,
      scale = "letterbox",
      audioPlayFrequency = 22050
    },
}
```

This tells the OpenAL system what sample rate to mix and playback at. For best results, set this no higher than you actually need. So if you never need better than 22,050 Hz playback, set this to 22,050. It produces quality speech recordings or middle-quality recordings of music. If you really do need high quality, then set this to 44,100 to produce audio CD type of quality at playback.

It is best to have all your audio files encoded at the same frequency when you have this set. The supported values are 11,025, 22,050, and 44,100.

Patents and royalties

For highly compressed formats, such as MP3 and AAC, AAC is the better option. AAC is the official successor to the MP3 by the MPEG Group. MP3 has patent and royalty issues that you may need to concern yourself with, if you distribute anything yourself. You might need to consult your lawyers for guidance. When AAC was ratified, it was agreed there would be no royalties required for distribution. If you prefer to use AAC over MP3, here's a tutorial on how to convert an MP3 to AAC or any file format of your preference at `http://support.apple.com/kb/ht1550`.

Ogg Vorbis is a royalty-free and patent-free format. However, this is not supported on iOS devices.

> More information on audio formats can be found at `http://www.nch.com.au/acm/formats.html`. Ray Wenderlich, a mobile developer, also has a tutorial available on file and data formats for audio at `http://www.raywenderlich.com/204/audio-101-for-iphone-developers-file-and-data-formats`.

Pop quiz – all about audio

Q1. What is the proper way of clearing audio files from the memory?

1. `audio.pause()`
2. `audio.stop()`
3. `audio.dispose()`
4. `audio.fadeOut()`

Q2. How many channels of audio can be played simultaneously in an application?

    1.   10

    2.   18

    3.   25

    4.   32

Q3. How do you make your audio file loop infinitely?

    1.   `loops = -1`

    2.   `loops = 0`

    3.   `loops = 1`

    4.   None of the above

Summary

You now understand the important aspects of using audio files in the Corona SDK. Now, you can go off adding your own sound effects and music to your games, or even add them to any of the samples you made in the previous chapters. By doing so, you add another part of the user experience that will draw players into the environment you have created.

Until now, you learned how to:

◆ Preload and play sound effects and music using `loadSound()` and `loadStream()`

◆ Control audio functions that pause, resume, stop, and rewind a music track under the Audio System API

◆ Dispose audio from memory when it is no longer in use

◆ Adjust volume in your audio files

In the next chapter, you will combine everything you have learned so far to create your final game in this book. You'll also be going over other ways to implement physical objects and collision mechanics that are popular in mobile games in the market today. More exciting information to learn awaits you. Let's power through!

7
Physics – Falling Objects

There are many variations on how to incorporate a physics engine using display objects. So far, we have worked on removing objects with collisions, moving objects through the stage area, and launching objects by applying force against gravity, just to name a few. Now, we will explore another mechanism that allows gravity to control the environment. The next game we'll create deals with falling physical objects.

In this chapter, we will:

◆ Work with more physics bodies

◆ Customize the body construction

◆ Track the objects caught

◆ Work with postcollisions

◆ Create falling objects

Here's to creating another fun, simple game in this chapter. Let's get cracking!

Creating our new game – Egg Drop

Every step taken so far has taught us more about game development on iOS/Android devices. In this new segment, our game will include sound effects, which will enhance the sensory experience in our games.

Make sure that you are using the latest stable build of Corona SDK.

The new game that we will create is called Egg Drop. The player controls the main character, which is a lumberjack with a frying pan. During game play, eggs start falling from the sky, and it is the lumberjack's job to catch the eggs in his frying pan and not let them hit the ground. Every egg caught earns 500 points. The player starts with three lives. When an egg fails to hit the frying pan and hits the ground, a life is lost. When all three lives are gone, the game is over.

When starting the new game project, be sure to grab the `Egg Drop` file from the `Chapter 7` folder. You can download the project files accompanying this book from the Packt Publishing website at `http://www.packtpub.com/`. It contains all the necessary files that are built out for you, such as the `build.settings`, `config.lua`, and audio files, and the art assets needed for the game. You'll then have to create a brand new `main.lua` file in the project folder before you start coding.

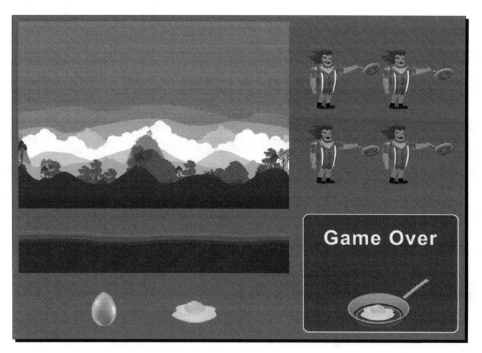

Starting variables

This will be our first full game setup, which will be filled with notable Corona SDK features. We'll combine our base knowledge of what we have learned so far with variables, display objects, the physics engine, touch/accelerometer events, and audio. Many of Corona's APIs are easy to use and understand. This shows the fast learning curve with Corona just by having basic to no knowledge of programming.

Time for action – setting up the variables

Let's get started with introducing the variables we'll be using to create our game. There will be a combination of display objects and integers to keep count; we also need to preload the main sound effects used during game play. Follow the steps to declare all the required variables:

1. Hide the status bar and add in the `display.newGroup()` group called `gameGroup`:

   ```
   display.setStatusBar( display.HiddenStatusBar )
   local gameGroup = display.newGroup()
   ```

2. Include the external modules in the game:

   ```
   local physics = require "physics"
   ```

3. Add in the display objects:

   ```
   local background
   local ground
   local charObject
   local friedEgg
   local scoreText
   local eggText
   local livesText
   local shade
   local gameOverScreen
   ```

4. Add in the variables:

   ```
   local gameIsActive = false
   local startDrop -- Timer object
   local gameLives = 3
   local gameScore = 0
   local eggCount = 0
   local mRand = math.random
   ```

5. Create the egg boundaries and density:

```
local eggDensity = 1.0
local eggShape = { -12,-13, 12,-13, 12,13, -12,13 }
local panShape = { 15,-13, 65,-13, 65,13, 15,13 }
```

6. Setup the accelerometer and audio:

```
system.setAccelerometerInterval( 100 )
local eggCaughtSound = audio.loadSound( "friedEgg.wav" )
local gameOverSound = audio.loadSound( "gameOver.wav" )
```

What just happened?

We continued creating a similar set up of our variables, like we did in the Panda Star Catcher game. It's more efficient to organize them by separating groups, display objects, audio, and so on.

Many of the variables displayed have designated integers that fulfill the goals of game play. This includes values such as gameLives = 3 and eggCount = 0.

Controlling the main character

Accelerometer events work best within the main scope of the game. It enables you to view the full real estate of the game environment, without having to interact with touches on the screen. Necessary touch events would make sense for user interface buttons such as pause, menu, play, and so on.

Time for action – moving the character

Eggs will be falling in all different areas of the screen from the sky. Let's prepare our main character to move through all the potential areas on the screen:

1. Set up a new local function called moveChar() with an event parameter:

```
local moveChar = function(event)
```

2. Add in the accelerometer movement for the character:

```
charObject.x = display.contentCenterX -
(display.contentCenterX* (event.yGravity*3))
```

3. Create character boundaries where it moves on the screen. This enables the character to stay within the game screen and not go past the offscreen boundaries:

```
if((charObject.x - charObject.width * 0.5) < 0) then
charObject.x = charObject.width * 0.5
elseif((charObject.x + charObject.width * 0.5) >
display.contentWidth) then
```

```
          charObject.x = display.contentWidth - charObject.width * 0.5
       end
    end
```

What just happened?

To make the accelerometer movement work with a device, we have to use yGravity.

 Accelerometer events are based on portrait scale when xGravity and yGravity are used accordingly. When display objects are designated for the landscape mode, the xGravity and yGravity values are switched to compensate for the events to work properly.

Notice that the code in step 3 keeps the charObject display object from going past any wall border boundaries.

Have a go hero – adding touch events

The character is currently controlled by the accelerometer. Another option to control the character is through a touch event. Try replacing the event listener with "touch" and using event parameters so that the touch event works properly.

If you remember how we incorporated the paddle movement with Breakout in *Chapter 3, Building Our First Game – Breakout* and *Chapter 4, Game Controls*, for the simulator, it should be very similar.

Updating the score

When the score is updated, it refers to our text display objects and translates the value from the number into a string.

Here is an example:

```
gameScore = 100
scoreText = display.newText( "Score: " .. gameScore, 0, 0, "Arial",
45 )
scoreText:setTextColor( 1, 1, 1)
scoreText.x = 160; scoreText.y = 100
```

In the previous example, you will notice that we set a value of 100 to gameScore. In the following lines for scoreText, gameScore is used to concatenate the "Score: " string and the value of gameScore. Doing so displays the value of gameScore in a string format by scoreText.

Time for action – setting the score

Who doesn't like some friendly competition? We're familiar with scoreboards from the games we made in the previous chapters. So, we are not strangers to tracking the score. Perform the following steps to set the score:

1. Create a local function called `setScore()` with a parameter called `scoreNum`:

```
local setScore = function( scoreNum )
```

2. Set the variables to count the score:

```
local newScore = scoreNum
gameScore = newScore
if gameScore < 0 then gameScore = 0; end
```

3. Have the score updated when points are earned in game play and close the function:

```
scoreText.text = "Score: " .. gameScore
scoreText.xScale = 0.5; scoreText.yScale = 0.5
scoreText.x = (scoreText.contentWidth * 0.5) + 15
scoreText.y = 15
end
```

What just happened?

When `setScore(scoreNum)` is called within any function, it will refer to all the methods using the `gameScore` variable. Assuming `gameScore = 0` at the start of the application, the value increments to what `gameScore` is set to.

In `scoreText.text = "Score: " .. gameScore`, `"Score: "` is the string that displays on the device during game play. The `gameScore` variable takes the current value given to the variable and displays it as a string.

Displaying the game environment

A logical setting for your display objects helps the player envision the relationship between the main character and the environment. Since our main character is a lumberjack, it would make sense to have him set in a forest or an area focused entirely on nature.

Time for action – drawing the background

In this section, we'll fill the screen with our environment display objects. This includes our background and ground objects, and we can also add physical elements to our ground so that we can designate collision events for it. To draw the background, perform the following steps:

1. Create a local function called `drawBackground()`:

   ```
   local drawBackground = function()
   ```

2. Add in the background image:

   ```
   background = display.newImageRect( "bg.png", 480, 320 )
   background.x = 240; background.y = 160
   gameGroup:insert( background )
   ```

3. Add in the ground elements and create the ground physical boundary. Close the function:

   ```
   ground = display.newImageRect( "grass.png", 480, 75 )
   ground.x = 240; ground.y = 325
   ground.myName = "ground"
   local groundShape = { -285,-18, 285,-18, 285,18, -285,18}
   physics.addBody( ground, "static", { density=1.0,
   bounce=0, friction=0.5, shape=groundShape } )
   gameGroup:insert( ground )
   end
   ```

What just happened?

The `background` and `ground` display objects are placed in the function called `drawBackground()`. The `display.newImageRect()` function is used since we are incorporating dynamic scaling on some of our images. The ground display object has a customized physical shape that is not of the same size as the original display object.

Our `background` object is centered to the dimensions of the device screen area and inserted in `gameGroup`.

The `ground` display object is placed near the bottom of the display area. It is assigned a name through `ground.myName = "ground"`. We'll use the name `"ground"` later on to determine collision events. A customized physical boundary is made for the ground through `groundShape`. This allows the body of the ground to affect the assigned dimensions of the display object. When `physics.addBody()` is initialized, we used `groundShape` as the shape parameter. Next, `ground` is set to `gameGroup` as well.

Displaying the heads-up display

In gaming, the **heads-up display (HUD)** is the method used to relay information visually to the player. In many games, the common features displayed are health/lives, time, weapons, menus, maps, and so on. This keeps your player alert to what is currently happening during game play. When it comes to tracking your lives, you want to be informed how many are left before your character runs out of chances to continue playing and the game ends.

Time for action – designing the HUD

While trying to make the player's gaming experience an enjoyable one, it's important that the information displayed is relevant to the game and placed strategically, so that it doesn't interfere with the main gaming area. So, to design the HUD, perform the following steps:

1. Create a new local function called hud():

```
local hud = function()
```

2. Display the text for the eggs that are caught during game play:

```
eggText = display.newText( "Caught: " .. eggCount, 0, 0,
"Arial", 45 )
eggText:setTextColor( 1, 1, 1 )
eggText.xScale = 0.5; eggText.yScale = 0.5
eggText.x = (480 - (eggText.contentWidth * 0.5)) - 15
eggText.y = 305
gameGroup:insert( eggText )
```

3. Add in text to track the lives:

```
livesText = display.newText( "Lives: " .. gameLives, 0,
0, "Arial", 45 )
livesText:setTextColor( 1, 1, 1 )--> white
livesText.xScale = 0.5; livesText.yScale = 0.5   --> for
clear retina display text
livesText.x = (480 - (livesText.contentWidth * 0.5)) - 15
livesText.y = 15
gameGroup:insert( livesText )
```

4. Add in text for the score and close the function:

```
scoreText = display.newText( "Score: " .. gameScore, 0,
0, "Arial", 45 )
scoreText:setTextColor( 1, 1, 1 )--> white
scoreText.xScale = 0.5; scoreText.yScale = 0.5   --> for
clear retina display text
```

```
        scoreText.x = (scoreText.contentWidth * 0.5) + 15
        scoreText.y = 15
        gameGroup:insert( scoreText )
    end
```

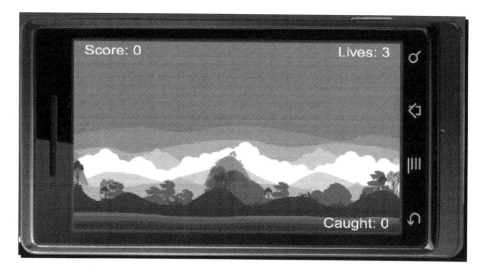

What just happened?

The `eggText` display object can be found near the bottom-right corner of the screen. It's still in view to the user while in game play and stays out of the main focus at the same time. Notice that `eggText = display.newText( "Caught: " .. eggCount, 0, 0, "Arial", 45 )` will refer to `eggCount` when the value is updated.

The `livesText` display object setup is similar to `eggText`. It is placed near the top-right corner of the screen. The placement for this object is rather prominent because of its importance in the game. It's in an area that is noticeable from the background and allows the player to refer to during the game. The `livesText` display object decrements the number when `gameLives` is updated.

The initial setup for `scoreText` starts in the `hud()` function. It is placed in the top-left corner of the screen, opposite to `livesText`.

Creating the game lives

If there are no consequences in a game, then there is no sense of urgency to complete the main objectives. To keep a player engaged during game play, introducing elements that add some challenging aspects will keep the competitiveness and excitement going. Adding consequences in a game creates tension for the player and gives them more motivation to stay alive.

Time for action – counting the lives

Tracking the lives left in the game keeps the player updated on how much sooner it will be till the game is over. To count the remaining lives in the game, perform the following steps:

1. Set up the function called `livesCount()`:

```
local livesCount = function()
```

2. Display the text for lives every time the number is decremented:

```
gameLives = gameLives - 1
livesText.text = "Lives: " .. gameLives
livesText.xScale = 0.5; livesText.yScale = 0.5  --> for
clear retina display text
livesText.x = (480 - (livesText.contentWidth * 0.5)) - 15
livesText.y = 15
print(gameLives .. " eggs left")
if gameLives < 1 then
  callGameOver()
end
end
```

What just happened?

The `livesCount()` function is a separate function that updates `gameLives`. It makes sure that you're aware that `gameLives = gameLives - 1`. This decreases the set value instantiated in the beginning of the code. When `gameLives` changes values, it displays the update through `livesText`. The `print` statement is used towards the end of the function to track the count in the terminal window.

When `gameLives < 1`, the `callGameOver()` function will be called and show the game over element of the game.

Have a go hero – adding images for the game lives

Currently, the game uses display text on screen to show how many lives are left during game play. A way to make the HUD display more appealing is by creating/adding small icons that correlate with the game, such as eggs or a frying pan.

Three separate display objects need to be created and placed in an orderly fashion so that when a life is taken away, the alpha of the object is reduced to 0.5.

A method needs to be created so that all the three display objects are affected when the game lives are reduced to zero.

Introducing the main character

Our main character will be animated for every action applied during game play. We will also create a complex body construction since the focus of its collision points will be on the object the character is holding, and not on their entire body.

Complex body construction

It is also possible to construct a body from multiple elements. Each body element is specified as a separate polygon shape with its own physical properties.

Since collision polygons in Box2D must be convex, any game object with a concave shape must be constructed by appending multiple body elements.

The constructor for a complex body is the same as the simple polygon body constructor, except that it has more than one body element listed:

```
physics.addBody( displayObject, [bodyType,] bodyElement1,
    [bodyElement2, ...] )
```

Each body element may have its own physical properties, along with a shape definition for its collision boundaries. Here is an example:

```
local hexagon = display.newImage("hexagon.png")
hexagon.x = hexagon.contentWidth
hexagon.y = hexagon.contentHeight
hexagonShape = { -20,-40, 20, -40, 40, 0, 20,40, -20,40, -40,0 }
physics.addBody( hexagon, "static", { density = 1.0, friction = 0.8,
bounce = 0.3, shape=hexagonShape } )
```

As in the simpler cases, the `bodyType` attribute is optional and will default to `"dynamic"`, if not specified.

Time for action – creating the character

The main character was created with a sprite sheet and needs to be set up to view the animation it provides. Other display images that will make an appearance include a cracked egg when a collision to a physical object has been made. To create the character, perform the following steps:

1. Create a new local function called `createChar()`:

    ```
    local createChar = function()
    ```

2. Create the sprite sheet for the main character:

```
local sheetData = { width=128, height=128, numFrames=4,
sheetContentWidth=256, sheetContentHeight=256 }
local sheet = graphics.newImageSheet( "charSprite.png",
sheetData )

    local sequenceData =
    {
       { name="move", start=1, count=4, time=400 }
    }

    charObject = display.newSprite( sheet, sequenceData )
    charObject:setSequence("move")
    charObject:play()
```

3. Set the starting position and physical properties for the main character:

```
charObject.x = 240; charObject.y = 250
physics.addBody( charObject, "static", { density=1.0,
bounce=0.4, friction=0.15, shape=panShape } )
charObject.rotation = 0
charObject.isHit = false -- When object is not hit
charObject.myName = "character"
```

4. Add in the transition image after the egg has made a collision:

```
friedEgg = display.newImageRect( "friedEgg.png", 40, 23 )
friedEgg.alpha = 1.0
friedEgg.isVisible = false
gameGroup:insert( charObject )
gameGroup:insert( friedEgg )
end
```

What just happened?

The image sheet being referred to is called `sheetData` and takes the first 4 frames of animation from `"charSprite.png"`. We created an animation set called `"move"`. Every time `"move"` is called, it starts the animation from frame 1 and plays 4 frames from the start at 400 milliseconds.

The main display object is called `charObject` and takes on the characteristics of `sheetData`. When it calls `setSequence("move")`, that animation sequence plays when the `play()` command is executed.

An important change to the physical body of the character is that its main collision point will be directed towards the frying pan used in the animation. Any collision detection on the character's body will not be read. The `charObject` display object is given a name called `"character"`, which will be used to detect the collision with the falling egg.

We have also placed the fried egg in this function, to prepare it for the collision.

Adding postcollisions

We want to make sure that when an object has interacted with another, an event type occurs right after. At the instance of a postcollision, we can confirm the collision force between two objects. This helps us determine that the object that was destroyed was completed with a set amount of force.

Collision handling

Be careful about how you handle the Box2D physics engine. It will crash during a collision if Corona code attempts to modify objects still involved in the collision, since Box2D is still working out iterated mathematics on them.

For crash-proof collision detection, do not have collisions occur immediately.

Do not modify/create/destroy physics objects during a collision, in order to prevent crashing.

If you need to modify/create/destroy an object as a result of a collision, your collision handler should set a flag or add a time delay so that the change can occur later, with `timer.performWithDelay()`.

Body properties

Many of the native Box2D methods have been made into simpler dot properties for display objects. The following examples show that a body, `newBody`, has been created using one of the constructor methods.

body.isAwake

This is a Boolean for the current awake state. By default, all bodies automatically *go to sleep* when there is no interaction with them for a couple of seconds. Bodies stop simulating until some kind of collision or other interaction wakes them up.

Here is an example:

```
newBody.isAwake = true
local object = newBody.isAwake
```

body.isBodyActive

This is a Boolean for the active state of a body. Inactive bodies are not destroyed, but they are removed from the simulation and cease to interact with other bodies.

Here is an example:

```
newBody.isBodyActive = true
local object = newBody.isBodyActive
```

body.isBullet

This is a Boolean for a body that is treated like a *bullet*. Bullets are subject to continuous collision detection. The default is `false`.

Here is an example:

```
newBody.isBullet = true
local object = newBody.isBullet
```

body.isSensor

This is a Boolean property that sets the `isSensor` property across all elements in the body. A sensor passes through other objects instead of bouncing off them, but detects some collision. This property acts across all body elements and will override any `isSensor` settings on the elements themselves.

Here is an example:

```
newBody.isSensor = true
```

body.isSleepingAllowed

This is a Boolean for a body that is allowed to go to sleep. A body that is awake is useful in cases such as tilt gravity, since sleeping bodies do not respond to changes in global gravity. The default is `true`.

Here is an example:

```
newBody.isSleepingAllowed = true
local object = newBody.isSleepingAllowed
```

body.isFixedRotation

This is a Boolean for a body whose rotation should be locked, even if the body is about to load or subjected to off-center forces. The default is `false`.

Here is an example:

```
newBody.isFixedRotation = true
local object = newBody.isFixedRotation
```

body.angularVelocity

This is the value of the current rotational velocity in degrees per second.

Here is an example:

```
newBody.angularVelocity = 50
local myVelocity = newBody.angularVelocity
```

body.linearDamping

This is the value for how much the linear motion of a body is damped. This is the rate of decrease of angular velocity over time. The default is zero.

Here is an example:

```
newBody.linearDamping = 5
local object = newBody.linearDamping
```

body.angularDamping

This is the value for how much the rotation of a body should be damped. The default is zero.

Here is an example:

```
newBody.angularDamping = 5
local object = newBody.angularDamping
```

body.bodyType

This is a string value for the type of physical body being simulated. The available values are `"static"`, `"dynamic"`, and `"kinematic"`, which are explained here:

- `static` bodies don't move or interact with each other. Examples of static objects would include the ground or the walls of a maze.
- `dynamic` bodies are affected by gravity and collisions with other body types.
- `kinematic` objects are affected by forces but not by gravity. Bodies that are draggable objects should be set to `"kinematic"` for the duration of the drag event.

The default body type is `"dynamic"`.

Here is an example:

```
newBody.bodyType = "kinematic"
local currentBodyType = newBody.bodyType
```

Time for action – creating the egg collision

We have handled collisions in the previous sample games we created. Handling postcollisions requires the introduction of force to execute the completion of a postcollision event:

1. Create a new local function called `onEggCollision()` with two parameters called `self` and `event`:

    ```
    local onEggCollision = function( self, event )
    ```

2. Create an `if` statement when the force is greater than 1 and include `not self.isHit`. Add in the `eggCaughtSound` sound effect:

    ```
    if event.force > 1 and not self.isHit then
        audio.play( eggCaughtSound )
    ```

3. Make `self` invisible and inactive, and replace it with the `friedEgg` display object:

    ```
    self.isHit = true
    print( "Egg destroyed!")
    self.isVisible = false
    friedEgg.x = self.x; friedEgg.y = self.y
    friedEgg.alpha = 0
    friedEgg.isVisible = true
    ```

4. Create a function that transitions the `friedEgg` display object and fades it off the stage by using the `onComplete` command:

    ```
    local fadeEgg = function()
        transition.to( friedEgg, { time=500, alpha=0 } )
    ```

```
end
transition.to( friedEgg, { time=50, alpha=1.0,
onComplete=fadeEgg } )
self.parent:remove( self )
self = nil
```

5. Using `if event.other.myName == "character"`, update `eggCount` when the main character catches the eggs. Also, update `gameScore` by `500` points for every collision. If the egg hits the ground, use `elseif event.other.myName == "ground"` and decrement the lives using `livesCount()`:

```
if event.other.myName == "character" then
  eggCount = eggCount + 1
  eggText.text = "Caught: " .. eggCount
  eggText.xScale = 0.5; eggText.yScale = 0.5  --> for
  clear retina display text
  eggText.x = (480 - (eggText.contentWidth * 0.5)) - 15
  eggText.y = 305
  print("egg caught")
  local newScore = gameScore + 500
  setScore( newScore )
elseif event.other.myName == "ground" then
  livesCount()
  print("ground hit")
end
end
end
```

What just happened?

Using onEggCollision(self, event), we set up the function with an if statement for event.force > 1 and not self.isHit. When both statements return true, the sound effect for the egg plays. The initial egg falling from the sky is removed from the scene upon collision and replaced by the friedEgg display object in the same location, using friedEgg.x = self.x; friedEgg.y = self.y.

The fadeEgg() function makes the newly replaced egg object appear in 50 milliseconds by transition.to(eggCrack, { time=50, alpha=1.0, onComplete=fadeCrack }) and then with the onComplete command, it returns the object to an invisible state with transition.to(eggCrack, { time=500, alpha=0 }).

When the name "character" is called from event.other.myName, every collision assigned to that name increments eggCount + 1. Therefore, eggText is updated with the eggCount value. The setScore(newScore) statement increments the score by 500 with every collision made to "character". When a collision is made to "ground", the livesCount() function is called, which subtracts life by 1.

Making the display objects fall

We will apply the main asset (egg object) by learning how to add physical objects to the scene and have them fall in random areas in the game. The physics engine will take into account a dynamic physics body that we will create for the egg display object.

Time for action – adding the egg object

Imagine a world, full of falling eggs. It's not entirely too realistic, but in this game, we're creating this element. At least, we'll be making sure that both gravity and real-world physics will be applied. To add the egg object, perform the following steps:

1. Create a new local function called eggDrop():

   ```
   local eggDrop = function()
   ```

2. Add in the egg display object properties:

   ```
   local egg = display.newImageRect( "egg.png", 26, 30 )
   egg.x = 240 + mRand( 120 ); egg.y = -100
   egg.isHit = false
   physics.addBody( egg, "dynamic",{ density=eggDensity,
   bounce=0, friction=0.5, shape=eggShape } )
   egg.isFixedRotation = true
   gameGroup:insert( egg )
   ```

3. Add in the `postCollision` event for the `egg` display object:

```
egg.postCollision = onEggCollision
egg:addEventListener( "postCollision", egg )
end
```

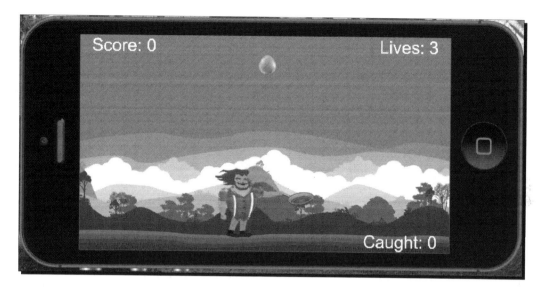

What just happened?

We have set the `egg` value for x with `240 + mRand( 120 )`. The `mRand` function is equal to `math.random`, which will allow the egg to appear in randomized places in an area of `120` pixels, starting at 50 in the *x* direction.

It is vital to make sure that `egg.isHit = false` for the collision event to apply correctly. The physics body is set to `"dynamic"` so that it reacts to gravity and makes the object fall. There is a customized density and shape made for the egg we have created, which was already made at the beginning of the code.

The last important detail for the collision to work is adding `egg` to the `onEggCollision()` function with `egg.postCollision = onEggCollision` and then making the event listener use the `"postCollision"` event with `egg:addEventListener( "postCollision", egg )`.

Time for action – making the egg drop

We're going to execute the timer for the eggs, so that they can start dropping on the screen. To make the egg drop, perform the following steps:

1. Create a local function called `eggTimer()` and use `timer.performWithDelay` to drop an egg every 1 second (`1000` milliseconds) repeatedly. Use `eggDrop()` to activate the drop:

   ```
   local eggTimer = function()
     startDrop = timer.performWithDelay( 1000, eggDrop, 0 )
   end
   ```

2. Within the first `if` statement in the `onEggCollision()` function, cancel the timer using the `timerID` and `startDrop` variables. Add the `if gameLives < 1` statement then to stop the eggs from falling:

   ```
   if gameLives < 1 then
     timer.cancel( startDrop )
     print("timer cancelled")
   end
   ```

What just happened?

In order for the eggs to start dropping from the sky, we created a function called `eggTimer()`. It activates the `eggDrop()` function by letting an egg drop after `1000` milliseconds (1 second) every time infinitely using `startDrop = timer.performWithDelay( 1000, eggDrop, 0 )`.

Backtracking to `onEggCollision()`, we want to check whether `gameLives` has reached less than 1. When this statement is true, the eggs will stop dropping. This is done using `timer.cancel( startDrop )`. The `timerID` we set in `eggTimer()` is `startDrop`.

Ending the game play

Every start of a game always has an ending, whether it is a simple *You Win* or *You Lose* or just a *Game Over*; all these give closure to the player. It's important to notify a player of such events, so that they can reflect on the achievements earned.

Time for action – calling game over

We will make sure that when a game over display screen pops up, any of our display objects that are currently in motion stop moving, and the event listeners are deactivated. Aside from the visual display of our game over screen, we'll be adding a sound notification that will also help to trigger the event. To end the game, perform the following steps:

1. Create a new local function called `callGameOver()` and place it after the `setScore()` function and before the `drawBackground()` function:

   ```
   local callGameOver = function()
   ```

2. Introduce the sound effects when the game over display pops up. Have `gameIsActive` set to `false` and pause the physics in the game:

   ```
   audio.play( gameOverSound )
   gameIsActive = false
   physics.pause()
   ```

3. Create a shade that overlays the current background:

   ```
   shade = display.newRect( 0, 0, 570, 320 )
   shade:setFillColor( 0, 0, 0 )
   shade.x = 240; shade.y = 160
   shade.alpha = 0   -- Getting shade ready to display at
   game end
   ```

4. Display the game over window and reiterate the final score:

   ```
   gameOverScreen = display.newImageRect( "gameOver.png",
   400, 300 )
   local newScore = gameScore
   setScore( newScore )
   gameOverScreen.x = 240; gameOverScreen.y = 160
   gameOverScreen.alpha = 0
   gameGroup:insert( shade )
   gameGroup:insert( gameOverScreen )
   transition.to( shade, { time=200, alpha=0.65 } )
   transition.to( gameOverScreen, { time=500, alpha=1 } )
   ```

5. Have the score display on the game over screen:

```
scoreText.isVisible = false
scoreText.text = "Score: " .. gameScore
scoreText.xScale = 0.5; scoreText.yScale = 0.5  --> for
clear retina display text
scoreText.x = 240
scoreText.y = 160
scoreText:toFront()  -- Moves to front of current display
group
timer.performWithDelay( 0,
   function() scoreText.isVisible = true; end, 1 )
end
```

What just happened?

Our `gameOver()` function triggers our `gameOverSound` sound effect that we preloaded at the beginning of our code. We made sure no events, such as the motion from the accelerometer, are disabled through `gameIsActive = false`.

The elements of our display objects appear at this point in time with `shade`, `gameOverScreen`, and `scoreText`.

If you notice, `scoreText` disappears when game play has ended by `scoreText.isVisible = false` and then reappears in a different area of the screen, using `timer.performWithDelay( 0, function() scoreText.isVisible = true; end, 1 )`.

Starting the game

We will activate all the remaining functions and have them run accordingly.

Time for action – activating the game

With all the game play elements set in place, it is time to get the application started by using the following steps:

1. Create a new local function called gameActivate() and insert gameIsActive = true. Place the function above the moveChar() function:

    ```
    local gameActivate = function()
      gameIsActive = true
    end
    ```

2. Initialize all the game actions by making a new function called gameStart():

    ```
    local gameStart = function()
    ```

3. Start the physics property and set the gravity for the falling object:

    ```
    physics.start( true )
    physics.setGravity( 0, 9.8 )
    ```

4. Activate all the functions instantiated. Add an event listener for the charObject, using the "accelerometer" event for the moveChar() function:

    ```
    drawBackground()
    createChar()
    eggTimer()
    hud()
    gameActivate()
    Runtime:addEventListener("accelerometer", moveChar)
    end
    ```

5. Instantiate the gameStart() function and return the gameGroup group:

    ```
    gameStart()
    return gameGroup
    ```

What just happened?

If you remember, in the beginning of our code, we set gameIsActive = false. We will now change this status through the gameActivate() function and make gameIsActive = true. We made the gameStart() function apply all the initial game play elements. This includes the start of the physics engine and gravity. At the same time, we took the remainder of all the functions and initialized them.

Once all the functions are activated, `gameGroup` needs to be returned so that all the display objects appear during the game play.

To make sure that your physical object boundaries for your display objects are in the right place, use `physics.setDrawMode( "hybrid" )` in the `gameStart()` function.

Pop quiz – animating the graphics

Q1. What retrieves or sets the text string of a text object?

1. `object.text`
2. `object.size`
3. `object:setTextColor()`
4. None of the above

Q2. What function converts any argument into a string?

1. `tonumber()`
2. `print()`
3. `tostring()`
4. `nil`

Q3. What body type is affected by gravity and collisions with the other body types?

1. dynamic
2. kinematic
3. static
4. None of the above

Summary

The game play construction of our application is now completed. Now that we're familiar with a variety of ways to use the physics engine, it goes to show the ease of using Box2D for designing other games that involve physics bodies.

We now have a better idea of:

◆ Applying the uses of dynamic and static physics bodies

◆ Constructing a customized shape for the physical properties of our display objects

◆ Tracking the number of objects caught using values from variables that are given

◆ Using postcollisions to switch out images

In the next chapter, we will complete the gaming experience by creating versatile menu screens by using the Composer API. You will also learn how to add the pause action, save high scores, and understand more about data saving and unloading files.

Using Corona SDK has helped us design and develop games in a minimal amount of time. Let's continue adding the final touches to our game!

8

Operation Composer

We've taken our game, Egg Drop, and explored ways to create game physics to react with collision detection and track other useful data, such as lives and a points system. We also worked with customizing physical bodies and created names for our display objects that apply to the game score count.

Next, we'll add a menu system that incorporates the introduction to the game, apply a pause menu during game play, and save high scores when the game is over.

We're on our way to completing an application that has the necessary elements to make it ready for the App Store and Google Play Store.

In this chapter, we will:

- ◆ Save and load high scores
- ◆ Add a pause menu
- ◆ Manage scenes with the Composer API
- ◆ Add a loading screen
- ◆ Add a main menu, options menu, and credits screen

So, let's get going!

Continuation of Egg Drop

We have finished the main game portion of Egg Drop as the main base of our application. Now, it's time for us to include how to pause action midgame and also save high scores. We will also add some new scenes that will help us introduce and transition to the game in an easy and quick fashion.

In the `Resources` folder of `Chapter 8`, grab all the image and file assets inside and copy them to your current `Egg Drop` project folder. You can download the project files accompanying this book from the Packt Publishing website. We will use these files to add the final touches to our game.

Data saving

Saving file information is used in many aspects of game development. We use it to save high scores and game settings, such as sound on/off, locking/unlocking levels, and so on. It is not necessary to have these features, but as they are good to have, maybe you'd like to include them in your applications.

In Corona SDK, applications are sandboxed; this means that your files (application images, data, and preferences) are stored in a location that no other application can access. Your files will reside in an app-specific directory for documents, resources, or temporary files. This restriction is related to the files on your device, not when you are coding on your Mac or PC.

BeebeGames class for saving and loading values

We'll be using the BeebeGames class created by Jonathan Beebe. It provides many easy and useful functions to use for games. Some of the notable functions included incorporate a simple way of saving and loading data that we'll be able add into our game. More documentation on the BeebeGames class can be found in the `Chapter 8` folder.

 You can also refer to https://github.com/lewisNotestine/luaCorona/blob/master/justATest/code/beebegames.lua to track updates on the class.

You can take a look at other methods relating to animation, transitions, timers, and so on if you would like to use them for future use. For now, we'll focus on the methods we can use to easily save and load values for our game.

Here is an example of saving and loading values:

```
-- Public Method: saveValue() --> save single-line file (replace
contents)

function saveValue( strFilename, strValue )
  -- will save specified value to specified file
  local theFile = strFilename
  local theValue = strValue

  local path = system.pathForFile( theFile,
  system.DocumentsDirectory)

  -- io.open opens a file at path. returns nil if no file found
  -- "w+": update mode, all previous data is erased
  local file = io.open( path, "w+" )
  if file then
  -- write game score to the text file
  file:write( theValue )
  io.close( file )
  end
end


-- Public Method: loadValue() --> load single-line file and store it
into variable

function loadValue( strFilename )
  -- will load specified file, or create new file if it doesn't exist

  local theFile = strFilename

  local path = system.pathForFile( theFile,
  system.DocumentsDirectory)

  -- io.open opens a file at path. returns nil if no file found
  -- "r": read mode
  local file = io.open( path, "r" )
  if file then
    -- read all contents of file into a string
    -- "*a": reads the whole file, starting at the current position
    local contents = file:read( "*a" )
    io.close( file )
    return contents
  else
```

```
        -- create file b/c it doesn't exist yet
        -- "w": write mode
        file = io.open( path, "w" )
        file:write( "0" )
        io.close( file )
        return "0"
    end
end
```

Getting paths to files

The paths to these files are unique to your application. To create file paths, you can use the `system.pathForFile` function. This function generates an absolute path to the icon file for your application, using the application's resource directory as the base directory for `Icon.png`:

```
local path = system.pathForFile( "Icon.png",
system.ResourceDirectory)
```

In general, your files must reside in one of the three possible base directories:

- `system.DocumentsDirectory`: This should be used for files that need to persist between application sessions.

- `system.TemporaryDirectory`: This is a temporary directory. Files written to this directory are not guaranteed to exist in subsequent application sessions. They may or may not exist.

- `system.ResourceDirectory`: This is the directory where all application assets exist. Note that you should never create, modify, or add files to this directory.

 More information on files can be found at `http://docs.coronalabs.com/api/library/system/index.html`.

Reading files

To read files, the `io` library is used. This library allows you to manage files, given an absolute path.

Writing files

To write files, you follow many of the steps that are the same as for reading a file. Instead of using a read method, you write data (strings or numbers) to a file.

Time for action – saving and loading the high score

When the **Game Over** screen displays, we will save and load the values of our final score and highest score. For this perform the following steps:

1. Open up your `main.lua` file that we created for Egg Drop. We'll continue using the same file and add in more code with the new alterations to the game.

2. Add in two new variables, `local highScoreText` and `local highScore` where all the other initialized variables are located, near the top of the code:

```lua
local highScoreText
local highScore
```

3. Introduce the `saveValue()` function after the preloaded sound files:

```lua
local saveValue = function( strFilename, strValue )
  -- will save specified value to specified file
  local theFile = strFilename
  local theValue = strValue

  local path = system.pathForFile( theFile,
  system.DocumentsDirectory )

  -- io.open opens a file at path. returns nil if no file
  found
  local file = io.open( path, "w+" )
  if file then
    -- write game score to the text file
    file:write( theValue )
    io.close( file )
  end
end
```

4. Add in the `loadValue()` function:

```lua
local loadValue = function( strFilename )
  -- will load specified file, or create new file if it
  doesn't exist

  local theFile = strFilename

  local path = system.pathForFile( theFile,
  system.DocumentsDirectory )

  -- io.open opens a file at path. returns nil if no file
  found
```

```
local file = io.open( path, "r" )
if file then
  -- read all contents of file into a string
  local contents = file:read( "*a" )
  io.close( file )
  return contents
else
  -- create file b/c it doesn't exist yet
  file = io.open( path, "w" )
  file:write( "0" )
  io.close( file )
  return "0"
end
end
```

5. At the end of the `callGameOver()` function, create an `if` statement to compare `gameScore` and `highScore`. Save the highest score by using the `saveValue()` function:

```
if gameScore > highScore then
  highScore = gameScore
  local highScoreFilename = "highScore.data"
  saveValue( highScoreFilename, tostring(highScore) )
end
```

6. Next, add in the `highScoreText` display text in the same `callGameOver()` function, to show the high score at the end of the game:

```
highScoreText = display.newText( "Best Game Score: " ..
tostring( highScore ), 0, 0, "Arial", 30 )
highScoreText:setTextColor( 1, 1, 1 )
highScoreText.xScale = 0.5; highScoreText.yScale = 0.5
highScoreText.x = 240
highScoreText.y = 120

gameGroup:insert( highScoreText )
```

7. At the end of the `gameStart()` function, have the high score loaded by using the `loadValue()` function:

```
local highScoreFilename = "highScore.data"
local loadedHighScore = loadValue( highScoreFilename )

highScore = tonumber(loadedHighScore)
```

What just happened?

After initializing the `saveValue()` and `loadValue()` functions at the game level, we created an `if` statement to compare `gameScore`, which is the current score during game play, and `highScore`, which is the highest score accrued so far. When the outcome of `gameScore` is higher, then it replaces the `highScore` data saved.

In order to save the value, a data file needs to be created. We created a variable called `local highScoreFilename = "highscore.data"`. We called the `saveValue()` function using `highScoreFilename` as a parameter. The `tostring(highScore)` parameter will convert the numeric value of `highScore` to a string.

When the **Game Over** screen is visible, `highScoreText` displays the value saved from `highScore` above the `gameScore` that is achieved. Adding a high score gives the player an incentive to top the highest score and adds the replay value to the game.

In the `gameStart()` function, it's important to have the value of `highScore.data` loaded at the start of game play. Using the same data file we created to save `highScore`, we can also load the value throughout the game. To load the value, `local highScore` calls `loadValue(highScoreFileName)`. This takes the information from `highScore.data`. To obtain the value, `tonumber(loadedHighScore)` converts it to an integer from a string and can be used to display the value of `highScore`.

Pausing the game

Have you ever found yourself in the middle of playing a game and all of a sudden you have to take a bathroom break or your hand cramps up? Obviously, any of these situations require you to deter your attention from your game progress, and you need to stop the current action temporarily to attend to those needs. This is when a pause button comes in handy so that you can stop the action in that moment in time and then continue where you left off when you're ready to play again.

Time for action – pausing the game

It's more than just making a button; it's also pausing all the action on screen, including physics and timers by performing the following steps:

1. Add in the `local pauseBtn` and `local pauseBG` variables where all the other variables are initialized near the beginning of the code. Preload the `btnSound` audio after `gameOverSound` near the top of the script:

    ```
    -- Place near other game variables
    local pauseBtn
    local pauseBG


    -- Place after gameOverSound
    local btnSound = audio.loadSound( "btnSound.wav" )
    ```

2. Within the `hud()` function and after the `scoreText` chunk, create another function that will run the event for the pause button. Call the `onPauseTouch(event)` function. Pause the physics in the game by setting `gameIsActive` to `false` and have the pause elements appear on screen:

    ```
    local onPauseTouch = function( event )
      if event.phase == "release" and pauseBtn.isActive then
        audio.play( btnSound )

        -- Pause the game

      if gameIsActive then

        gameIsActive = false
        physics.pause()

        local function pauseGame()
          timer.pause( startDrop )
          print("timer has been paused")
        end
    ```

```
timer.performWithDelay(1, pauseGame)

-- SHADE
if not shade then
  shade = display.newRect( 0, 0, 570, 380 )
  shade:setFillColor( 0, 0, 0 )
  shade.x = 240; shade.y = 160
  gameGroup:insert( shade )
end
shade.alpha = 0.5

-- SHOW MENU BUTTON
if pauseBG then
  pauseBG.isVisible = true
  pauseBG.isActive = true
  pauseBG:toFront()
end

pauseBtn:toFront()
```

3. When the game is unpaused, have the physics become active again and remove all the pause display objects:

```
else

  if shade then
    display.remove( shade )
    shade = nil
  end

  if pauseBG then
    pauseBG.isVisible = false
    pauseBG.isActive = false
  end

  gameIsActive = true
  physics.start()

  local function resumeGame()
  timer.resume( startDrop )
  print("timer has been resumed")
end
timer.performWithDelay(1, resumeGame)

    end
  end
end
```

4. Add the pauseBtn UI button and pauseBG display object after the onPauseTouch() function:

```
pauseBtn = ui.newButton{
   defaultSrc = "pausebtn.png",
   defaultX = 44,
   defaultY = 44,
   overSrc = "pausebtn-over.png",
   overX = 44,
   overY = 44,
   onEvent = onPauseTouch,
   id = "PauseButton",
   text = "",
   font = "Helvetica",
   textColor = { 255, 255, 255, 255 },
   size = 16,
   emboss = false
}

pauseBtn.x = 38; pauseBtn.y = 288
pauseBtn.isVisible = false
pauseBtn.isActive = false

gameGroup:insert( pauseBtn )

pauseBG = display.newImageRect( "pauseoverlay.png", 480,
320 )
pauseBG.x = 240; pauseBG.y = 160
pauseBG.isVisible = false
pauseBG.isActive = false

gameGroup:insert( pauseBG )
```

5. In order for pauseBtn to display during game play, make it visible and active in the gameActivate() function:

```
pauseBtn.isVisible = true
pauseBtn.isActive = true
```

6. When the game is over, disable pauseBtn in the callGameOver() function Place the code right after the physics.pause() line:

```
pauseBtn.isVisible = false
pauseBtn.isActive = false
```

What just happened?

We created the onPauseTouch(event) function to control all the pause events that occur within the game play. To pause all the motion in the game, we changed the Boolean of gameIsActive to false and the physics.pause() function to stop all the eggs that are falling from moving. Next, the timer is paused for startDrop so that any eggs falling from the sky won't accumulate over time as long as the pause function is still active.

A slightly transparent overlay called shade is called to appear when the pause button is pressed. This will deter the attention from the game scene and allow the user to differentiate when the game play is not active.

The **Game Paused** banner also displays on the top of the screen by making it visible and active. The pauseBG object is pushed ahead of the display hierarchy by pauseBG:toFront().

To unpause the game, we reversed the process of how the pause display items appeared. When pauseBtn is pressed for the second time, shade is taken away by display. remove(shade); shade = nil. The pauseBG.isVisible and pauseBG.isActive properties are both set to false.

Remember that we had set gameIsActive to false earlier Well, it's now time to set it back to true. This also means resuming physics with physics.start(). The timer is resumed by the resumeGame() local function and calls timer.resume(startDrop) within the function.

The pauseBtn and pauseBG display objects are inserted at the end of the if statement block. The pauseBtn object is then shown as visible and active once the game is playable. It is invisible and inactive when the **Game Over** screen appears so that there are no other touch events that can interfere when the game is over.

The Composer API

The Composer API provides an easy solution for developers to control scenes with or without transitions. This is a great scene-management library to display menu systems and even managing multiple levels in a game. Composer also comes with a variety of transition effects. More information can be found on the Corona Docs at http://docs.coronalabs.com/api/library/composer/index.html.

Our scene management will look similar to the scene template displayed at http://docs.coronalabs.com/api/library/composer/index.html#scene-template.

Game development with the Composer API

You may wonder how we're going to apply Composer with Egg Drop. It's really simple. We'll have to alter some lines in our game code to make it compatible with Composer and create some new scenes for the menu system that is applied before game splay.

Time for action – altering the game file

We will rename our current main.lua file to maingame.lua and add some additional lines to our game code. Be sure to *change* the file name within your Egg Drop project folder. To rename the file follow these steps:

1. Remove the following lines near the top of the code. We'll hide the status bar in another scene that we'll create later on in this chapter. The gameGroup display group will be altered to fit within the Composer parameters:

```
display.setStatusBar( display.HiddenStatusBar )
local gameGroup = display.newGroup()
```

2. At the very top of the code, implement Composer by adding local composer = require("composer") and local scene = composer.newScene() so that we can call the scene events:

```
local composer = require( "composer" )
local scene = composer.newScene()
```

3. After `local loadValue = function( strFilename )`, add in the `create()` event. We will also add back in our `gameGroup` display group, but under the scene's view property. Also, add in `composer.removeScene( "loadgame" )`. The `"loadgame"` scene will be introduced later on in this chapter:

```
-- Called when the scene's view does not exist:
function scene:create ( event )
  local gameGroup = self.view

  -- completely remove loadgame's view
  composer.removeScene( "loadgame" )

  print( "\nmaingame: create event")
end
```

4. After the `create()` event, create the `show()` event and add it before the `gameActivate()` function. The `show()` event will transition all our game play functions onscreen. Include `gameGroup` in the scene's view property as well:

```
-- Called immediately after scene has moved onscreen:
function scene:show( event )
  local gameGroup = self.view
```

5. After the `gameStart()` function, remove the `return gameGroup` line:

```
return gameGroup -- Code will not run if this line is not removed
```

6. Next, close `function scene: show( event )` with end:

```
  print( "maingame: show event" )

end
```

7. Create the `hide()` and `destroy()` events:

```
-- Called when scene is about to move offscreen:
function scene:hide( event )

  print( "maingame: hide event" )

end

-- Called prior to the removal of scene's "view" (display
group)
function scene:destroy( event )

  print( "destroying maingame's view" )

end
```

8. Finally, create event listeners for all the scene events and add `return scene` at the end of the code:

```
-- "create" event is dispatched if scene's view does not exist
scene:addEventListener( "create", scene )

-- "show" event is dispatched whenever scene transition has
finished
scene:addEventListener( "show", scene )

-- "hide" event is dispatched before next scene's transition
begins
scene:addEventListener( "hide", scene )

-- "destroy" event is dispatched before view is unloaded, which
can be
scene:addEventListener( "destroy", scene )

return scene
```

What just happened?

Using the Composer API will help us transition scenes a lot easier and quicker. Every time you want to load a new scene into view, `require("composer")` needs to be added. The `local scene = composer.newScene()` statement will allow us to call the scene events, `create()`, `show()`, `hide()`, and `destroy()`.

At the very end of the game code, we added event listeners for all the scene events and for `return scene`.

The format of how each scene is managed with Composer will look similar to the preceding code. Most of the game code will be dispatched when a scene is displayed by the `create()` and `show()` events. When you want to clean or unload listeners, audio, assets, and so on, the `hide()` and `destroy()` events are used.

Organizing the game

We've been used to having `main.lua` as our main source file to show every detail of our game code. It's time to organize it efficiently with the help of the Composer API.

Time for action – adding the new main.lua file

While using Composer, our `main.lua` file is still vital since it is the first thing that Corona SDK looks at to launch an application in the simulator. We're going to add some lines of code that will change scenes for our game:

1. Create a brand new file called `main.lua` and let's add it back in our status bar:

```
display.setStatusBar( display.HiddenStatusBar )
```

2. Import Composer and load the first scene called `loadmainmenu`. We will create this scene in the next couple of sections:

```
-- require controller module
local composer = require ( "composer" )

-- load first screen
composer.gotoScene( "loadmainmenu" )
```

What just happened?

In order to incorporate Composer throughout the application, we called the `local composer = require ( "composer" )` module. The scene will be changed with `composer.gotoScene( "loadmainmenu" )`, which is a loading screen directing the user to the main menu screen.

New game transitions

Now that we have introduced the Composer API, we can apply some long-awaited transitions that will be helpful for our game. One way to approach this is by transitioning out of the game once it is over.

Time for action – changing screens after the game is over

Now that we have renamed our game file, let's add in a scene transition so that our game is not stuck at the **Game Over** screen once game play is over. To change the screen, perform the following steps:

1. In our `maingame.lua` file, add in a new variable called `local menuBtn`, where all the other variables are initialized in the beginning of the code. Inside the `callGameOver()` function, add the following lines after the `highScoreText` code:

```
local onMenuTouch = function( event )
  if event.phase == "release" then
```

```
          audio.play( btnSound )
          composer.gotoScene( "mainmenu", "fade", 500  )

       end
    end

    menuBtn = ui.newButton{
      defaultSrc = "menubtn.png",
      defaultX = 60,
      defaultY = 60,
      overSrc = "menubtn-over.png",
      overX = 60,
      overY = 60,
      onEvent = onMenuTouch,
      id = "MenuButton",
      text = "",
      -- Can use any font available per platform
      font = "Helvetica",
      textColor = { 255, 255, 255, 255 },
      size = 16,
      emboss = false
    }

    menuBtn.x = 100; menuBtn.y = 260

    gameGroup:insert( menuBtn )
```

What just happened?

In order to transition out of the game over screen, a menu button was created to change scenes. Inside the onMenuTouch() function, upon the release of the button, we called composer.gotoScene("mainmenu", "fade", 500). This will allow the application to transition to the main menu in 500 milliseconds using a fade, which we will create later on in this chapter.

Have a go hero – restarting the game

Now that you're well aware of how the Composer API works with changing scenes and using UI buttons to transition between them, how about creating a button that restarts the game after the game over screen appears? So far, the application allows the user to go back to the menu screen once the game has reached an end.

Within the callGameOver() function, a new local function needs to be created that will run an event using the UI button system to change scenes with Composer. Note that you can't call the same scene over if you're currently in it.

Creating a loading screen

Loading screens provide feedback that the program is in the process of loading. This is helpful by informing the user that the next screen is underway, so that they don't assume that the application has crashed, especially if the next screen is loading a large amount of data.

Time for action – adding the loading screen

We'll place loading screens when the application launches and before the game level starts. This tells the user that more content or information is on its way.

1. Create a new file called loadmainmenu.lua in your project folder.

2. Import Composer and add in the composer.newScene() function:

```
local composer = require( "composer" )
local scene = composer.newScene()
```

3. Create two local variables called `myTimer` and `loadingImage`. Add in the `create()` event and a `sceneGroup` display group:

```
local myTimer
local loadingImage

-- Called when the scene's view does not exist:
function scene:create( event )
  local sceneGroup = self.view

  print( "\nloadmainmenu: create event" )
end
```

4. Create the `show()` event and add in a `sceneGroup` display group:

```
  -- Called immediately after scene has moved onscreen:
function scene:show( event )
  local sceneGroup = self.view

  print( "loadmainmenu: show event" )
```

5. Introduce the `loadingImage` display object:

```
  loadingImage = display.newImageRect( "loading.png", 480, 320)
  loadingImage.x = 240; loadingImage.y = 160
  sceneGroup:insert( loadingImage )
```

6. Create another local function called `goToMenu()` and call `composer.gotoScene( "mainmenu", "zoomOutInFadeRotate", 500 )` to change the scene to `"mainmenu"`:

```
    local goToMenu = function()
      composer.gotoScene( "mainmenu", "zoomOutInFadeRotate",
      500)
    end
```

7. Use the `timer` function and have it call `goToMenu()` once every 1,000 milliseconds. Define it with the `myTimer` timer ID. Close the `show()` event with `end`:

```
    myTimer = timer.performWithDelay( 1000, goToMenu, 1 )
  end
```

8. Call the `hide()` and `destroy()` events. In the `hide()` event, cancel `myTimer`:

```
-- Called when scene is about to move offscreen:
function scene:hide()

  if myTimer then timer.cancel( myTimer ); end
```

```
      print( "loadmainmenu: hide event" )

end

-- Called prior to the removal of scene's "view" (display
group)
function scene:destroy( event )

  print( "destroying loadmainmenu's view" )
end
```

9. Add event listeners for all the scene events and for `return` scene. **Save and close the file:**

```
-- "create" event is dispatched if scene's view does not exist
scene:addEventListener( "create", scene )

-- "show" event is dispatched whenever scene transition has
finished
scene:addEventListener( "show", scene )

-- "hide" event is dispatched before next scene's transition
begins
scene:addEventListener( "hide", scene )

-- "destroy" event is dispatched before view is unloaded, which
can be
scene:addEventListener( "destroy", scene )

return scene
```

10. Create a new file called `loadgame.lua` in your project folder. We'll make another loading screen that occurs right before the game scene, `maingame.lua`. Use `composer.gotoScene( "maingame", "flipFadeOutIn", 500 )` **to** transition scenes. Save and close your file:

```
local composer = require( "composer" )
local scene = composer.newScene()

local myTimer
local loadingImage

-- Called when the scene's view does not exist:
function scene:create( event )
  local sceneGroup = self.view
```

```
    -- completely remove mainmenu
    composer.removeScene( "mainmenu" )

    print( "\nloadgame: create event" )
end



-- Called immediately after scene has moved onscreen:
function scene:show( event )
    local sceneGroup = self.view

    print( "loadgame: show event" )

    loadingImage = display.newImageRect( "loading.png", 480, 320)
    loadingImage.x = 240; loadingImage.y = 160
    sceneGroup:insert( loadingImage )

    local changeScene = function()
        composer.gotoScene( "maingame", "flipFadeOutIn", 500 )
    end
    myTimer = timer.performWithDelay( 1000, changeScene, 1 )

end

-- Called when scene is about to move offscreen:
function scene:hide()

    if myTimer then timer.cancel( myTimer ); end

    print( "loadgame: hide event" )

end

-- Called prior to the removal of scene's "view" (display
group)
function scene:destroy( event )

    print( "destroying loadgame's view" )
end

-- "create" event is dispatched if scene's view does not exist
scene:addEventListener( "create", scene )
```

```
-- "show" event is dispatched whenever scene transition has
finished
scene:addEventListener( "show", scene )

-- "hide" event is dispatched before next scene's transition
begins
scene:addEventListener( "hide", scene )

-- "destroy" event is dispatched before view is unloaded, which
can be
scene:addEventListener( "destroy", scene )

return scene
```

What just happened?

In the `loadmainmenu.lua` file, once `loadingImage` was added to the screen, we created the `goToMenu()` function to change scenes to `"mainmenu"` and use the `"zoomOutInFadeRotate"` transition that zooms out and rotates the loading screen image as it fades to the background. The `myTimer = timer.performWithDelay( 1000, goToMenu, 1 )` statement performs the function in 1,000 milliseconds (one second) and runs it once. This is long enough to view the image and have it fade out.

All display objects enter the scene by `function scene:show( event )`. The `loadingImage` object is placed in `sceneGroup`. To make sure we have no timers running after the scene change, `myTimer` stops running with the use of `timer.cancel(myTimer)` under `function scene:hide()`.

The code for `loadgame.lua` is similar to `loadmainmenu.lua`. For this file, Composer transitions scenes to `maingame.lua`, the game play file.

Creating a main menu

A main menu or title screen is one of the first impressions a player sees before playing the game. It usually shows small snippets of images or scenery that correlate with the actual game and also displays the title of the application.

There are buttons such as **Start** or **Play** that urge the player to go into the game if they choose to and some secondary buttons such as **Options** to view settings and other information.

Time for action – adding a main menu

We will create the frontend of our game by introducing the game title and the **Play** and **Options** buttons that will transition throughout different scenes in the application with ease.

1. Create a new file called `mainmenu.lua` and import Composer and the UI modules, the `composer.newScene()` function, and the variables for timer and audio:

```
local composer = require( "composer" )
local scene = Composer.newScene()

local ui = require("ui")

local btnAnim

local btnSound = audio.loadSound( "btnSound.wav" )
```

2. Create the `create()` event. Add in the `composer.removeScene( "maingame" )` and `composer.removeScene( "options" )` lines, which will remove the `"maingame"` and `"options"` scenes. You can remove `"maingame"` after the player has transitioned from the main game screen and is sent to the main menu screen. You can remove `"options"` after the player has transitioned from the options screen and is sent to the main menu screen:

```
-- Called when the scene's view does not exist:
function scene:create( event )
  local sceneGroup = self.view
```

```
    -- completely remove maingame and options
    composer.removeScene( "maingame" )
    composer.removeScene( "options" )

    print( "\nmainmenu: create event" )
end
```

3. Add in the `show()` event and the `backgroundImage` display object;

```
-- Called immediately after scene has moved onscreen:
function scene:show( event )
    local sceneGroup = self.view

    print( "mainmenu: show event" )

    local backgroundImage = display.newImageRect(
    "mainMenuBG.png", 480, 320 )
    backgroundImage.x = 240; backgroundImage.y = 160
    sceneGroup:insert( backgroundImage )
```

4. Introduce the `playBtn` display object and create a function called `onPlayTouch(event)` that uses `composer.gotoScene()` to change the scene to `"loadgame"`. Use the `"fade"` effect to change scenes:

```
local playBtn

local onPlayTouch = function( event )
    if event.phase == "release" then

        audio.play( btnSound )
        composer.gotoScene( "loadgame", "fade", 300  )

    end
end

playBtn = ui.newButton{
    defaultSrc = "playbtn.png",
    defaultX = 100,
    defaultY = 100,
    overSrc = "playbtn-over.png",
    overX = 100,
    overY = 100,
    onEvent = onPlayTouch,
    id = "PlayButton",
    text = "",
```

```
      font = "Helvetica",
      textColor = { 255, 255, 255, 255 },
      size = 16,
      emboss = false
   }


   playBtn.x = 240; playBtn.y = 440
      sceneGroup:insert( playBtn )
```

5. Transition the `playBtn` display object to y = 260 in 500 milliseconds using the `easing.inOutExpo` transition. Have it initialized through `btnAnim`:

```
btnAnim = transition.to( playBtn, { time=1000, y=260,
transition=easing.inOutExpo } )
```

6. Introduce the `optBtn` display object and create a function called `onOptionsTouch(event)`. Use `composer.gotoScene()` to transition the scene to `"options"` using the `"crossFade"` effect:

```
local optBtn

   local onOptionsTouch = function( event )
      if event.phase == "release" then

         audio.play( btnSound )
         composer.gotoScene( "options", "crossFade", 300)

      end
   end

   optBtn = ui.newButton{
      defaultSrc = "optbtn.png",
      defaultX = 60,
      defaultY = 60,
      overSrc = "optbtn-over.png",
      overX = 60,
      overY = 60,
      onEvent = onOptionsTouch,
      id = "OptionsButton",
      text = "",
      font = "Helvetica",
      textColor = { 255, 255, 255, 255 },
      size = 16,
```

```
    emboss = false
  }
  optBtn.x = 430; optBtn.y = 440
  sceneGroup:insert( optBtn )
```

7. Transition the `optBtn` display object to $y = 280$ in 500 milliseconds using the `easing.inOutExpo` transition. Have it initialized through `btnAnim`. Close the `scene:show( event )` function with `end`:

```
  btnAnim = transition.to( optBtn, { time=1000, y=280,
  transition=easing.inOutExpo } )
```

```
end
```

8. Create the `hide()` event and cancel the `btnAnim` transition. Also, create the `destroy()` event:

```
-- Called when scene is about to move offscreen:
function scene:hide()

  if btnAnim then transition.cancel( btnAnim ); end

  print( "mainmenu: hide event" )

end
```

```
-- Called prior to the removal of scene's "view" (display
group)
function scene:destroy( event )

  print( "destroying mainmenu's view" )
end
```

9. Add the event listeners for all the scene events and for `return` scene. Save and close your file:

```
-- "create" event is dispatched if scene's view does not exist
scene:addEventListener( "create", scene )
```

```
-- "show" event is dispatched whenever scene transition has
finished
scene:addEventListener( "show", scene )
```

```
-- "hide" event is dispatched before next scene's transition
begins
scene:addEventListener( "hide", scene )

-- "destroy" event is dispatched before view is unloaded, which
can be
scene:addEventListener( "destroy", scene )

return scene
```

What just happened?

On the main menu screen, we added an image that displayed the game title and the **Play** and **Options** buttons. The **Options** button is still not functional at this time. The onPlayTouch() function transitions the scene to "loadgame". This will change scenes to loadgame.lua. The **Play** button is placed at x = 240; y = 440, (middle and offscreen). When the scene loads, playBtn transitions to y = 260, so it pops up from the bottom of the screen in 1000 milliseconds.

The **Options** button does a similar thing. The optBtn object is placed to the right of the stage and pops up at y = 280 in 500 milliseconds.

The btnAnim transition is cancelled by transition.cancel(btnAnim) through the scene:hide() function. It is important to clean timers, transitions, and event listeners every time you change scenes so that potential memory leaks do not occur while in the application.

Creating an options menu

An options menu allows users to change various settings in the game or include other information that can't be displayed in the main menu. Games can vary from having many options to only having a few. Sometimes, an options menu can be called a settings menu, which offers the same type of customization to the player's experience.

Time for action – adding an options menu

We'll add an options menu that can be accessed through the main menu. We're going to add a new UI button called **Credits**, which will direct the user to the credits screen once it is pressed. To add an option menu perform the following steps:

1. Create a new file called `options.lua` and import Composer and the UI modules, the `composer.newScene()` function, and the variables for timer and audio:

```
local composer = require( "composer" )
local scene = composer.newScene()

local ui = require("ui")

local btnAnim

local btnSound = audio.loadSound( "btnSound.wav" )
```

2. Create the `create()` event. Add in `composer.removeScene( "mainmenu" )`, which will remove the `"mainmenu"` scene. This will occur after the player has transitioned from the main menu screen and is sent to the options screen. Next, add in `composer.removeScene( "creditsScreen" )`. This will remove `"creditsScreen"` after the player has transitioned from the credits screen back to the options screen:

```
-- Called when the scene's view does not exist:
function scene:create( event )
  local sceneGroup = self.view

  -- completely remove mainmenu and creditsScreen
  composer.removeScene( "mainmenu" )
  composer.removeScene( "creditsScreen" )

  print( "\noptions: create event" )
end
```

3. Add in the `show()` event and the `backgroundImage` display object:

```
-- Called immediately after scene has moved onscreen:
function scene:show( event )
  local sceneGroup = self.view

  print( "options: show event" )

  local backgroundImage = display.newImageRect(
  "optionsBG.png", 480, 320 )
  backgroundImage.x = 240; backgroundImage.y = 160
  sceneGroup:insert( backgroundImage )
```

4. Create a button for the credits screen. Transition the `creditsBtn` display object to `y = 260` in **1000** milliseconds using the `easing.inOutExpo` transition. Have it initialized through `btnAnim`:

```
local creditsBtn

local onCreditsTouch = function( event )
  if event.phase == "release" then

    audio.play( btnSound )
    Composer.gotoScene( "creditsScreen", "crossFade", 300 )

  end
end

creditsBtn = ui.newButton{
  defaultSrc = "creditsbtn.png",
  defaultX = 100,
  defaultY = 100,
  overSrc = "creditsbtn-over.png",
  overX = 100,
  overY = 100,
  onEvent = onCreditsTouch,
  id = "CreditsButton",
  text = "",
  font = "Helvetica",
  textColor = { 255, 255, 255, 255 },
  size = 16,
  emboss = false
}
```

```
creditsBtn.x = 240; creditsBtn.y = 440
sceneGroup:insert( creditsBtn )

btnAnim = transition.to( creditsBtn, { time=1000, y=260,
transition=easing.inOutExpo } )
```

5. Create the **Close** button that loads the main menu. Close the `scene:show( event` `) with` end:

```
local closeBtn

local onCloseTouch = function( event )
  if event.phase == "release" then
    audio.play( tapSound )
    composer.gotoScene( "mainmenu", "zoomInOutFadeRotate",
    500 )
  end
end

closeBtn = ui.newButton{
  defaultSrc = "closebtn.png",
  defaultX = 60,
  defaultY = 60,
  overSrc = "closebtn-over.png",
  overX = 60,
  overY = 60,
  onEvent = onCloseTouch,
  id = "CloseButton",
  text = "",
  font = "Helvetica",
  textColor = { 255, 255, 255, 255 },
  size = 16,
  emboss = false
}

closeBtn.x = 50; closeBtn.y = 280
sceneGroup:insert( closeBtn )
end
```

6. Create the `hide()` event and cancel the `btnAnim` transition. Also, create the `destroy()` event. Add the event listeners for all the scene events and the `return` scene statement. Save and close your file:

```
-- Called when scene is about to move offscreen:
function scene:hide()
```

```
    if btnAnim then transition.cancel( btnAnim ); end

    print( "options: hide event" )

end

-- Called prior to the removal of scene's "view" (display
group)
function scene:destroy( event )

    print( "destroying options's view" )
end


-- "create" event is dispatched if scene's view does not exist
scene:addEventListener( "create", scene )

-- "show" event is dispatched whenever scene transition has
finished
scene:addEventListener( "show", scene )

-- "hide" event is dispatched before next scene's transition
begins
scene:addEventListener( "hide", scene )

-- "destroy" event is dispatched before view is unloaded, which
can be
scene:addEventListener( "destroy", scene )

return scene
```

What just happened?

In this scene, `creditsBtn` will operate in a manner similar to how our main menu was created. The **Credits** button is still not functional at this time. In the `onCreditsTouch()` function, the scene is transitioned to `"creditsScreen"` and uses `"crossFade"` as the effect. From the off-screen position, `creditsBtn` transitions to y=260 in 1,000 milliseconds when the scene is loaded.

A **Close** button is created for this scene so that the user will have a way to go back to the previous screen. With the `onCloseTouch()` function, Composer changes the scene to `"mainmenu"` upon the release of `closeBtn`. The main menu screen will display when you press the close button. The `btnAnim` transition is canceled through the `scene:hide()` function.

Creating a credits screen

A credits screen usually shows and lists all the people involved in the production of the game. It can include other information in the form of thanking certain individuals and programs used to create the final project.

Time for action – adding a credits screen

The credits screen that we'll create will be based on a touch event that transitions to the previous screen from which it was introduced. To add a credits screen, perform the following steps:

1. Create a new file called `creditsScreen.lua` and import Composer, the `composer.newScene()` function, and the `backgroundImage` variable:

```
local composer = require( "composer" )
local scene = composer.newScene()

local backgroundImage
```

2. Create the `create()` event. Add in the `composer.removeScene("options")` line, which will remove the `"options"` scene. This will occur after the player has transitioned from the options screen and is sent to the credits screen:

```
-- Called when the scene's view does not exist:
function scene:create( event )
  local sceneGroup = self.view

  -- completely remove options
  composer.removeScene( "options" )

  print( "\ncreditsScreen: create event" )
end
```

3. Add in the `show()` event and the `backgroundImage` display object:

```
-- Called immediately after scene has moved onscreen:
function scene:show( event )
  local sceneGroup = self.view

  print( "creditsScreen: show event" )

  backgroundImage = display.newImageRect( "creditsScreen.png",
  480, 320 )
  backgroundImage.x = 240; backgroundImage.y = 160
  sceneGroup:insert( backgroundImage )
```

4. Create a local function called `changeToOptions()` with an event parameter. Have the function change the scene with Composer back to the options screen, using a touch event on `backgroundImage`. Close the `scene:show(event)` function with `end`:

```
  local changeToOptions = function( event )
    if event.phase == "began" then

      composer.gotoScene( "options", "crossFade", 300  )

    end
  end

  backgroundImage:addEventListener( "touch", changeToOptions)
end
```

5. Create the `hide()` and `destroy()` events. Add the event listeners for all the scene events and the `return` scene statement. Save and close your file:

```
-- Called when scene is about to move offscreen:
function scene:hide()

  print( "creditsScreen: hide event" )

end

-- Called prior to the removal of scene's "view" (display
group)
function scene:destroy( event )
```

```
    print( "destroying creditsScreen's view" )
end

-- "create" event is dispatched if scene's view does not exist
scene:addEventListener( "create", scene )

-- "show" event is dispatched whenever scene transition has
finished
scene:addEventListener( "show", scene )

-- "hide" event is dispatched before next scene's transition
begins
scene:addEventListener( "hide", scene )

-- "destroy" event is dispatched before view is unloaded, which
can be
scene:addEventListener( "destroy", scene )

return scene
```

What just happened?

The credits screen works with an event listener. The `changeToOptions(event)` function will tell Composer to change the scene to `"options"` using `composer.gotoScene( "options", "crossFade", 500 )`. At the end of the function, `backgroundImage` will activate the event listener when the screen is touched. The `backgroundImage` object is inserted into the `sceneGroup` under the `scene:show( event )` function. Egg Drop is now fully operable using Composer. Run the game in the simulator. You'll be able to transition to all the scenes that we created in this chapter, as well as play the game.

Have a go hero – adding more levels

Now that Egg Drop is completed and has a working menu system, challenge yourself by creating more levels. Minor alterations will have to be added to add some placement for additional levels. Remember to apply Composer when changing scenes.

Try creating the following:

- Level select screen
- Level number buttons to add additional levels

When creating new levels, refer to the format shown in `maingame.lua`. New levels can be altered by changing the interval of how fast the egg falls from the sky, or maybe by adding other game assets that fall but have to be dodged in order to avoid getting a penalty. There are so many possibilities of adding your own spin with this game framework. Give it a try!

Pop quiz – game transitions and scenes

Q1. What function do you call to change scenes with Composer?

1. `composer()`
2. `composer.gotoScene()`
3. `composer(changeScene)`
4. None of the above

Q2. What function converts any argument into a number or nil?

1. `tonumber()`
2. `print()`
3. `tostring()`
4. `nil`

Q3. How do you pause a timer?

1. `timer.cancel()`
2. `physics.pause()`
3. `timer.pause( timerID )`
4. None of the above

Q4. How do you resume a timer?

1. `resume()`
2. `timer.resume( timerID )`
3. `timer.performWithDelay()`
4. None of the above

Summary

Congratulations! We have a game that is complete and can go into the App Store or Google Play Store. Of course, we will not use this exact game, but you have learned enough to create one. It's a great accomplishment to have completed the game framework, especially in the short amount of time it took to create something so simple.

Here are some skills you learned in this chapter:

- Saving high scores using saveValue() and loadValue()
- Understanding how to pause physics/timers
- Displaying the pause menu
- Change scenes with the Composer API
- Creating transitions between scenes using loading screens
- Using a main menu to introduce the game title and submenus

We have achieved an important milestone in this chapter. Everything that we have gone over in the previous chapters was applied to this sample game. The great thing about it is that it took us less than a day's worth of development to code. The art assets, on the other hand, are a different story.

We still have a few more things to learn with regard to what Corona SDK is capable of. In the next chapter, we'll go into more detail on how to optimize our game assets for high-resolution devices. We will also see how to post messages on Facebook and Twitter through your application.

9
Handling Multiple Devices and Networking Your Apps

Allowing your application to integrate with social networks is a great way to promote your finished product. Many games enable the player to upload their high scores and share them among other users who are playing the same title. Some provide challenges that need to be completed successfully in order to unlock achievements. Social networks enhance the gaming experience and provide great exposure for the developer.

We'll also go into more detail about build configuration since we're getting more accustomed to programming. Understanding the importance of configuring your device build is vital for cross-platform development. This is a capability that Corona SDK can handle with ease across iOS and Android devices.

In this chapter, we will learn the following topics:

- Revisiting configuration settings
- Posting messages to Twitter
- Posting messages to Facebook

Let's add in these finishing touches!

Return to configuration

Build settings and runtime configuration were briefly discussed in *Chapter 2, Lua Crash Course and the Corona Framework*. Let's get into more specific details on how to handle a variety of devices that work on the iOS and Android platforms.

Build configuration

There are a variety of ways to handle device orientation to match the settings your game design requires.

Orientation support (iOS)

There are scenarios in which you want the native user interface (UI) elements to autorotate or to be oriented in a certain way, but you also need to maintain a fixed coordinate system within Corona.

To lock Corona's orientation while allowing the native iPhone UI elements to rotate, add a content parameter in `build.settings` as follows:

```
settings =
{
  orientation =
  {
    default = "portrait",
    content = "portrait",
    supported =
    {
      "landscapeLeft", "landscapeRight", "portrait",
      "portraitUpsideDown",
    },
  },
}
```

To lock Corona's internal coordinate system to portrait orientation while locking iPhone UI elements to the landscape orientation, you could do the following in `build.settings`:

```
settings =
{
  orientation =
  {
    default ="landscapeRight",
    content = "portrait",
    supported =
    {
```

```
        "landscapeRight", "landscapeLeft",
      },
    },
  }
```

Orientation support (Android)

The Android platform supports portrait and landscape orientations. The orientation *portraitUpsideDown* may not be available on some Android devices. Also, autorotation is not currently supported on Android. The default orientation doesn't affect Android devices. The orientation is initialized to the actual orientation of the device (unless only one orientation is specified).

Here is an example of an Android-specific `build.settings` file (you might also combine Android and iPhone settings in the same file):

```
settings =
{
  android =
  {
    versionCode = "2",
    versionName = "2.0"

    usesPermissions =
    {
      "android.permission.INTERNET",
    },
  },

  orientation =
  {
    default = "portrait"
  },
}
```

Version code and version name (Android)

The `versionCode` and `versionName` fields can be set within an optional `"android"` table in `build.settings`.

The `versionCode` field is defaulted to `"1"`, while the `versionName` field is defaulted at `"1.0"` if it's not set in the `build.settings` file. When an updated version of an application is submitted to the Google Play Store, the `versionCode` and `versionName` fields also have to be updated. All version numbers for `versionCode` have to be whole numbers. The `versionCode` field cannot contain any decimal numbers, while the `versionName` field can contain decimals.

For more information, see *android:versionCode* and *android:versionName* at `http://developer.android.com/guide/topics/manifest/manifest-element.html#vcode`.

> The `versionCode` attribute is an internal number used to distinguish application releases for the Google Play Store. It is not the same as the version provided by the Corona build dialog. The `versionName` attribute is the version number shown to users.

Application permissions (Android)

An optional `"usesPermissions"` table can be used to specify permissions, using string values as given in the Android manifest reference: `http://developer.android.com/reference/android/Manifest.permission.html`.

Developers should use permissions that match their application requirements. For example, if network access is required, the Internet permission needs to be set.

> For more useful information on the `android.permission` keys applied in Corona SDK, refer to `http://docs.coronalabs.com/guide/distribution/buildSettings/index.html#permissions`.

Content scaling on an easier level

Content scaling throughout multiple devices can be frustrating at times if you've never addressed them before in your `config.lua` file. There are many individual screen sizes. The size of iPhone 5 is 640 x 1136 px, and that of iPad 2 is 768 x 1024 px. The size of Droid is 480 x 854 px, and that of the Samsung Galaxy tablet is 600 x 1024 px, just to name a few. Memory can run out easily due to image size boundaries.

When setting up your `config.lua`, like we've done in the previous chapters, we had our content set to `width = 320`, `height = 480`, and `scale = "letterbox"`. If building for Android devices, `"zoomStretch"` works best to accommodate varying screen sizes on the platform. This creates a common build for iOS and Android and presents display images that are large enough to fit on a variety of screen sizes.

If you want to scale for larger screen sizes and then scale down, use the screen size of the iPad 2. Your `config.lua` would look similar to the following code:

```
application =
{
    content =
```

```
  {
    width = 768,
    height = 1024,
    scale = "letterbox"
  }
}
```

While the preceding example is another solution to scale content, it's important to remember the limitations in texture memory involved with larger (high resolution) images. While devices such as the iPad with Retina display, iPhone 5s, and the Samsung Galaxy Tab 4 tablet will handle this just fine, the iPhone 4s and older devices will have far less texture memory available to handle large graphics.

A way to resolve this potential problem is to use dynamic image resolution to substitute assets that are better suited for low-end devices and high-end devices. We will discuss this topic in more detail later in this section.

The best of both worlds

As you may have noticed, some of the background images we used in our sample apps are scaled at 380 x 570. This happens to be the size that fills the entire screen on all common devices for both iOS and Android. Better yet, it is a middle ground to compensate for higher- and lower-resolution images on any device.

In order for your content to be displayed as evenly as possible, the following must be set up accordingly:

Settings for `config.lua` are as follows:

```
application =
{
  content =
  {
    width = 320,
    height = 480,
    scale = "letterbox"
  }
}
```

In any file that contains any of your display images, a typical background would be displayed as follows:

```
local backgroundImage = display.newImage( "bg.png", true )
backgroundImage.x = display.contentCenterX
backgroundImage.y = display.contentCenterY
```

Any content with a size of 320 x 480 is considered the focus area. Anything outside of the area is cropped, but will fill the screen with content on any device.

The deeper meaning of dynamic image selection

We know we can swap base images used for smaller devices (iPhone 4s) and larger devices (iPhone 6 and Kindle Fire HD). This occurs when trying to scale multiple devices in the same build.

A file-naming scheme is available for use to handle such devices for iOS and Android. Knowing how to handle the scaling of assets affected for the device proposed is half the battle. We'll have to define what resolution scale needs to be addressed for Corona to access the assets they're directed toward.

Using the line `display.newImageRect( [parentGroup,] filename [, baseDirectory] w, h )` will call out your dynamic resolution images.

Typically, we've used `["@2x"] = 2` to call out the higher resolution image when available in our project for iOS devices:

```
application =
{
  content =
  {
    width = 320,
    height = 480,
    scale = "letterbox",

    imageSuffix =
    {
      ["@2x"] = 2,
    },
  },
}
```

The preceding example will only work for iPhone 4s and iPad 2 since it surpasses the base size of 320 x 480 on both devices. If we wanted to make it accessible to the Droid 2, the scale threshold would be 1.5. For an Android tablet to work, such as the Samsung Galaxy tablet, the scale threshold is 1.875. So how do we figure out these numbers? Simple. Take the width of the higher-end device and divide it by 320 (the base size). For example, the Droid 2 dimensions are 480 x 854. Divide 480 by 320 and it equals 1.5.

The Samsung Galaxy Tab 4 tablet's dimensions are 800 x 1280. Divide 800 by 320 and it equals 2.5.

If trying to manage both iOS and Android devices in the same project, you can change your `imageSuffix` in `config.lua`, as shown in the following code:

```
imageSuffix =
{
  ["@2x"] = 1.5, -- this will handle most Android devices such as
    the Droid 2, Nexus, Galaxy Tablet, etc...
}
```

Alternatively, you could use the following code:

```
imageSuffix =
{
  ["@2x"] = 2.5, -- this will handle the Galaxy Tab 4 and similar
    sized devices
}
```

Using either of the preceding examples will trigger the proposed Android devices to display the higher-resolution image.

The `imageSuffix` string doesn't necessarily have to be `"@2x"`; it can be anything like `"@2"`, `"_lrg"`, or even `"-2x"`. As long as your higher-resolution image has the intended suffix after the primary image name, it'll work just fine.

High-resolution sprite sheets

High-resolution sprite sheets are not handled the same way as dynamic image selections. While you can continue using the same naming convention to differentiate your high-resolution images from your basic images, the image will not be able to use `display.newImageRect()` when referring to sprite sheets.

If your current content scale is `width = 320`, `height = 480`, and `scale = "letterbox"` in your `config.lua` file, then the scale output for the following devices will demonstrate the following:

- iPhone = 1
- iPhone 4s = 0.5
- Droid 2 = 0.666666668653488
- iPad 2 = 0.46875

Applying a basic sprite sheet that matches the scale for an iPhone will display sharp and clean images. When the same sprite sheet is applied to the iPhone 4, the display will match the content scale of the device, but the sprite sheet will look slightly pixilated and blurry around the edges. Using `display.contentScaleX` and calling some methods will solve that problem for you. Notice that `displayScale < 1` will access the high-resolution sprite sheet based on the preceding device scale:

```
local sheetData
local myObject

local displayScale = display.contentScaleX -- scales sprite
sheets down
if displayScale < 1 then -- pertains to all high-res devices

   sheetData = { width=256, height=256, numFrames=4,
   sheetContentWidth=512, sheetContentHeight=512 }
else
   sheetData = { width=128, height=128, numFrames=4,
   sheetContentWidth=256, sheetContentHeight=256 }
end

local sheet = graphics.newImageSheet( "charSprite.png",
sheetData)

local sequenceData =
{
   { name="move", start=1, count=4, time=400 }
}

myObject = = display.newSprite( sheet, sequenceData )

if displayScale < 1 then --scale the high-res sprite sheet if
you're on a high-res device.
   myObject.xScale = .5; myObject.yScale = .5
end

myObject.x = display.contentWidth / 2
myObject.y = display.contentHeight / 2

myObject.x = 150; myObject.y = 195

myObject: setSequence("move")
myObject:play()
```

Networking your apps

When you have completed developing your main game framework, it's good to think about how to network it if you decide to do this.

At some point in our lives, all of us have used some kind of networking tool, such as Twitter or Facebook. You probably use these applications currently, but the point is that you read updates from other users about a new game that was launched, or someone is spreading the word to download a game and compete with them. You can be that developer and develop the game they're talking about!

Incorporating networking mechanisms in your game does not have to be a hassle. It only takes several lines of code to get it working.

Posting to Twitter

Tweet, tweet, tweet... Twitter is a networking tool that connects you to the latest information that appeals to your interests. It is also a great tool to share information with others about your business and, of course, your game. Reach out to the game development audience by promoting your application.

The user who will be sharing a post to Twitter will need to create an account at `http://twitter.com/` and will also need to make sure they're logged in.

Time for action – adding Twitter to your apps

We're going to implement Twitter in our apps by accessing a web service through UI buttons.

1. In the `Chapter 9` folder, copy the `Twitter Web Pop-Up` project folder to your desktop. All the configuration, libraries, and assets needed are already included. You can download the project files that accompany this book from the Packt Publishing website.

2. Create a new `main.lua` file and save it to the project folder.

3. Set the following variables at the beginning of the code:

   ```
   display.setStatusBar( display.HiddenStatusBar )

   local ui = require("ui")

   local openBtn
   local closeBtn
   local score = 100
   ```

4. Create a local function called onOpenTouch() with an event parameter. Add an if statement so that the event receives a "release" action:

```
local onOpenTouch = function ( event )
  if event.phase == "release" then
```

5. Using the local variable called message, add in the following string statement and concatenate score:

```
local message = "Posting to Twitter from Corona SDK and got a
final score of " ..score.. "."
```

6. Add in local myString and apply string.gsub() for message to replace space instances:

```
local myString = string.gsub(message, "( )", "%%20")
```

7. Introduce the native.showWebPopup() function that links to the Twitter account. Concatenate myString to include the preloaded message. Close the function:

```
      native.showWebPopup(0, 0, 320, 300,
      "http://twitter.com/intent/tweet?text="..myString)


    end
end
```

8. Set up the openBtn UI function:

```
      openBtn = ui.newButton{
      defaultSrc = "openbtn.png",
      defaultX = 90,
      defaultY = 90,
      overSrc = "openbtn-over.png",
      overX = 90,
      overY = 90,
      onEvent = onOpenTouch,
    }

    openBtn.x = 110; openBtn.y = 350
```

9. Create a local function called onCloseTouch() with an event parameter. Add an if statement with event.phase == "release" to activate native.cancelWebPopup():

```
local onCloseTouch = function ( event )
  if event.phase == "release" then

    native.cancelWebPopup()

  end
end
```

10. Set up the `closeBtn` UI function:

```
closeBtn = ui.newButton{
defaultSrc = "closebtn.png",
defaultX = 90,
defaultY = 90,
overSrc = "closebtn-over.png",
overX = 90,
overY = 90,
onEvent = onCloseTouch,
}

closeBtn.x = 210; closeBtn.y = 350
```

11. Save the file and run the project in the simulator. Make sure you're connected to the Internet to see the results.

 If you're currently not logged in to your Twitter account, you'll be asked to log in before you see the results of the tweet from our code.

What just happened?

Near the top of the code, we set a variable `local score = 100`. This will be used in our Twitter message.

In the `onOpenTouch(event)` function, a web popup will load on the release of `openBtn`. The text that will be posted is displayed in a string format under the variable, `local message`. You will notice that we concatenate `score` into the string so that it displays the value in the message post.

`local myString` and `string.gsub()` are used to replace all the instances indicated in a pattern inside the string. In this case, it takes the string inside a message and searches for every empty space between each word and replaces it with `%20`. `%20` encodes URL parameters to indicate spaces. The extra `%` acts as an escape character.

The `native.showWebPopup()` function displays at dimensions 320 x 300, which is about half the screen size on a device. The URL to display the Twitter message dialog is added and concatenates `myString`.

When the web pop up no longer needs to be used and needs to be closed, `onCloseTouch(event)` is called by `closeBtn`. This will take the `event` parameter `"release"` and call `native.cancelWebPopup()`. This particular function will dismiss the current web popup.

Posting to Facebook

Another social networking tool that can be used to share information about your game is Facebook. You can easily customize a post to link information about your game or share messages about high scores and to encourage other users to download it.

In order to post messages to Facebook, you need to be logged in to your Facebook account or create one at `https://www.facebook.com/`. You will have to obtain an App ID from the Facebook Developer website at `https://developers.facebook.com/`. The App ID is a unique identifier for your site that determines what the right level of security is in place between the user and the app page/website.

Once you have created an App ID, you will also need to edit the App information and choose how you want it to integrate with Facebook. You are given several choices, such as Website, Native iOS App, and Native Android App, just to name a few. The website integration must be selected and filled in with a valid URL in order for Facebook to redirect to the specified URL for posts that deal with web popups.

Time for action – adding Facebook to your apps

Similar to our Twitter example, we'll be incorporating Facebook posts with a web popup as well:

1. In the `Chapter 9` folder, copy the `Facebook Web Pop-Up` project folder to your desktop. All the configuration, libraries, and assets needed are already included. You can download the project files that accompany this book from the Packt Publishing website.

2. Create a new `main.lua` file and save it to the project folder.

3. Set the following variables at the beginning of the code:

```
display.setStatusBar( display.HiddenStatusBar )

local ui = require("ui")

local openBtn
local closeBtn
local score = 100
```

4. Create a local function called `onOpenTouch()` with an event parameter. Add an `if` statement when the event receives a `"release"` action:

```
local onOpenTouch = function( event )
    if event.phase == "release" then
```

5. Add the following local variables that include the strings that we'll be implementing in the Facebook post:

```
local appId = "0123456789" -- Your personal FB App ID from
the facebook developer's website

local message1 = "Your App Name Here"
local message2 = "Posting to Facebook from Corona SDK and got
a final score of " ..score.. "."
local message3 = "Download the game and play!"

local myString1 = string.gsub(message1, "( )", "%%20")
local myString2 = string.gsub(message2, "( )", "%%20")
local myString3 = string.gsub(message3, "( )", "%%20")
```

6. Introduce the native web popup function that links to the Facebook account. Include parameters for the Facebook dialog box that redirects the URL of your preferred website, the display with a touch mode that connects to your app URL, and an image URL that presents your app icon or company logo. Concatenate all variables with string methods to output all messages. Close the function. Add in the `openBtn` UI function. You will need to replace all of the following URL information with your own:

```
native.showWebPopup(0, 0, 320, 300,
"http://www.facebook.com/dialog/feed?app_id=" .. appId ..
"&redirect_uri=http://www.yourwebsite.com&display=touch&link=ht
tp://www.yourgamelink.com&picture=http://www.yourwebsite.com/im
age.png&name=" ..myString1.. "&caption=" ..myString2..
"&description=".. myString3)

    end
end

    openBtn = ui.newButton{
    defaultSrc = "openbtn.png",
    defaultX = 90,
    defaultY = 90,
    overSrc = "openbtn-over.png",
    overX = 90,
    overY = 90,
    onEvent = onOpenTouch,
}
openBtn.x = 110; openBtn.y = 350
```

 More information pertaining to the Facebook Dialog can be found on the Facebook Developers website at `http://developers.facebook.com/docs/reference/dialogs/`.

7. Create a local function called `onCloseTouch()` with an event parameter. Add an `if` statement with `event.phase == "release"` to activate `native.cancelWebPopup()`. Set up the `closeBtn` UI function:

```
local onCloseTouch = function( event )
    if event.phase == "release" then

        native.cancelWebPopup()

    end
end
```

```
closeBtn = ui.newButton{
defaultSrc = "closebtn.png",
defaultX = 90,
defaultY = 90,
overSrc = "closebtn-over.png",
overX = 90,
overY = 90,
onEvent = onCloseTouch,
}

closeBtn.x = 210; closeBtn.y = 350
```

8. Save the file and run the project in the simulator. Make sure you're connected to the Internet and your Facebook account to see the results.

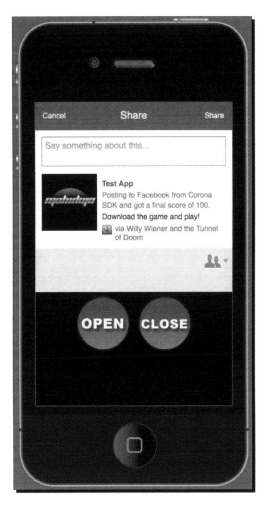

What just happened?

Within the `onOpenTouch(event)` function, several variables are called when `openBtn` is pressed and released. Notice that `local appId` indicates a string of numbers that you can obtain after creating an app on the Facebook Developers website.

`message1`, `message2`, and `message3` are the strings that display the message post. `myString1`, `myString2`, and `myString3` help replace the spaces indicated in `message1`, `message2`, and `message3`.

The `native.showWebPopup()` function displays with a dimension of 320 x 300 and presents the dialog URL to Facebook. The following parameters display accordingly:

- `app_id`: This is your unique ID created on the Facebook Developer website. For example, `"1234567"`.
- `redirect_uri`: The URL to redirect to after the user clicks on a button on the dialog. This is required in the parameters.
- `display`: This displays the mode to render the dialog.
- `touch`: This is used on smart phone devices such as iPhone and Android. This fits the dialog screen within small dimensions.
- `link`: This is the link attached to the post.
- `picture`: This is the URL of a picture to the post.
- `name`: This is the name of the link attachment.
- `caption`: This is the caption of the link (appears beneath the link name).
- `description`: This is the description of the link (appears beneath the link caption).

When the web popup is no longer required and needs to be closed, `onCloseTouch(event)` is called by `closeBtn`. This will take the event parameter `"release"` and call `native.cancelWebPopup()`. This particular function will dismiss the current web popup.

Facebook Connect

This library supplies a number of functions that provide access to `http://www.facebook.com` through the official Facebook Connect interface.

Time for action – posting scores using Facebook Connect

Facebook Connect is another way to post on the wall feed by using the native Facebook UI features. We'll be creating a different way to post messages and scores to the newsfeed. In order to see how Facebook Connect operates, you need to load the build to a device to view the results. It will not run in the simulator.

1. In the `Chapter 9` folder, copy the `Facebook Connect` project folder to your desktop. All the configuration, libraries, and assets needed are already included. You can download the project files that accompany this book from the Packt Publishing website.

2. Create a new `main.lua` file and save it to the project folder.

3. Set up the following variables at the beginning of the code:

```
display.setStatusBar( display.HiddenStatusBar )

local ui = require("ui")
local facebook = require "facebook"

local fbBtn
local score = 100
```

4. Create a local function called `onFBTouch()` with an event parameter. Add an `if` statement that contains `event.phase == release`. Also, include your Facebook app ID in a string format:

```
local onFBTouch = function( event )
    if event.phase == "release" then

        local fbAppID = "0123456789" -- Your FB App ID from
        facebook developer's panel
```

5. Create another local function within `onFBTouch(event)` called `facebookListener()` with an event parameter as well. Include an `if` statement that refers to `"session" == event.type`:

```
local facebookListener = function( event )
    if ( "session" == event.type ) then
```

6. Add in another `if` statement where `"login"` equals to `event.phase`. Include a local variable called `theMessage` to display the message you want to share with other Facebook users:

```
if ( "login" == event.phase ) then

    local theMessage = "Got a score of " .. score .. " on
    Your App Name Here!"
```

7. Add the `facebook.request()` function that will post the following messages to the user's Facebook wall. Close any remaining `if` statements with `end` in the `facebookListener(event)` function:

```
facebook.request( "me/feed", "POST", {
    message=theMessage,
    name="Your App Name Here",
    caption="Download and compete with me!",
    link="http://itunes.apple.com/us/app/your-app-name/
id382456881?mt=8",
        picture="http://www.yoursite.com/yourimage.png"} )
    end
  end
end
```

The `link` parameter demonstrates a URL for an iOS application. You can direct the URL to an Android application that will look something like `https://play.google.com/store/apps/details?id=com.yourcompany.yourappname` or a general website URL of your choosing.

8. Call the `facebook.login()` function that includes your App ID, listener, and permissions to post on a user's Facebook wall. Close the remainder of the `onFBTouch(event)` function:

```
facebook.login(fbAppID, facebookListener, {"publish_actions"})

    end
end
```

9. Enable the `fbBtn` UI function and save your file:

```
fbBtn = ui.newButton{
  defaultSrc = "facebookbtn.png",
  defaultX = 100,
  defaultY = 100,
  overSrc = "facebookbtn-over.png",
  overX = 100,
  overY = 100,
  onEvent = onFBTouch,
}

fbBtn.x = 160; fbBtn.y = 160
```

10. Create a new device build for either iOS or Android. Load the build to your device and run the application. You will be asked to log in to your Facebook account before you can see the results from the application.

 Michelle Fernandez
Got a score of 100 on Your App Name Here!

 **Your App Name Here**
Download and compete with me!

 Like · Comment · 13 seconds ago via WWTD

What just happened?

One of the most important things that need to be done is `require "facebook"` in order to have the Facebook API to work. We also created a local variable called `score` with the value of 100.

The `onFBTouch(event)` function will initiate the event parameter on `"release"` of `fbBtn`. Within the function, `fbAppID` is included with characters in a string format. This will be a unique set of numbers that you must obtain from the Facebook Developers website. The App ID will be created for you when you make an App page on the site.

Another function, `facebookListener(event)`, is created, and it will initiate all `fbConnect` events. The `if` statement that contains (`"login" == event.phase`) will request to post a message to your feed through `"me/feed, "POST"`. The feed contains the following:

- `message=theMessage`: This refers to the string that belongs to the variable. It also concatenates scores, so it displays the value as well.

- `name`: This is a message that includes your app name or subject matter.

- `caption`: This is a short persuasive message to catch other users' attention about playing the game.

- `link`: This provides the URL to download the game from either the App Store or Google Play Store.

- `picture`: This is a URL that contains your image that displays your app icon or a visual representation of the game.

After the parameters are set, `facebook.login()` will refer to `fbAppID` and `facebookListener()` to see if a valid application ID is being used to post on Facebook. On success, the post is published through `"publish_actions"`.

Have a go hero – create a dialog box

See if you can figure out how to display a dialog box using Facebook Connect and using the same setup as shown in the preceding example. The following line will display this as:

```
facebook.showDialog( {action="stream.publish"} )
```

Now, see where in the code `facebook.showDialog()` can be accessed. This is another way of posting messages to Facebook.

Pop quiz – handling social networks

Q1. What is the specific API that scales down high-resolution sprite sheets?

1. `object.xScale`
2. `display.contentScaleX`
3. `object.xReference`
4. None of the above

Q2. What are the publishing permissions called that allow posting on a user's wall on Facebook?

1. `"publish_stream"`
2. `"publish_actions"`
3. `"post"`
4. `"post_listener"`

Q3. Which parameter(s) is required for `facebook.login()`?

1. `appId`
2. `listener`
3. `permissions`
4. All of the above

Summary

We have covered several more areas on enhancing configuration settings and integrating three of the most popular social networks in today's media in our apps.

We also took an in-depth look into the following:

- ◆ Build settings
- ◆ Dynamic content scaling and dynamic image resolution
- ◆ High-resolution sprite sheets
- ◆ Posting message feeds to Twitter and Facebook

In the next chapter, we will go over the process on how to submit our games to the App Store and Google Play Store. You don't want to miss this for the world!

10

Optimizing, Testing, and Shipping Your Games

Developing a game to the point of completion is a great accomplishment. It's one step closer to sharing it with the rest of the world, so that other people can play your new game. The benefit of creating your game with Corona SDK is that you have the option to build for iOS and/or Android. You want to ensure that your application is ready for submission so that it can be distributed in the mobile platform you're developing in. We'll go over the process of what it takes to prepare your game for its release.

 The application interface used here is frequently updated; however, you will be able to perform all the steps irrespective of the interface you're using.

In this chapter, we will cover the following topics:

◆ Improve the performance of your application

◆ Set up a distribution provisioning profile for the App Store

◆ Manage application information in iTunes Connect

◆ Learn how to submit an application to the Application Loader for the App Store

◆ Sign applications for Android

◆ Learn how to submit an application to the Google Play Store

Understanding memory efficiency

As you develop your application, you should always consider how your design choices affect the performance of your application. The device memory still has its constraints even though there are improvements in the computing power and memory. Performance and optimization within the device will not only achieve faster response times, but also help minimize memory usage and maximize battery life. A link to an example on how to check memory usage can be found at `https://gist.github.com/JesterXL/5615023`.

Memory is an important resource on mobile devices. When too much memory is being consumed, devices may be forced to quit your application when you least expect it. Here are some things to be aware of while developing:

- **Eliminate memory leaks**: Allowing leaks to exist means having extra used memory in your application that takes up valuable space. Even though Lua does automatic memory management, memory leaks can still occur in your code. For example, when you introduce global variables into your application, it is your job to tell Lua when they are not needed anymore so that memory can be freed. This is done through using `nil` in your code (`myVariable = nil`).

- **Display images should be small in file size as much as possible**: You may want to have many display images in your scene, but they may take up too much texture memory. Sprite sheets can take a toll on the memory in your apps. They should be created as small as conveniently possible and have an appropriate number of frames that demonstrate the animation clearly. For all items that you have displayed, plan out which elements are constantly in your background and foreground. If there is a way to combine several images together so that they don't move, do so. It'll save some memory when adding multiple display images.

- **Do not load all your resources at once**: Avoid loading resource files until they are actually needed. This will help save memory and keep your application from crashing while trying to load too many things at once.

- **Remove objects from the display hierarchy**: When a display object is created, it is implicitly added to a display hierarchy. When you no longer need a display object, you should remove it from the display hierarchy, especially when the objects contain images. This can be done using `display.remove( myImage ); myImage = nil` or `myImage:removeSelf()`.

  Here is an example:

```
local box = display.newRect( 0, 50, 100, 100)
box:setFillColor( 1, 1, 1)
box.alpha = 1

local function removeBox()
   if box.alpha == 1 then
```

```
      print("box removed")
      display.remove( box )
      box = nil
  end
end
timer.performWithDelay( 1000, removeBox, 1 ) -- Runs timer to
1000 milliseconds before calling the block within removeBox()
```

◆ **Sound files should be made as small as possible**: Use a free program, such as Audacity at , or your preferred audio software to compress music or sound effects and build for the device. It is best to compare untouched audio with compressed audio to hear the difference in quality. This will help you determine a good median between sound quality and file size.

Graphics

Display images have a way of taking up a lot of texture memory if you're not paying attention to the size and number of images being used all at once.

Group objects

If a property of several objects is set to the same value, it's preferable to add the objects to a group and then modify the property of the group. It'll make it much easier for you to code, and it optimizes your animation.

Turning off animations when they're not being used

It's easy to forget to stop animations from running in the background when they're not needed or when you've made them invisible.

When you include a listener such as `"enterFrame"` and the objects registered under the listener have been set to `.isVisible = false`, it'll continue to run in the background even though it is not seen on screen. Make sure that listeners are removed when they are not needed.

Optimizing image sizes

When you have large file sizes, especially full-screen images, the responsiveness of your application will slow down because of the time it takes to load, and plus, it uses up a lot of memory. When using large images, try compressing the file size as much as you can with an image-editing tool, such as Photoshop or ImageOptim (`https://imageoptim.com`). It'll help reduce the file size and save you the pain of application lag. Compressing large image sizes will benefit you in the long run. If images are backgrounds, consider switching to tiled images.

Distributing iOS applications

Once your game is finally debugged and completed, what's next? Assuming you're already registered in the iOS Developer Program, there are some guidelines that have to be followed before an application can be submitted to the App Store.

Prepping your app icons

There are various image sizes and naming conventions required for your app icon, depending on which iOS devices your application is developed for. You can find the latest information under the **App Icon** subsection of the **Icon and Image Design** section of the iOS Human Interface Guidelines, on the Apple Developer website at `https://developer.apple.com/library/ios/documentation/UserExperience/Conceptual/MobileHIG/AppIcons.html#//apple_ref/doc/uid/TP40006556-CH19-SW1`.

The following are the app icon requirements, which also need to be in a noninterlaced `.png` format:

- `iTunesArtwork@2x`: This is a 1024 x 1024 px image. The `.png` extension needs to be removed for this image.
- `Icon-60@2x.png`: This is a 120 x 120 px image, which is used for Retina iPhone.
- `Icon-60@3x.png`: This is a 180 x 180 px image, which is used for iPhone 6 Plus.
- `Icon-76.png`: This is a 76 x 76 px image, which is used for iPad.
- `Icon-76@2x.png`: This is a 152 x 152 px image, which is used for Retina iPad.
- `Icon-Small-40.png`: This is a 40 x 40 px image, which is used for iPad 2 and iPad mini search.
- `Icon-Small-40@2.png`: This is an 80 x 80 px image, which is used for Retina iPhone/iPad search.
- `Icon-Small-40@3x.png`: This is a 120 x 120 px image, which is used for iPhone 6 Plus search.
- `Icon-Small.png`: This is a 29 x 29 px image, which is used for iPad 2 and iPad mini settings.
- `Icon-Small@2x.png`: This is a 58 x 58 px image, which is used for Retina iPhone/iPad settings.
- `Icon-Small@3x.png`: This is an 87 x 87 px image, which is used for iPhone 6 Plus settings.

In your `build.settings` file, you will need to include the icon references for all the devices you are building for in your application. Here is an example of how to set up your file if you are creating universal builds:

```
settings =
{
  orientation =
  {
    default = "landscapeRight",
  },

  iphone =
    {
      plist =
      {
        CFBundleIconFiles = {
          "Icon-60@2x.png",
          "Icon-60@3x.png",
          "Icon-76.png",
          "Icon-76@2x.png",
          "Icon-Small-40.png",
          "Icon-Small-40@2x.png",
          "Icon-Small-40@3x.png",
          "Icon-Small.png",
          "Icon-Small@2x.png",
          "Icon-Small@3x.png",
        },

      },
    },

}
```

You do not need to include the `iTunesArtwork@2x` image in the `plist`, but make sure that it's inserted in your base project folder of the app.

Time for action – setting up your distribution certificate and provisioning profile for the App Store

We have focused on creating development certificates and provisioning profiles to test and debug our apps on a device. Now, we have to create a distribution version of them in order to submit an iOS application. Be aware that Apple can change the design of their website at any time. So, don't get frustrated if the steps and screenshots do not match up:

1. Log in to your Apple Developer account and go to **Certificates, Identifiers, & Profiles**. Click on **App IDs**. Create a new App ID by selecting the **+** icon in the upper-right corner and create a description that pertains to your application so that you can identify it. If you have an existing App ID that you have been using during development, you can disregard this step.

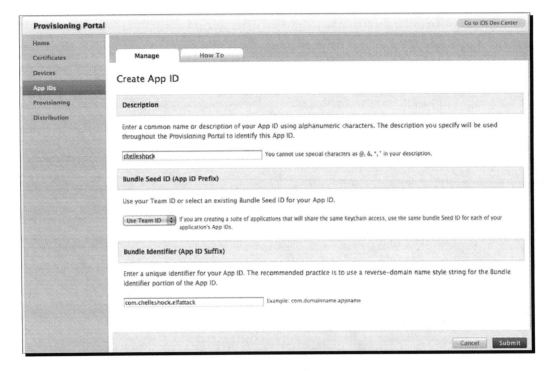

2. Click on **Distribution** under **Provisioning Profile**. Select the **+** button and select **App Store** under the **Distribution** section. Press **Continue**.

3. Select the App ID you want to associate with the file and click on **Continue**. Next, select the certificate that will be associated with your provisioning profile and click on **Continue**.

4. Provide a profile name for your provisioning profile and select the **Generate** button.

5. On the next screen, click on the **Download** button and double-click on the file to install it on your machine.

What just happened?

The App ID you use is imperative to identify your app that will be submitted. It is best to have a unique reverse-domain style string. Make sure that you create explicit App IDs for Corona apps. Do not use wildcard App IDs.

In order to distribute for the App Store, you need to create an App Store Distribution Provisioning Profile and a Production Certificate. Any development profile will not be accepted. The process is similar to making a development provisioning profile and development certificate.

You can find more information on distribution provisioning profiles on the Apple Developer site at `https://developer.apple.com/ios/manage/distribution/index.action` (you will be asked to log in to your Apple Developer account if you haven't done so already) and the Corona Labs site at `http://docs.coronalabs.com/guide/distribution/iOSBuild/index.html`.

iTunes Connect

iTunes Connect is a suite of web-based tools that allows you to submit and manage your applications for distribution on the App Store. In iTunes Connect, you will be able to check the status of your contracts; set up your tax and banking information; obtain sales and finance reports; request promotional codes; and manage users, applications, metadata, and your In-App Purchase catalog.

Contracts, tax, and banking

If you plan on selling your app, you need to have a paid commercial agreement in place so that it can be posted to the App Store. You will have to request a contract pertaining to iOS Paid Applications. All this is done through iTunes Connect under the **Contracts**, **Tax**, and **Banking** links.

When requesting contracts, beware of potential issues that can occur, such as delays when Apple processes your information for the first time and/or issues when changing your current contact information in iTunes Connect (that is, change of address if you have moved to a different location). It is your responsibility to regularly contact Apple for support to make sure that the information is always up to date in your contracts.

Time for action – managing your application in iTunes Connect

We will now go over how to set up our application information in iTunes Connect. Any other information pertaining to user accounts, contracts, and banking that you would like to set up can be found at `https://developer.apple.com/app-store/review/`.

1. Log in to iTunes Connect at `http://itunesconnect.apple.com/`. Your login information is the same as your iOS Developer account. Once logged in, select **Manage Your Applications**. Click on the **Add New App** button. **App Name** is the name of your application. **SKU Number** is a unique alphanumeric identifier for the app. **Bundle ID** is the one you created in the iOS Provisioning Portal. Fill in the information and click on **Continue**:

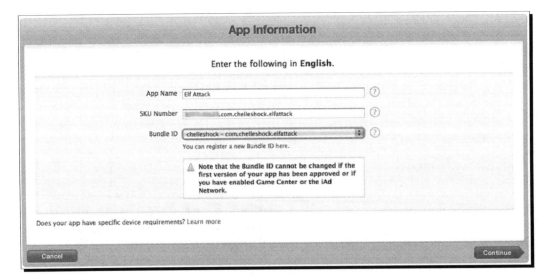

2. The next step is to select the date on which you want your application to be live in the App Store and **Price Tier** that you want to charge. There is an optional checkbox for **Discount for Educational Institutions**. This is only if you want your app to be discounted for educational institutions that want to purchase multiple copies at the same time. Click on **Continue** when done:

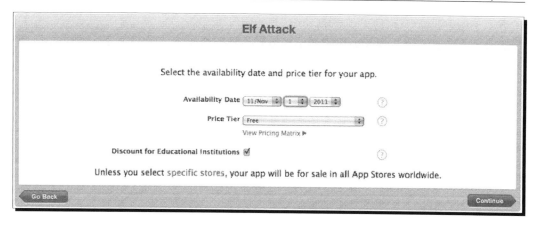

3. Next, fill in the **Metadata** section about your application. This includes the version number, description of your game, categories, keywords pertaining to your app, copyright, contact information, and support URL:

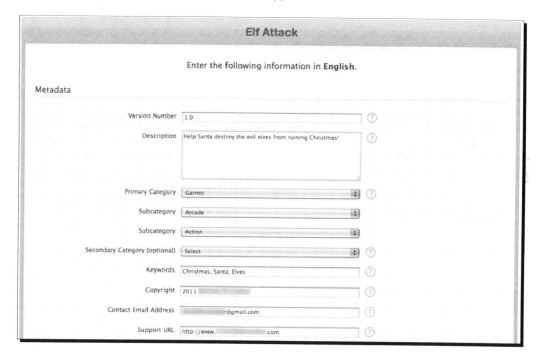

4. The **Rating** section is based on the content of your application. For each description, choose the level of frequency that best describes your app. There are certain content types that will result in automatic rejection, such as realistic violence portrayed in your app or personal attacks to a target individual or group. You can learn more about *App Store Review Guidelines* at `https://developer.apple.com/appstore/resources/approval/guidelines.html`.

Rating

For each content description, choose the level of frequency that best describes your app.

App Rating Details ▶

Apps must not contain any obscene, pornographic, offensive or defamatory content or materials of any kind (text, graphics, images, photographs, etc.), or other content or materials that in Apple's reasonable judgment may be found objectionable.

Apple Content Descriptions	None	Infrequent/Mild	Frequent/Intense
Cartoon or Fantasy Violence	○	●	○
Realistic Violence	●	○	○
Sexual Content or Nudity	●	○	○
Profanity or Crude Humor	●	○	○
Alcohol, Tobacco, or Drug Use or References	●	○	○
Mature/Suggestive Themes	●	○	○
Simulated Gambling	●	○	○
Horror/Fear Themes	●	○	○
Prolonged Graphic or Sadistic Realistic Violence	●	○	○
Graphic Sexual Content and Nudity	○	○	○

9+

App Rating

---

5. As discussed earlier in the **Uploads** section, you will need a large version of your app icon, that is, iPhone/iPod Touch screenshots and iPad screenshots (if your app runs on iPad) of the content in your application.

6. You will be greeted with a page summary of your application information. Check to make sure that the information displayed is correct and then click on **Done**:

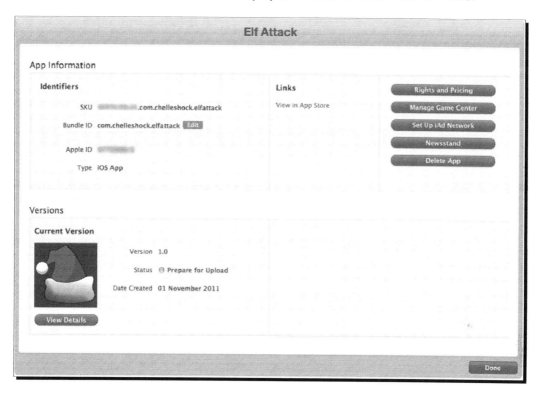

7. You will be sent back to your version details page. Notice a button that says **Ready to Upload Binary**. Click on the button, and you will be required to answer a couple of questions about **Export Compliance**. Once completed, you will have the permission to upload your binary through **Application Loader**.

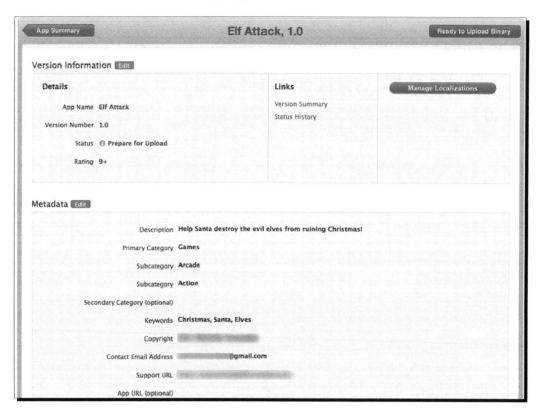

What just happened?

iTunes Connect is where you'll be managing your application from here on out when distributing it to the App Store. Every single piece of information you want to display about your app is done through iTunes Connect.

Once you're in the section pertaining to **App Information**, make sure that your **SKU Number** is unique and that it relates to your app, so that you can identify it later down the line. Also, make sure that **Bundle ID** you designated for your app is the correct one.

The app availability in the **Rights and Pricing** section controls when you want your app to go live once it's approved. It's good to set it for a date a couple of weeks in the future from when you submit it. It can take a couple of days to a couple of weeks for the review process to go from **Under Review** to **Ready for Sale** as long as there are no problems with the submission. The price tier is where you set the price for your app, or it can be set to **Free**. You can click on **View Pricing Matrix** to determine the price you're aiming to sell your app for.

The information in the **Metadata** section is what the customer will see in the App Store. The **Rating** section pertains to Apple Content Descriptions. Make sure that the level of frequency is checked off as close as possible to the content of your application.

The **Uploads** section is where you include your 1024 x 1024 px app icon and screenshots that best suit your app visually. Make sure that you provide the correct image sizes. Once you have transitioned back to the **Application Information** screen, you'll notice that the status says **Prepare for Upload**. When you click on the **Ready to Upload Binary** button on the **Version Details** page, you will answer questions about **Export Compliance**. Soon after, the status will change to **Waiting for Upload**.

More information relating to iTunes Connect can be found at `http://developer.apple.com/library/ios/iTunesConnectGuide`.

Building an iOS application for distribution in Corona

We have come to the homestretch in getting your iOS application submitted to the App Store. Assuming that you have already tested your application and debugged it with your development provisioning profile, you're ready to create a distribution build that will create a binary ZIP file of your app.

Time for action – building your application and uploading it to the Application Loader

Time to create the final game build for iOS distribution and upload it to the Application Loader for review under Apple's board.

1. Launch the Corona simulator, navigate to the application project folder, and run it. Go to the Corona simulator menu bar and then to **File | Build | iOS**. Fill in all your application details. Make sure that your **Application Name** and **Version** fields match what is displayed in your iTunes Connect account. Choose **Device** to build an app bundle. Next, select the target device (iPhone or iPad) your app is created for from the **Supported Devices** drop-down menu. Under the **Code Signing Identity** drop-down menu, choose the **Distribution Provisioning Profile** option you created in the iOS Provisioning Portal. In the **Save to folder** section, click on **Browse** and choose where you would like your application to be saved. Click on the **Build** button when done:

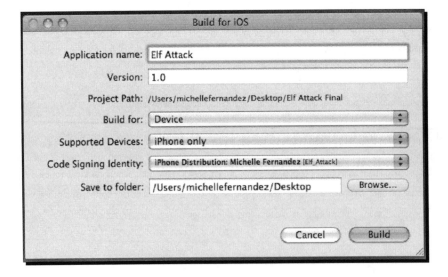

2. When the build has been compiled, you will be greeted with a display that your application is ready for distribution. Select the **Upload to App Store** button.

3. When the **Welcome to Application Loader** window pops up, log in with your iTunes Connect information. You will then be brought to another window with the **Deliver Your App** or **Create New Package** option. Choose **Deliver Your App.** The next window displays a drop-down menu; choose the name of the application you will be submitting and then click on the **Next** button.

4. The available application information found in iTunes Connect is displayed. Verify that it is correct and then click on the **Choose** button.

5. Click on the ellipsis (**...**) button to replace the current file before submitting it and then select the **Send** button.

6. The Application Loader will begin submitting your application binary file to the App Store.

7. You will get a confirmation that your binary was delivered to the App Store if it uploaded successfully. You can check on the status of your application in iTunes Connect when it goes to review, ready for sale, live, and so on. An e-mail will be sent to you upon every status change of your application. That's it! This is how you submit an app to the App Store!

8. When your application has been reviewed and approved by the App Store, you can go into iTunes Connect and adjust the availability date if it is approved before your proposed launch date. Your app will be live in the App Store instantly:

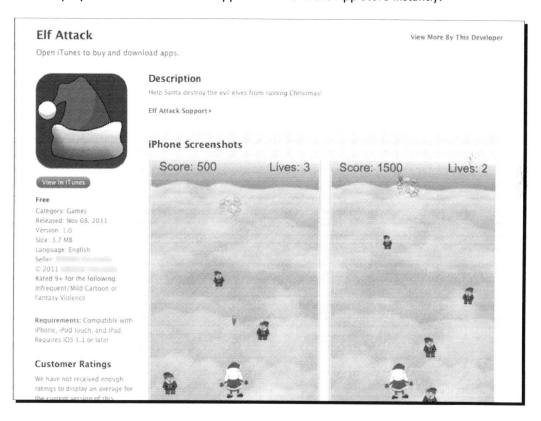

What just happened?

It's important that when you build your app under **Code Signing Identity**, you select your distribution provisioning profile that was created for your distribution build. Upon the compilation of your build, you can launch the Application Loader. Make sure that you have Xcode installed. The Application Loader will launch readily after you select the **Upload to App Store** button.

While you're in the Application Loader, the name of your app will be displayed in the dropdown once you have completed loading the binary information to iTunes Connect. When you deliver your app, select the zipped-up binary from the location you saved your file at.

As soon as the file is uploaded, a confirmation window will appear and an e-mail will be sent to the Apple ID assigned to your Apple account. Your binary will be shown with a **Waiting for Review** status in iTunes Connect.

After all these steps, you now know how to submit an iOS application to the App Store. Hooray!

Have a go hero – making a universal iOS build

If you developed an application for iPhone only, try implementing it as an iPad version as well so that it can become a universal build. Take the lessons you learned from the previous chapters using your `build.settings` and `config.lua` files to resize your application. Also, don't forget about what is required of your app icon as well. It's like hitting two birds with one stone!

The Google Play Store

The Google Play Store is a publishing platform that helps you publicize, sell, and distribute your Android applications to users around the world.

To register as a Google Play Developer and get started with publishing, visit the Google Play Android Developer Console publisher site. You can sign up for an account at `https://play.google.com/apps/publish/`.

Creating launcher icons

A launcher icon is a graphic that represents your application. Launcher icons are used by applications and appear on the user's home screen. They can also be used to represent shortcuts in your application. These are similar to the icons created for iOS applications. The following are the launcher icon requirements, which also need to be in a 32-bit `.png` format:

+ `Icon-ldpi.png`: This is a 36 x 36 px image at 120 dpi, which is used for low-density screen

+ `Icon-mdpi.png`: This is a 48 x 48 px image at 160 dpi, which is used for medium-density screen

+ `Icon-hdpi.png`: This is a 72 x 72 px image at 240 dpi, which is used for high-density screen

+ `Icon-xhdpi.png`: This is a 96 x 96 px image at 320 dpi, which is used for x-high-density screen

+ `Icon-xxhdpi.png`: This is a 144 x 144 px image at 480 dpi, which is used for xx-high-density screen

+ `Icon-xxxhdpi.png`: This is a 192 x 192 px image at 640 dpi, which is used for xxx-high-density screen.

Launcher icons need to be placed in your project folder at the time you build your application. The Google Play Store also requires you to have a 512 x 512 px version of your icon, which can be uploaded in the developer console at the upload time of your build. For more information on launcher icons, visit `http://developer.android.com/guide/practices/ui_guidelines/icon_design_launcher.html`.

Time for action – signing your app for the Google Play Store

The Android system requires all the installed applications to be digitally signed with a certificate whose private key is held by the application's developer. The Android system uses the certificate as a means of identifying the author of an application and establishing a relationship of trust between applications. The certificate is not used to control which applications the user can install. The certificate does not need to be signed by a certificate authority; it can be self-signed. Certificates can be signed on either Mac or Windows systems.

1. On the Mac, go to **Applications | Utilities | Terminal**. On Windows, go to **Start Menu | All Programs | Accessories | Command Prompt**. Using the `keytool` command, add in the following lines and press *Enter*:

```
keytool -genkey -v -keystore my-release-key.keystore -alias
aliasname -keyalg RSA -validity 999999
```

Replace `my-release-key` with the name of your application and `aliasname` with a similar or equal alias name. Also, if you add any extra numbers past `999999` (that is, extra 9s), the application will appear broken.

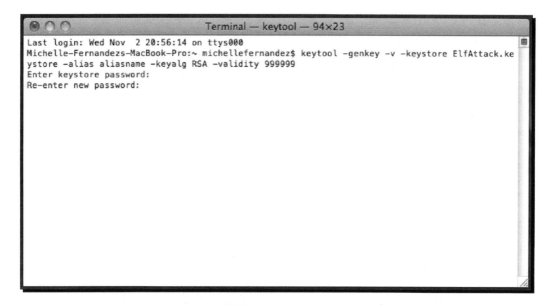

2. You will be asked to enter a keystore password. From here, you will create a unique password that you, as the developer, must come up with. You will be asked to re-enter it. The remaining questions that will be asked pertain to your developer/ company information, location, and so on. Fill it all in. Once you have filled in the required information, you have generated a key to sign your Android build. For more information pertaining to app signing, visit http://developer.android.com/ tools/publishing/app-signing.html.

3. Launch the Corona simulator, navigate to the application project folder and run it. Go to the Corona simulator menu bar and then to **File** | **Build** | **Android**. Fill in the information for **Application Name**, **Version Code**, and **Version Name** pertaining to your app. Specify a **Package** name using the Java scheme. Select **Google Play** from the **Target App Store** menu. Under **Keystore**, select the **Browse** button to locate your signed private key and then from the pull-down menu, select your generated key for your release build. You will be prompted to enter your keystore password you used to sign your application in the `keytool` command. Under **Key Alias**, choose the alias name you created for your key from the pull-down menu and enter your password when prompted. Select the **Browse** button to choose a location for your app build. Choose the **Build** button when finished:

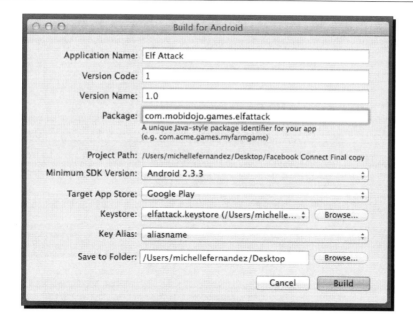

What just happened?

The `keytool` command generates the keystore as a file called `my-release-key.keystore`. The keystore and key are protected by the passwords you entered. The keystore contains a single key, which is valid for 999999 days. The alias is a name that you will use later to refer to this keystore when signing your application.

Your keystore password is something that you create and must remember when you build your app in Corona. There will be an option if you want to use a different password for the alias name. You can press *Enter* to use the same one while you're in the Terminal or Command Prompt.

When you create your build in Corona, make sure that your version number is an integer with no special characters. Also, you will have to make sure that your `build.settings` file includes the `versionCode` as well. This will be the same number as your version number. Refer to *Chapter 9, Handling Multiple Devices and Networking Your Apps* for more information.

The Java scheme in your build is the reverse of your domain name with the name of your product/company appended and the name of your app, for example, `com.mycompany.games.mygame`.

When you have built your app by using your private key and you have selected an alias name, the `.apk` file will be created and will be ready to be published on the Google Play Store.

Time for action – submitting an app to the Google Play Store

We'll use the Developer Console. This is where your developer profile will be created to publish to the Google Play Store.

1. Once you're logged in to the Developer Console, click on the Android icon and select the button that says **Add new application**. You will be greeted with a pop-up window that will allow you to upload your build. Select your default language from the drop-down menu and enter the name of your app under **Title**. Click on the **Upload APK** button to proceed to the next page.

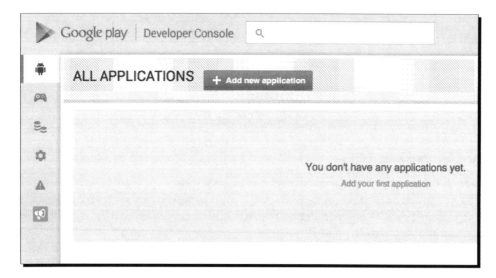

2. Click on **Upload your first APK to Production** and then on **Browse files** to locate the .apk file of your application. Select the **Open** button to upload your file.

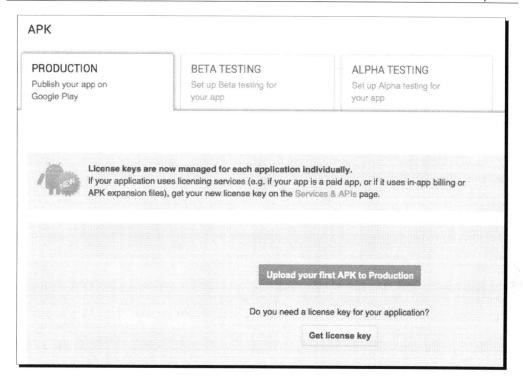

3. After your `.apk` file is uploaded, select the **Store Listing** tab. Fill out the information with the details of your app, including **Title**, **Short description**, and **Full description**:

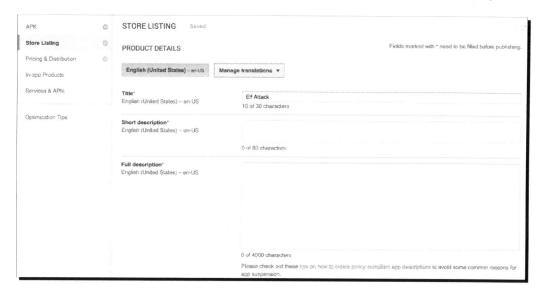

4. In the Graphic Assets section, add in your app screenshots. At least two screenshots are required to submit your app. Other mandatory graphics that are needed are **Hi-res icon** and **Feature Graphic**.

5. The Categorization, Contact Details, and Privacy Policy sections need to be addressed. Make sure that you complete these sections and click on the **Save** button at the top of the page before proceeding to the next tab.

6. Select the **Pricing & Distribution** tab. Select the information that pertains to your app. The pricing default setting is **Free**. If you want to make a paid version, you must set up a merchant account with Google Checkout. Click on **Save** when you're finished:

7. After filling out all the information pertaining to your app, make sure that the APK, Store Listing, and Pricing & Distribution tabs have a green check mark next to them.

8. Finally, click on the **Ready to Publish** button and select **Publish this app** in the drop-down menu. Congratulations! You have just published your app to the Google Play Store!

What just happened?

The Developer Console page displays a simple step-by-step process on how to publish your `.apk` file.

The assets required to publish an app show the acceptable resolution and image types next to each section. It is optional to include a promotional graphic, feature graphic, and promotional video, but it would be in your best interest to add enough substance to your app page. This will make it appealing to potential customers.

After all the information related to your app is completed, make sure that you save your progress. Once you select the **Publish this app** menu, you're done! You should be able to see your app in the Google Play Store within the hour you published it.

Have a go hero – adding more promos

The Google Play Store gives you many options on how to promote your application. Additional assets can be included from the Developer Console. Try the following:

♦ Add a promotional graphic as a marketing vehicle to showcase your app.

♦ Add a feature graphic.

♦ Create a promotional video of your app. A website such as YouTube is a good way to share a trailer of your game.

Pop quiz – publishing applications

Q1. When creating an iOS Distribution Provisioning file, what distribution method do you need to use?

1. Development
2. App Store
3. Ad hoc
4. None of the above

Q2. Where do you refer to for the status of the submitted iOS applications?

1. iTunes Connect
2. iOS Provisioning Portal
3. The Application Loader
4. None of the above

Q3. What is required to build an app for the Google Play Store?

1. Create a private key under the `keytool` command
2. Sign your application with a debug key
3. Sign your application with your private key
4. a and c

Summary

We have accomplished a huge milestone with this chapter. We know how to submit not only to one but two major app markets! Publishing your applications to the App Store and Google Play Store is not scary, after all.

We have covered the following topics:

- The importance of memory efficiency
- Creating provision profiles for distribution to the App Store
- Managing iTunes Connect
- Submitting a binary to the Application Loader
- Signing a release build for Android applications
- Submitting .apk files to the Google Play Store

In the next chapter, we'll take a look at In-App Purchases in the Apple iTunes Store for the iOS platform.

11

Implementing In-App Purchases

In-App Purchase is an optional feature that developers can use to embed a store directly within an app. Sometimes, you may want to extend some features in your current game to keep your consumers interested in playing. Here's your chance, and possibly, more revenue in your pocket!

This chapter is only concerned with In-App Purchases in the Apple iTunes Store for the iOS platform. Android developers who want to implement In-App Purchases in their apps can refer to for reference. The set up for In-App Purchase is done in a similar fashion for iOS and Android. There are, however, some differences that need to be set up in your `build.settings` file and code.

 The application interface used here is frequently updated. However, you will be able to perform all the steps irrespective of the interface you're using.

We'll cover the following in this chapter:

- Consumable, nonconsumable, and subscription purchases
- Making transactions
- Restoring purchased items
- Initializing Corona's store module
- Creating and testing In-App Purchases on a device

Ready, set, go!

The wonders of In-App Purchase

The purpose of implementing In-App Purchase is to add an in-app payment functionality to collect payment for enhanced functionality or additional content usable in your game. The following are options of incorporating this feature:

- ◆ A game that offers new level packs to play outside the default content
- ◆ A freemium game that allows you to purchase virtual currency to create or build new assets during game play
- ◆ Adding additional characters or special power ups to enhance game elements

These are some examples that can be implemented with In-App Purchases.

In-App Purchases allow users to purchase additional content within an application. The App Store manages transaction information only. Developers cannot use the App Store to deliver content. So, either you bundle content with your app when you ship it (it will be unlocked on purchase), or you have to work out your own system to download the data, if you wish to deliver content.

Types of In-App Purchases

There are several In-App Purchase types that you can apply in your apps.

You can find more information on In-App Purchases on the Apple website at `https://developer.apple.com/library/ios/documentation/LanguagesUtilities/Conceptual/iTunesConnectInAppPurchase_Guide/Chapters/CreatingInAppPurchaseProducts.html`.

- ◆ **Consumable**: These are products that must be purchased each time the user needs that item. They're typically one-time services, such as money in an app where you need to pay for supplies to build structures.
- ◆ **Nonconsumable**: These are products that only need to be purchased once by the user. These could be additional level packs in a game.
- ◆ **Auto-renewing subscriptions**: These are products that allow the user to purchase in-app content for a set duration of time. An example of an auto-renewable subscription would be a magazine or newspaper that takes advantage of the auto-renewing functionality built into iOS.

◆ **Free subscriptions**: These are used to put free subscription content in Newsstand. Once a user signs up for a free subscription, it will be available on all devices associated with that user's Apple ID. Note that free subscriptions do not expire and can only be offered in Newsstand-enabled apps.

◆ **Non-renewing subscriptions**: Similar to auto-renewable subscriptions, these are non-renewing subscriptions that require a user to renew each time the subscription is due to expire. Your app must contain code that recognizes when the expiration occurs. It must also prompt the user to purchase a new subscription. An auto-renewable subscription eliminates these steps.

Corona's store module

Applying In-App Purchases in your application can be a little mind-boggling and tedious process. Integrating it with Corona requires calling the store module:

```
store = require("store")
```

The store module is already incorporated to the Corona API, similar to Facebook and Game Network. You can find more information on Corona's store module at http://docs.coronalabs.com/daily/guide/monetization/IAP/index.html.

store.init()

The store.init() function must be called when handling store transactions to your app. It activates In-App Purchases and allows you to receive callbacks with the listener function you specify:

```
store.init( listener )
```

The only parameter here is listener. It's a function that handles transaction callback events.

The following blocks determine the transaction states that can occur during an In-App Purchase. The four different states are purchased, restored, cancelled, and failed:

```
function transactionCallback( event )
  local transaction = event.transaction
  if transaction.state == "purchased" then
    print("Transaction successful!")
    print("productIdentifier", transaction.productIdentifier)
    print("receipt", transaction.receipt)
    print("transactionIdentifier", transaction.identifier)
    print("date", transaction.date)
```

```
        elseif  transaction.state == "restored" then
        print("Transaction restored (from previous session)")
        print("productIdentifier", transaction.productIdentifier)
        print("receipt", transaction.receipt)
        print("transactionIdentifier", transaction.identifier)
        print("date", transaction.date)
        print("originalReceipt", transaction.originalReceipt)
        print("originalTransactionIdentifier",
        transaction.originalIdentifier)
        print("originalDate", transaction.originalDate)

        elseif transaction.state == "cancelled" then
        print("User cancelled transaction")

        elseif transaction.state == "failed" then
        print("Transaction failed, type:", transaction.errorType,
        transaction.errorString)

        else
        print("unknown event")
        end

        -- Once we are done with a transaction, call this to tell the
        store
        -- we are done with the transaction.
        -- If you are providing downloadable content, wait to call this
        until
        -- after the download completes.
        store.finishTransaction( transaction )
    end

    store.init( "apple", transactionCallback )
```

event.transaction

The event.transaction object contains the transaction.

The transaction object supports the following read-only properties:

- ◆ "state": This is a string containing the state of the transaction. Valid values are "purchased", "restored", "cancelled", and "failed".

- ◆ "productIdentifier": This is the product identifier associated with the transaction.

- ◆ "receipt": This is a unique receipt returned from the App Store. It is returned as a hexadecimal string.

- ◆ `"signature"`: This is a string used to verify the purchase. For Google Play, it is returned by `"inapp_signature"`. In iOS, it returns `nil`.

- ◆ `"identifier"`: This is a unique transaction identifier returned from the App Store. It is a string.

- ◆ `"date"`: This is the date the transaction occurred.

- ◆ `"originalReceipt"`: This is a unique receipt returned from the App Store from the original purchase attempt. It is mostly relevant in the case of a restore. It is returned as a hexadecimal string.

- ◆ `"originalIdentifier"`: This is a unique transaction identifier returned from the Store from the original purchase attempt. This is mostly relevant in the case of a restore. It is a string.

- ◆ `"originalDate"`: This is the date of the original transaction. It is mostly relevant in the case of a restore.

- ◆ `"errorType"`: This is the type of error that occurred when the state is `"failed"` (a string).

- ◆ `"errorString"`: This is a descriptive error message of what went wrong in the `"failed"` case.

store.loadProducts()

The `store.loadProducts()` function retrieves information about items available for sale. This includes the price of each item, a name, and a description:

```
store.loadProducts( arrayOfProductIdentifiers, listener )
```

Its parameters are as follows:

- ◆ `arrayOfProductIdentifiers`: This is an array with each element containing a string of the product ID of the In-App product you want to know about

- ◆ `listener`: This is a callback function that is invoked when the store finishes retrieving the product information

The following block displays the list of products that are available in the app. Information about the product can be retrieved from the `loadProductsCallback()` function and determines whether it is valid or invalid:

```
-- Contains your Product ID's set in iTunes Connect
local listOfProducts =
{
  "com.mycompany.InAppPurchaseExample.Consumable",
  "com.mycompany.InAppPurchaseExample.NonConsumable",
  "com.mycompany.InAppPurchaseExample.Subscription",
```

```
    }

    function loadProductsCallback ( event )
      print("showing valid products", #event.products)
      for i=1, #event.products do
        print(event.products[i].title)
        print(event.products[i].description)
        print(event.products[i].price)
        print(event.products[i].productIdentifier)
      end

      print("showing invalidProducts", #event.invalidProducts)
        for i=1, #event.invalidProducts do
          print(event.invalidProducts[i])
    end
    end

    store.loadProducts( listOfProducts, loadProductsCallback )
```

event.products

When a requested list of products is returned by `store.loadProducts()`, the array of product information can be accessed through the `event.products` property.

Product information, such as title, description, price, and the product identifier, is contained in a table:

```
    event.products
```

Each entry in the `event.products` array supports the following fields:

- ◆ `title`: This is the localized name of the item
- ◆ `description`: This is the localized description of the item
- ◆ `price`: This is the price of an item (as a number)
- ◆ `productIdentifier`: This is the product identifier

event.invalidProducts

When `store.loadProducts()` returns its requested list of products, any products you requested that are not available for sale will be returned in an array. You can access the array of invalid products through the `event.invalidProducts` property.

This is a Lua array containing the product identifier string requested from `store.loadProducts()`:

```
    event.invalidProducts
```

store.canMakePurchases

The `store.canMakePurchases` function returns true if purchases are allowed, and false otherwise. Corona's API can check whether purchasing is possible. iOS devices provide a setting that disables purchasing. This can be used to avoid purchasing apps accidentally.

```
if store.canMakePurchases then
  store.purchase( listOfProducts )
else
  print("Store purchases are not available")
end
```

store.purchase()

The `store.purchase()` function initiates a purchase transaction on a provided list of products.

This function will send purchase requests to the store. The listener specified in `store.init()` will be invoked when the store finishes processing the transaction:

```
store.purchase( arrayOfProducts )
```

Its only parameter is `arrayOfProducts`, an array specifying the products you want to buy:

```
store.purchase{ "com.mycompany.InAppPurchaseExample.Consumable"}
```

store.finishTransaction()

This function notifies the App Store that a transaction is complete.

After you finish handling a transaction, you must call `store.finishTransaction()` on the transaction object. If you don't do this, the App Store will think your transaction was interrupted and will attempt to resume it on the next application launch.

Syntax:

```
store.finishTransaction( transaction )
```

Parameters:

Transaction: The `transaction` object belonging to the transaction you want to mark as finished.

Example:

```
store.finishTransaction( transaction )
```

store.restore()

Any previously purchased items that have been wiped clean from a device or upgraded to a new device can be restored on the user's account without paying for the product again. The `store.restore()` API initiates this process. Transactions can be restored by the `transactionCallback` listener, which is registered with `store.init()`. The transaction state will be `"restored"` and your app may then make use of the `"originalReceipt"`, `"originalIdentifier"`, and `"originalDate"` fields of the transaction object:

```
store.restore()
```

The block will run through the `transactionCallback()` function and determine whether a product has been previously purchased from the application. If the result is true, `store.restore()` will initiate the process of retrieving the product without asking the user to pay for it again:

```
function transactionCallback( event )
  local transaction = event.transaction
  if transaction.state == "purchased" then
    print("Transaction successful!")
    print("productIdentifier", transaction.productIdentifier)
    print("receipt", transaction.receipt)
    print("transactionIdentifier", transaction.identifier)
    print("date", transaction.date)

  elseif  transaction.state == "restored" then
    print("Transaction restored (from previous session)")
    print("productIdentifier", transaction.productIdentifier)
    print("receipt", transaction.receipt)
    print("transactionIdentifier", transaction.identifier)
    print("date", transaction.date)
    print("originalReceipt", transaction.originalReceipt)
    print("originalTransactionIdentifier",
    transaction.originalIdentifier)
    print("originalDate", transaction.originalDate)

  elseif transaction.state == "cancelled" then
      print("User cancelled transaction")
```

```
elseif transaction.state == "failed" then
  print("Transaction failed, type:", transaction.errorType,
  transaction.errorString)

else
  print("unknown event")
end


-- Once we are done with a transaction, call this to tell the store
-- we are done with the transaction.
-- If you are providing downloadable content, wait to call this until
-- after the download completes.
store.finishTransaction( transaction )
end

store.init( transactionCallback )
store.restore()
```

Create an In-App Purchase

Before reading on, make sure you know how to create an App ID and Distribution Provisioning Profile from the iOS Provisioning Portal. Also, make sure you know how to manage new applications in iTunes Connect. If you're unsure, refer to *Chapter 10, Optimizing, Testing, and Shipping Your Games*, for more information. Here are the things that need to be ready in your app before creating an In-App Purchase:

◆ A Distribution Certificate already made for your app.

◆ An explicit App ID for your application, for example, com.companyname.appname. Do not substitute a wildcard character (asterisk: "*"). The Bundle ID needs to be completely unique in order to use the In-App Purchase function.

◆ An ad hoc Distribution Provisioning Profile (used to test In-App Purchases). When you're ready to submit an app with In-App Purchase, an App Store Distribution Provisioning Profile is required.

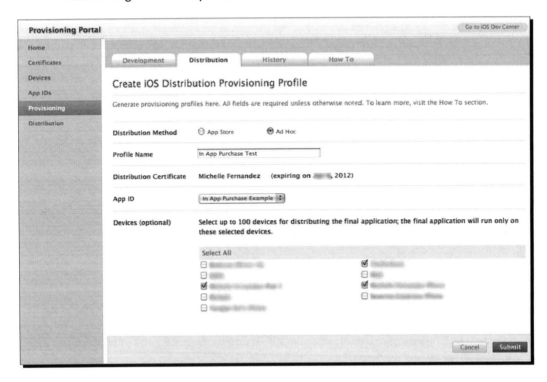

◆ Your application information must be set up in iTunes Connect. You do not need to get your binary uploaded to create or test In-App Purchases.

◆ Make sure that you have an iOS Paid Applications contract in effect with Apple. If you don't, you'll need to request it in **Contracts, Tax, and Banking** located on the iTunes Connect home page. You will need to provide your banking and tax information in order to offer In-App Purchases in your apps.

Time for action – creating the In-App Purchase in iTunes Connect

We'll be implementing an In-App Purchase through iTunes Connect and create a scenario in a sample application that will call a transaction. Let's create the Product ID that will be used in our In-App Purchase:

1. Log in to iTunes Connect. On the home page, select **Manage Your Applications**. Select the application you plan to add an In-App Purchase to.

2. Once you're on the app summary page, click on the **Manage In-App Purchases** button and then click on the **Create New** button in the top-left corner.

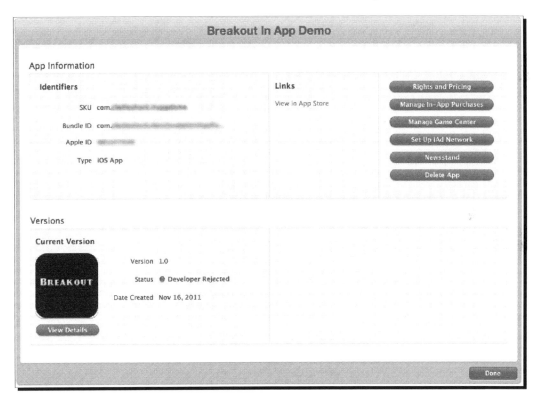

3. You will be brought to a page that shows you a summary of the types of In-App Purchases that you can create. For this example, **Non-Consumable** is selected. We'll be creating a product that needs to be purchased only once.

4. In the next page is the area where you fill in the information about the product. The information applies to consumable, nonconsumable, and non-renewing subscription In-App Purchases. Fill the **Reference Name** and **Product ID** fields for your product. The Product ID needs to be a unique identifier and can be any alphanumeric sequence of letters and numbers (for example, `com.companyname.appname.productid`).

 Auto-renewing subscriptions require you to generate a shared secret. If you are to use auto-renewing subscriptions in your app, then on the **Manage in-App Purchases** page, click on the **View or generate a shared secret** link. You will be brought to a page to generate the shared secret. Click on the **Generate** button. The shared secret will display a string of 32 randomly generated alphanumeric characters. When you choose auto-renewing subscriptions, the difference from the other In-App Purchase types is that you have to choose the duration between auto-renewals of your product. For more information on auto-renewing subscriptions, go to `http://developer.apple.com/library/ios/iTunesConnectGuide`.

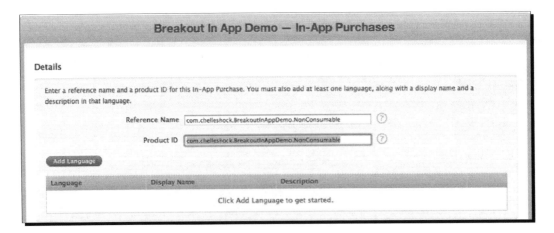

5. Click on the **Add Language** button. Select the language that will be used for the In-App Purchase. Add a display name for your product and a short description about it. When you're done, click on the **Save** button.

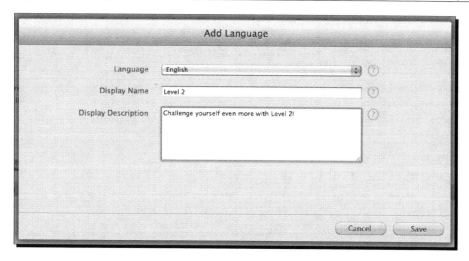

6. In **Pricing and Availability**, ensure that **Yes** is selected for **Cleared for Sale**. In the **Price Tier** drop-down menu, select the price you plan to sell your In-App Purchase for. In this example, **Tier 1** is selected. In **Screenshot for Review**, you'll need to upload a screenshot of your In-App Purchase. If you're testing on an ad hoc build, the screenshot is not necessary. Once you're ready for distribution, the screenshot is required so that the In-App Purchase can be reviewed upon submittal. Click on the **Save** button when done.

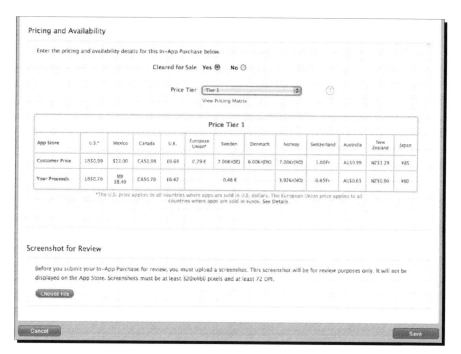

7. You will see a summary of the In-App Purchase that you created on the next page. Click on the **Done** button if all of the information looks correct.

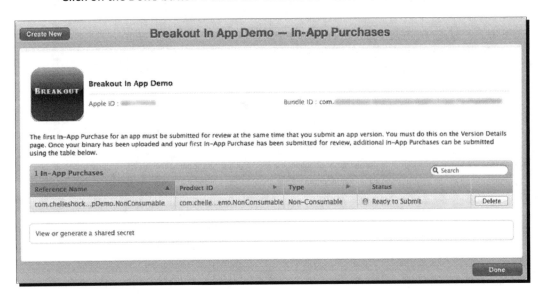

What just happened?

Adding a new In-App Purchase is a very simple process. The information contained in the Product ID is what will be called upon during a transaction. Managing the type of In-App Purchase entirely depends on what type of product you want to sell in your game. This example demonstrates the purpose of taking a nonconsumable product that represents purchasing/unlocking a new level in a game. This is a common scenario for users who to want to sell level packs.

Your application does not have to be completed to test In-App Purchases. All that is required is to have your application information set up in iTunes Connect so that you can manage the features of In-App Purchase.

Time for action – using the Corona store module to create an In-App Purchase

Now that we have set up our Product ID for our In-App Purchase in iTunes Connect, we can implement it in our app to purchase the product we're going to sell. A sample menu app of Breakout was created to demonstrate how to purchase levels within an application. The app contains two levels in the level select screen. The first is available by default. The second is locked and can only be unlocked by purchasing it for $0.99. We're going create a level select screen so that it acts in that manner:

1. In the `Chapter 11` folder, copy the `Breakout In-App Purchase Demo` project folder to your desktop. You can download the project files accompanying this book from the Packt Publishing website. You will notice that the configuration, libraries, assets, and `.lua` files needed are included.

2. Create a new `levelselect.lua` file and save it to the project folder.

3. Set up the scene with the following variables and saving/loading functions. The most important variable of all is `local store = require("store")`, which calls the store module for In-App Purchases:

```lua
local composer = require( "composer" )
local scene = composer.newScene()

local ui = require("ui")
local movieclip = require( "movieclip" )
local store = require("store")


-------------------------------------------------------------------
---------------
-- BEGINNING OF YOUR IMPLEMENTATION
-------------------------------------------------------------------
---------------


local menuTimer

-- AUDIO
local tapSound = audio.loadSound( "tapsound.wav" )

--*************************************************

-- saveValue() --> used for saving high score, etc.

--*************************************************
local saveValue = function( strFilename, strValue )
  -- will save specified value to specified file
  local theFile = strFilename
  local theValue = strValue

  local path = system.pathForFile( theFile,
  system.DocumentsDirectory )

  -- io.open opens a file at path. returns nil if no file found
  local file = io.open( path, "w+" )
  if file then
    -- write game score to the text file
```

```
      file:write( theValue )
      io.close( file )
    end
  end


  --*****************************************************

  -- loadValue() --> load saved value from file (returns loaded
  value as string)

  --*****************************************************
  local loadValue = function( strFilename )
    -- will load specified file, or create new file if it doesn't
  exist

    local theFile = strFilename

    local path = system.pathForFile( theFile,
    system.DocumentsDirectory )

    -- io.open opens a file at path. returns nil if no file found
    local file = io.open( path, "r" )
    if file then
      -- read all contents of file into a string
      local contents = file:read( "*a" )
      io.close( file )
      return contents
    else
      -- create file b/c it doesn't exist yet
      file = io.open( path, "w" )
      file:write( "0" )
      io.close( file )
      return "0"
    end
  end


  -- DATA SAVING
  local level2Unlocked = 1
  local level2Filename = "level2.data"
  local loadedLevel2Unlocked = loadValue( level2Filename )
```

4. Create the `create()` event and remove the `"mainmenu"`, `"level1"`, and `"level2"` scenes:

```
  -- Called when the scene's view does not exist:
```

```
function scene:create( event )
  local sceneGroup = self.view

  -- completely remove maingame and options
  composer.removeScene( "mainmenu" )
  composer.removeScene( "level1" )
  composer.removeScene( "level2" )

  print( "\nlevelselect: create event" )
end
```

5. Next, create the `show()` event and an array that contains a string of **Product ID** set as an In-App Purchase in iTunes Connect:

```
function scene:show( event )
  local sceneGroup = self.view

  print( "levelselect: show event" )

  local listOfProducts =
  {
    -- These Product IDs must already be set up in your store
    -- Replace Product ID with a valid one from iTunes Connect
    "com.companyname.appname.NonConsumable", -- Non Consumable
    In-App Purchase
  }
```

6. Add a local blank table for `validProducts` and `invalidProducts`. Create a local function called `unpackValidProducts()` that checks valid and invalid Product IDs:

```
  local validProducts = {}
  local invalidProducts = {}

  local unpackValidProducts = function()
    print ("Loading product list")
    if not validProducts then
      native.showAlert( "In-App features not available",
      "initStore() failed", { "OK" } )
    else
      print( "Found " .. #validProducts .. " valid items ")
        for i=1, #invalidProducts do
          -- Debug:  display the product info
            native.showAlert( "Item " .. invalidProducts[i]
            .. " is invalid.",{ "OK" } )
            print("Item " .. invalidProducts[i] .. " is
            invalid.")
```

```
                    end


             end
      end
```

7. Create a local function called `loadProductsCallback()` with an `event` parameter. Set up the handler to receive product information with print statements:

```
local loadProductsCallback = function ( event )
  -- Debug info for testing
     print ("loadProductsCallback()")
     print ("event, event.name", event, event.name)
     print (event.products)
     print ("#event.products", #event.products)

     validProducts = event.products
     invalidProducts = event.invalidProducts
     unpackValidProducts ()
  end
```

8. Create a local function called `transactionCallback()` with an `event` parameter. Add several cases of results that are supposed to occur for every `transaction.state` event. When the store is done with the transaction, call `store.finishTransaction(event.transaction)` before the end of the function. Set up a another local function called `setUpStore()` with an `event` parameter to call `store.loadProducts(listOfProducts, loadProductsCallback)`:

```
local transactionCallback = function ( event )
  if event.transaction.state == "purchased" then
    print ("Transaction successful!")
      saveValue ( level2Filename, tostring(level2Unlocked)
  elseif event.transcation.state == "restored" then
    print ("productIdentifier",
    event.transaction.productIdentifier)
    print ("receipt", event.transaction.receipt)
    print ("transactionIdentifier",
    event.transaction.transactionIdentifier)
    print ("date", event.transaction.date)
    print ("originalReceipt",
    event.transaction.originalReceipt)
  elseif event.transaction.state == "cancelled" then
    print ("Transaction cancelled by user.")
  elseif event.transaction.state == "failed" then
    print ("Transaction failed, type: ",
    event.transaction.errorType,
    event.transaction.errorString)
```

```
      local alert = native.showAlert("Failed ", infoString,{
      "OK" })
    else
      print("Unknown event")
      local alert = native.showAlert("Unknown ", infoString,{
      "OK" })
    end
    -- Tell the store we are done with the transaction.
    store.finishTransaction( event.transaction )
    end

    local setupMyStore = function(event)
      store.loadProducts( listOfProducts, loadProductsCallback)
      print ("After store.loadProducts(), waiting for
      callback")
    end
```

9. Set up the display objects for the background and level **1** button:

```
local backgroundImage = display.newImageRect(
"levelSelectScreen.png", 480, 320 )
backgroundImage.x = 240; backgroundImage.y = 160
sceneGroup:insert( backgroundImage )

local level1Btn = movieclip.newAnim({"level1btn.png"}, 200,
60)
level1Btn.x = 240; level1Btn.y = 100
sceneGroup:insert( level1Btn )

local function level1touch( event )
  if event.phase == "ended" then
    audio.play( tapSound )
    composer.gotoScene( "loadlevel1", "fade", 300  )
  end
end
level1Btn:addEventListener( "touch", level1touch )
level1Btn:stopAtFrame(1)
```

10. Set up the level **2** button placement:

```
-- LEVEL 2
local level2Btn =
movieclip.newAnim({"levelLocked.png","level2btn.png"}, 200,
60)
level2Btn.x = 240; level2Btn.y = 180
sceneGroup:insert( level2Btn )
```

11. Use the local onBuyLevel2Touch(event) function and create an if statement to check event.phase == ended and level2Unlocked ~= tonumber(loadedLevel2Unlocked) so that the scene changes to mainmenu.lua:

```
local onBuyLevel2Touch = function( event )
  if event.phase == "ended" and level2Unlocked ~=
  tonumber(loadedLevel2Unlocked) then
    audio.play( tapSound )
    composer.gotoScene( "mainmenu", "fade", 300  )
```

12. Within the same if statement, create a local function called buyLevel2() with a product parameter to call the store.purchase() function:

```
local buyLevel2 = function ( product )
  print ("Congrats! Purchasing " ..product)


  -- Purchase the item
  if store.canMakePurchases then
    store.purchase( {validProducts[1]} )
  else
    native.showAlert("Store purchases are not available,
    please try again later",  { "OK" } ) - Will occur only
    due to phone setting/account restrictions
  end
end
-- Enter your product ID here
-- Replace Product ID with a valid one from iTunes Connect
buyLevel2("com.companyname.appname.NonConsumable")
```

13. Add an elseif statement to check when level 2 has been purchased and unlocked, once the transaction has been completed:

```
elseif event.phase == "ended" and level2Unlocked ==
tonumber(loadedLevel2Unlocked) then
  audio.play( tapSound )
  composer.gotoScene( "loadlevel2", "fade", 300  )
  end
end
level2Btn:addEventListener( "touch", onBuyLevel2Touch )

if level2Unlocked == tonumber(loadedLevel2Unlocked) then
  level2Btn:stopAtFrame(2)
end
```

14. Activate the In-App Purchase with `store.init()` and call `transactionCallback()` as the parameter. Also call `setupMyStore()` with a timer set at 500 milliseconds:

```
store.init( "apple", transactionCallback)
    timer.performWithDelay (500, setupMyStore)
```

15. Create the **Close** UI button and a local function called `onCloseTouch()` with an event parameter. Have the function transition scenes to `loadmainmenu.lua` upon release of the **Close** button. Close the `enterScene()` event with end:

```
local closeBtn

local onCloseTouch = function( event )
    if event.phase == "release" then

        audio.play( tapSound )
        composer.gotoScene( "loadmainmenu", "fade", 300  )

    end
end

closeBtn = ui.newButton{
    defaultSrc = "closebtn.png",
    defaultX = 100,
    defaultY = 30,
    overSrc = "closebtn.png",
    overX = 105,
    overY = 35,
    onEvent = onCloseTouch,
    id = "CloseButton",
    text = "",
    font = "Helvetica",
    textColor = { 255, 255, 255, 255 },
    size = 16,
    emboss = false
}

closeBtn.x = 80; closeBtn.y = 280
closeBtn.isVisible = false
sceneGroup:insert( closeBtn )

menuTimer = timer.performWithDelay( 200, function()
closeBtn.isVisible = true; end, 1 )

end
```

16. Create the `hide()` and `destroy()` events. Within the `hide()` event, cancel the `menuTimer` timer. Add all the event listeners for the scene events and `return scene`:

```
-- Called when scene is about to move offscreen:
function scene:hide()

  if menuTimer then timer.cancel( menuTimer ); end

    print( "levelselect: hide event" )

  end



-- Called prior to the removal of scene's "view" (display
group)
function scene:destroy( event )

  print( "destroying levelselect's view" )
end

-- "create" event is dispatched if scene's view does not exist
scene:addEventListener( "create", scene )

-- "show" event is dispatched whenever scene transition has
finished
scene:addEventListener( "show", scene )

-- "hide" event is dispatched before next scene's transition
begins
scene:addEventListener( "hide", scene )

-- "destroy" event is dispatched before view is unloaded, which
can be
scene:addEventListener( "destroy", scene )

return scene
```

17. Save the file and run the project in the Corona simulator. When you select the **Play** button, you will notice a **1** button and a **Locked** button on the level select screen. When you press the **Locked** button, it calls the store to make a transaction. You will notice a print statement in the terminal that displays what **Product ID** is being referred to for purchase. Full In-App Purchase features cannot be tested in the simulator. You will have to create a distribution build and upload it on an iOS device to initiate a purchase in the store.

What just happened?

In this example, we used the `saveValue()` and `loadValue()` functions from BeebeGames Class to implement how our locked level will go from locked to unlocked mode using movie clips as buttons. The array in `local listOfProducts` displays **Product ID** in a string format. The Product ID in this example needs to be a nonconsumable In-App Purchase type and has to be an existing one in iTunes Connect.

The `unpackValidProducts()` function checks how many valid and invalid items are in the In-App Purchase. The `loadProductsCallback()` function receives the product information in the store. The `transactionCallback(event)` function checks every state: `"purchased"`, `"restored"`, `"cancelled"`, and `"failed"`. When a `"purchased"` state is achieved within the In-App Purchase, the `saveValue()` function is called to change the value of `level2.data`. When the transaction is completed, `store.finishTransaction(event.transaction)` needs to be called to tell the store that you are done with your purchase.

The `setupMyStore(event)` function calls `store.loadProducts(listOfProducts, loadProductsCallback)` and checks the available Product ID (or IDs) in the application. The event is handled once `store.init(transactionCallback)` is initialized and `setupMyStore()` is called.

The `onBuyLevel2Touch(event)` function allows us to check when an In-App Purchase has been made for the locked level. When the user is able to purchase and when they accept the In-App Purchase, the transaction is processed and the value of `level2Unlocked` will match that of `tonumber(loadedLevel2Unlocked)`. The `buyLevel2(product)` function validates the purchased item with `store.purchase()` once the Product ID returns valid.

After the In-App Purchase, the screen transitions to the main menu to allow the **Locked** button to change to the level **2** button. Once the button has changed to frame 2, level 2 is accessible.

Have a go hero – handling multiple Product IDs

Now that you know how to create an In-App Purchase for one product, try adding more than one product to the same application. The scenarios are open ended.

You can add the following:

- More levels for purchases
- A variety of characters the user can play as if your game has a main character
- New background scenes for your application

How you handle new products for your store is up to you.

Testing In-App Purchases

You would want to ensure that the purchases work correctly. Apple provides a sandbox environment that allows you to test your app In-App Purchases. The sandbox environment uses the same model as the App Store, but does not process actual payments. Transactions return as if payments were processed successfully. It is a requirement to test In-App Purchases in a sandbox environment before submitting them for a review by Apple.

When testing in the sandbox environment, you'll need to create a separate user test account that is different from your current iTunes Connect account. Using your current account is not allowed for testing your store in the sandbox.

User test accounts

While you're logged in to your iTunes Connect account, you'll have to select the **Manage Users** link from the Home page. Select **Test User** on the **Select User Type** page. Add a new user and ensure that the test account uses an e-mail address that is not associated with any other Apple account. All test accounts should only be used in the test environment when testing In-App Purchases. Click on the **Save** button when all of the information is filled in.

Once your user test account is created, you'll have to make sure that you've signed out of your Apple account in the **Store** settings of your device. This will keep non-test accounts from being used when testing In-App Purchases. You're only allowed to sign in to your user test account when prompted in the In-App Purchase sandbox to test your application. Do not sign in to your test account before the application is launched. This will prevent it from invalidating your test account.

Time for action – testing the In-App Purchase with the Breakout In-App Purchase Demo

Before you can test an In-App Purchase on an iOS device, make sure that you have a test user account in iTunes Connect. Also, make sure that you've created a distribution build using an ad hoc Distribution Provisioning Profile for the app to test In-App Purchase's features. If you followed all the earlier steps in this chapter, testing a purchase through the store will work accordingly:

1. In the Corona simulator, create a distribution build of the Breakout In-App Purchase Demo. Once the build has been compiled, upload the build on your iOS device.

2. Keep your device connected to your machine and launch Xcode. From the toolbar, go to **Windows | Organizer**. Once you're in **Organizer**, select the device that is connected in the **Devices** section and then select **Console**. This will allow you to check the console output of your device to catch debug messages from your code (that is, print statements) and any application crashes.

3. Before launching the application, you'll need to select the **Settings** icon on your device. Scroll up until you see the **Store** icon and select it.

4. Sign out of your iTunes Store account if you're logged in, so that you can test In-App Purchases in the sandbox environment.

5. Launch the Breakout In-App Purchase Demo from your device. Select the **Play** button and then select the **Locked** button. The screen will transition back to the main menu, and a window will pop up to confirm your In-App Purchase. Press **OK** to continue with the purchase.

6. Next, you will be greeted with another window to sign in with your Apple ID. This is where you will log in with the test user account you created in iTunes Connect. Do not sign in with your actual Apple account that was used to log in to iTunes Connect.

7. Once you've logged in, select the **Play** button again. You will notice that the **2** button has been unlocked. When you select it, you will have access to that scene.

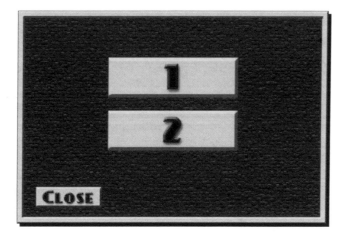

8. Exit the app and refer to the console. You will notice the output from the device and some familiar print statements from your code. The console log displays the Product ID used for the In-App Purchase and informs you whether it is valid and whether the transaction is successful.

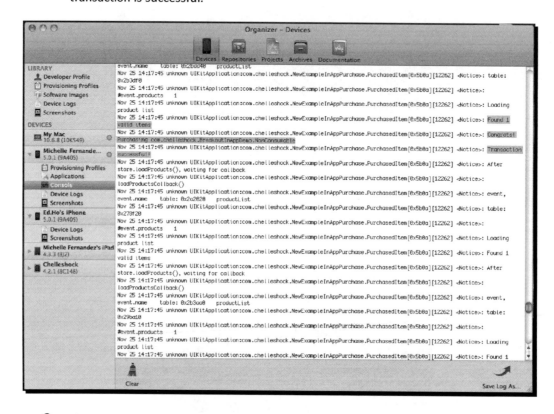

9. If you want to ensure that the In-App Purchase actually worked, delete the application from your device and log out of your user test account. Upload the same build on your device—there's no need to create a new one. Launch the application and run the In-App Purchase again. Log in using the same user test account. You should receive a pop-up window that mentions that you've already purchased the product, and asks you whether you want to download it again for free. Receiving a notification means your In-App Purchase was successful.

What just happened?

It is important to follow the In-App Purchase test steps properly. To make sure you're getting accurate results in the sandbox environment, signing out of your Apple account from the **Store** settings is the key to this entire process.

Once you launch the application and call the store function by pressing the Locked button, you will notice the display name and price of the In-App Purchase. It should match with what you created in iTunes Connect, if you have implemented it correctly.

When you log in by using the test user account you created in iTunes Connect, the transaction should go through without any errors, assuming that there are no server issues on Apple's side or connection problems on the device. Level 2 on the level select screen will be unlocked and accessible. Congratulations! You have created an In-App Purchase.

Have a go hero – using other In-App Purchase types

In the Breakout In-App Purchase Demo, we focused more on nonconsumable In-App Purchases. Try integrating consumable, auto-renewing, or non-renewing subscriptions with your own apps.

Apps that feature consumable products are games that require currency to buy or build things in a free-to-play environment. Subscription products can be focused towards games that are never-ending and are constantly updated with new levels or games that may require an online server to interact in a multiplayer environment. See what you can come up with!

Pop quiz – all about In-App Purchases

Q1. What are nonconsumable purchases?

    1.   Products that only need to be purchased once by the user.

    2.   Products that need to be purchased each time the user needs the item.

    3.   Products that allow the user to purchase content for a set duration of time.

    4.   A subscription that requires a user to renew each time it expires.

Q2. What is true about testing In-App Purchases?

    1.   You need to be logged in to your account at all times.

    2.   Your Apple account is used to test In-App Purchases.

    3.   Login to your user test account when prompted in In-App Purchase sandbox.

    4.   d. None of the above.

Q3. What type of Provisioning Profile must be used to test In-App Purchases?

    1.   Development Provisioning Profile.

    2.   Ad Hoc Distribution Provisioning Profile.

    3.   App Store Distribution Provisioning Profile.

    4.   None of the above.

Summary

We can finally see the light at the end of the tunnel. By now, you should have an idea on how to implement In-App Purchases in your games. It is a very lengthy process to organize, set up the code, and test accurate purchases in the sandbox environment.

The following were taught in this chapter:

- How to set up product IDs for In-App Purchases in iTunes Connect
- Implementing purchase items using Corona's store module
- Adding test user accounts in iTunes Connect
- Testing In-App Purchases on a device

Grasping the concept of In-App Purchasing can take some time. It is best to study the sample code and review the functions pertaining to Corona's store module.

Please check out Apple's *In-App Purchase Programming Guide* at: `https://developer.apple.com/library/ios/documentation/NetworkingInternet/Conceptual/StoreKitGuide/StoreKitGuide.pdf` and the In-App Purchases in the API Reference section of Corona Labs site: for more references pertaining to this topic.

After 11 chapters, we have reached the end of this book. You now have obtained enough knowledge to create your own applications to sell in the Apple App Store or Google Play Store. Hopefully all the information you have acquired has been helpful. I look forward to hearing about the games you have developed using Corona SDK!

Pop Quiz Answers

Chapter 1 – Getting Started with Corona SDK

Pop quiz – understanding Corona

Q1 What is true about using the Corona simulator?	1
Q2 How many iOS devices can you use for development in the iPhone Developer Program?	4
Q3 What does the version code have to be when building for Android in Corona SDK?	2

Chapter 2 – Lua Crash Course and the Corona Framework

Pop quiz – basics of Lua

Q1 Which of the following are values?	4
Q2 Which relational operator is false?	3
Q3 What is the correct way to scale an object in the x direction?	4

Chapter 3 – Building Our First Game – Breakout

Pop quiz – building a game

Q1 When adding the physics engine in your code, which functions are valid to add to your application?	4
Q2 Which is correct when adding an event listener?	4
Q3 What is the correct way to have the following display object transition to $x = 300$, $y = 150$, and have the alpha changed to 0.5, in 2 seconds?	1

Chapter 4 – Game Controls

Pop quiz – working with game controls

Q1 How do you properly remove a display object from the stage?	3

Q2 What is the correct way to make the following display object into a physics object?
 	
`local ball = display.`
`newImage("ball.png")`
	3

Q3 What best represents what `"began"` means in the following function?
 	
`local function onCollision(`
`event )`
`  if event.phase == "began"`
`and event.object1.myName ==`
`"Box 1" then`
 	
`    print( "Collision made."`
`)`
 	
`  end`
`end`
	4

Chapter 5 – Animating Our Game

Pop quiz – animating graphics

Q1 What is the proper way to pause the animation of an image sheet?	1
Q2 How do you make an animation sequence loop forever?	3
Q3 How do you create a new image sheet?	4

Chapter 6 – Playing Sounds and Music

Pop quiz – all about audio

Q1 What is the proper way of clearing audio files from the memory?	3
Q2 How many channels of audio can be played simultaneously in an application?	4
Q3 How do you make your audio file loop infinitely?	1

Chapter 7 – Physics – Falling Objects

Pop quiz – animating the graphics

Q1 What retrieves or sets the text string of a text object?	1
Q2 What function converts any argument into a string?	3
Q3 What body type is affected by gravity and collisions with the other body types?	1

Chapter 8 – Operation Composer

Pop quiz – game transitions and scenes

Q1 What function do you call to change scenes with Composer?	2
Q2 What function converts any argument into a number or nil?	1
Q3 How do you pause a timer?	3
Q4. How do you resume a timer?	2

Chapter 9 – Handling Multiple Devices and Networking Your Apps

Pop quiz – handling social networks

Q1 What is the specific API that scales down high-resolution sprite sheets?	2
Q2 What are the publishing permissions called that allow posting on a user's wall on Facebook?	2
Q3 Which parameter(s) is required for `facebook.login()`?	4

Chapter 10 – Optimizing, Testing, and Shipping Your Games

Pop quiz – publishing applications

Q1 When creating an iOS Distribution Provisioning file, what distribution method do you need to use?	2
Q2 Where do you refer to for the status of the submitted iOS applications?	1
Q3 What is required to build an app for the Google Play Store?	4

Chapter 11 – Implementing In-App Purchases

Pop quiz – all about In-App Purchases

Q1 What are nonconsumable purchases?	1
Q2 What is true about testing In-App Purchases?	3
Q3 What type of Provisioning Profile must be used to test In-App Purchases?	2

Index

volume control, audio system
 audio.getMaxVolume() function 183
 audio.getMinVolume() function 182
 audio.getVolume() function 182
 audio.setMaxVolume() function 181
 audio.setMinVolume() function 181
 audio.setVolume() function 180

W

win condition
 creating 123, 124
Windows
 Corona, activating on 5, 6
 Corona, setting up on 5, 6
 simulator, used on 7
workflow
 memory, using 72
 optimizing 72

X

Xcode
 about 22
 downloading 10, 11
 installing 10, 11

Thank you for buying
Corona SDK Mobile Game Development Beginner's Guide
Second Edition

About Packt Publishing

Packt, pronounced 'packed', published its first book, *Mastering phpMyAdmin for Effective MySQL Management*, in April 2004, and subsequently continued to specialize in publishing highly focused books on specific technologies and solutions.

Our books and publications share the experiences of your fellow IT professionals in adapting and customizing today's systems, applications, and frameworks. Our solution-based books give you the knowledge and power to customize the software and technologies you're using to get the job done. Packt books are more specific and less general than the IT books you have seen in the past. Our unique business model allows us to bring you more focused information, giving you more of what you need to know, and less of what you don't.

Packt is a modern yet unique publishing company that focuses on producing quality, cutting-edge books for communities of developers, administrators, and newbies alike. For more information, please visit our website at www.PacktPub.com.

Writing for Packt

We welcome all inquiries from people who are interested in authoring. Book proposals should be sent to author@packtpub.com. If your book idea is still at an early stage and you would like to discuss it first before writing a formal book proposal, then please contact us; one of our commissioning editors will get in touch with you.

We're not just looking for published authors; if you have strong technical skills but no writing experience, our experienced editors can help you develop a writing career, or simply get some additional reward for your expertise.

Corona SDK Mobile Game Development Beginner's Guide

ISBN: 978-1-84969-188-8   Paperback:408 pages

Create monetized games for iOS and Android with minimum cost and code

1. Build once and deploy your games to both iOS and Android.

2. Create commercially successful games by applying several monetization techniques and tools.

3. Create three fun games and integrate them with social networks such as Twitter and Facebook.

Corona SDK Application Design

ISBN: 978-1-84969-736-1   Paperback: 98 pages

A quick and easy guide to creating your very own mobile apps with Corona SDK

1. Build apps that can be used on multiple platforms.

2. Test your apps and publish them on GooglePlay and Apple's App store.

3. Develop your own apps with the help of interactive examples.

Please check **www.PacktPub.com** for information on our titles

Source SDK Game Development Essentials

ISBN: 978-1-84969-592-3   Paperback: 294 pages

Develop engaging and immersive mods with Source SDK

1. Create maps and mods using the tools provided with Source SDK.

2. Learn how to use Hammer to create your own game worlds.

3. Create goal-driven A.I. sequences and scripts.

4. Master Source SDK tools with ease with step by step tutorials.

Developing Mobile Games with Moai SDK

ISBN: 978-1-78216-506-4   Paperback: 136 pages

Learn the basics of Moai SDK through developing games

1. Develop games for multiple platforms with a single code base.

2. Understand the basics of Moai SDK.

3. Build two prototype games including one with physics.

Please check **www.PacktPub.com** for information on our titles

Made in the USA
Lexington, KY
14 October 2015